CW00497322

A PRIMROSE PATH

For Sue,
With all best wishes

A PRIMROSE PATH

THE GILDED LIFE OF LORD ROSEBERY'S FAVOURITE SON

MARTIN GIBSON

ARUM
PRESS

CONTENTS

LIST OF ILLUSTRATIONS

INTRODUCTION AND ACKNOWLEDGEMENTS

Perhaps unsurprisingly the publication of this book, and the research I conducted behind it, arose out of the centenary of World War One. Before then, in the summer of 2014 when I was living in the village of Elm, close to Wisbech in Cambridgeshire, it came to my notice that Wisbech's serving Member of Parliament, Neil Primrose, had been killed in action in Palestine in 1917. Even though he was the son of a former Prime Minister, and had himself served as a minister in both the Asquith and Lloyd George wartime coalition governments, I discovered there was remarkably little out there about him in print, or online. Even the *Oxford Dictionary of National Biography* is silent on Neil, while now containing articles on his brother the 6th Earl of Rosebery (1882-1974), and both of his sisters Lady Sybil Grant (1879-1955) and Peggy, Lady Crewe (1881-1967). This omission of his youngest child, whom he considered by far the most able and politically astute of his children, would undoubtedly have astounded the 5th Earl of Rosebery.

Immediately following his death, Neil's sacrifice and the snuffed-out promise of his future political career were widely compared to that of another Prime Minister's son, Raymond Asquith; but a century on the former is largely forgotten, while the latter remains fairly widely known. The explanation for this is, at least in part, that Lord Rosebery strongly opposed memorialising his deceased younger son in print, whereas the Asquiths were content to keep Raymond's flame burning following his 1916 death in action. Rosebery freely admitted to the King in November 1917 that Neil was "my greatest friend and confidant", and the idea that his son's uniquely precious life should be further scrutinised publicly in print appalled him.

In the light of this unusual lacuna, in October 2014 I started to research Neil's life and a year later my thirty-page booklet *Captain Neil Primrose*

MP 1882-1917 was published by the Wisbech Society and Preservation Trust Limited.

The historian Michael Bloch was an early admirer of what he generously called my "excellent monograph" and most kindly made mention of it in his 2016 paperback edition of *Closet Queens*. Michael also informed me that his researches into the life of Jeremy Thorpe and West Country Liberalism had brought up the name of Neil's great associate, the long-dead MP Thomas Agar-Robartes (1880-1915). He informed me that Thomas's twin sister Everilda (1880-1969) had been a warm admirer of another Liberal MP for Bodmin, Peter Bessell, in the 1960s and had apparently even made arrangements for Bessell to inherit Thomas's papers, which she had carefully treasured and preserved at Lanhydrock House ever since his death from wounds sustained during the 1915 battle of Loos, over fifty years earlier.

My pamphlet also led me to the distinguished historian Dr Cameron Hazlehurst who, on learning of my work, emailed from Australia to say "Primrose has been on my radar for 50 years". In many follow-up emails Cameron has suggested numerous published sources and archives worthy of investigation. Cameron's involvement has also culminated in the greatest kindness, his editing the manuscript of this book and in his encouraging me to get it published.

However prior to the production of a manuscript, let alone its publication, I needed to unearth sufficient additional material to generate one.

My additional research started at the Parliamentary Archive at Westminster, where I found much of use in the Lloyd George papers and to a lesser extent in the Bonar Law papers. At the British Library I found a few letters from Neil to his friend Rufus Isaacs, among the large amount of private papers of Lord Reading that are held there. At Cambridge University Library there are three long and important letters that Neil wrote from France to his brother-in-law Lord Crewe in the final months of 1914. Also in Cambridge, at the Churchill Archives Centre, I made the perhaps surprising discovery, given their friendship, that they hold nothing relating to Neil and Winston Churchill. His Honour Lord Parmoor kindly wrote to say that he has nothing relating to Neil in the surviving papers of his great-uncle Fred Cripps that could add to what is written about Neil in his 1957 memoir *Life's a Gamble*.

At Oxford in the Weston Library of the Bodleian, I found a surprisingly rich seam of relevant material among the papers of Herbert Fisher, Neil's New College tutor. Also in Oxford, at Balliol College, among the Jowett papers are Lord Rosebery's letters to Benjamin Jowett, concerning the recruitment of private tutors for his young sons and a private secretary for himself.

My greatest discovery of material was made in November 2016 quite by chance when I read about the new and virtually unknown archive building at Windmill Hill, Waddesdon, Buckinghamshire. The archive houses the papers of the former owners of Waddesdon Manor including Neil's great friend and relation James de Rothschild (1878-1957), and his wife Dorothy (1895-1988), who inherited Waddesdon in 1922 and bequeathed it to the National Trust in 1957. The Head Archivist informed me that they did have some letters from Neil to James and Dorothy de Rothschild and vice versa. However in addition they had to my surprise all of Neil's surviving political and financial papers, as well as 96 letters that Neil received from his father between 1902 and 1915. How all of these papers came into James de Rothschild's possession remains something of a mystery, as on Neil's death they were inherited and then closely guarded by his father. However as James de Rothschild's candidacy and election as MP for Neil's former constituency co-incided with Lord Rosebery's death in May 1929, it seems safe to speculate that Rosebery's heirs felt it appropriate to hand Neil's papers over to James.

So far as the 5th Earl of Rosebery's own papers are concerned, they reside in two locations, the National Library of Scotland and Dalmeny House. In November 2017 the current Lord Dalmeny informed me that, as the material his parents have is uncatalogued and as they have no archivist, "we are not certain if there are letters of Neil's to his father at Dalmeny". Perhaps understandably in these circumstances they have decided to no longer provide access to researchers, following their last doing so for Leo McKinstry when he was researching his 2005 biography *Rosebery Statesman in Turmoil*.

Therefore I must concede that the possibility remains that there is relevant material at Dalmeny House that may, in time, become available. Certainly the few pieces of relevant material on Neil in the Rosebery papers held at the National Library of Scotland are tantalising: a single letter from Thomas Agar-Robartes to Neil when he was away in North America in

1905, and Rosebery's highly emotional and revealing reflection on his learning of Thomas's death in France.

I regret that I have failed to unearth any letters between Neil and his wife Lady Victoria during those parts of 1915-17 when they were separated by his military service. All I have found, at Windmill Hill, are two brief notes from Lady Victoria to Dorothy de Rothschild written while Neil was in Egypt in 1915-16. On checking with the Borthwick Institute for Archives at York University, I was told that while the Hickleton papers do contain a small number of Lady Victoria's letters, none pre-date 1920 and those they do have make no reference to Neil.

Another historian who has advised me, Lord Lexden, told me to pursue Cornish leads, and while I have endeavoured to do so, my efforts have not borne fruit. Paul Holden, then National Trust House and Collections Manager at Lanhydrock, informed me that they do not have any papers of Thomas Agar-Robartes. What they do have is a substantial collection of photographs, including images of Neil and Thomas together at Bullingdon Club dinners and on Varsity polo fields. Also and intriguingly they have the photographs of several hundred Eton College boys, taken in the school in the 1890s, including several of Neil and of his brother Harry, Lord Dalmeny. Quite how, by who, and why this extraordinary collection was assembled remains unclear.

The fact that the National Trust has nothing more than photographs is perhaps unsurprising, because on Thomas's death in 1915 his entire estate went to his beloved twin sister Everilda. Following Everilda's death in 1969, Thomas's surviving personal and political papers were apparently handed to the then Liberal MP for Bodmin, Peter Bessell (this is asserted in print by Bessell in his 1980 book *Cover Up, The Jeremy Thorpe Affair*). Although I succeeded in contacting Peter's son Paul, this led to nothing more than his confirmation that these papers no longer exist, and his belief that they were lost, with much else, following his father's flight to America in 1974 and the subsequent creditors' re-possession of his house.

My archival researches concluded in West Sussex, with the Petworth House Archive and Rosebery's voluminous correspondence with his sister Constance, Lady Leconfield. There on page after page I found a most moving testament to a father's lifelong devotion to his younger son, and of the all-consuming grief that followed his heroic death.

I must acknowledge the gracious permission of Her Majesty the Queen to quote from material relating to Neil that is in the Royal Archives, at Windsor Castle. Julie Crocker of the Royal Archives was immensely kind and helpful and sent me scans and transcripts of everything that was relevant. I am also grateful to the Earl and Countess of Rosebery for their kind permission to reproduce two photographs from their family collection and to their son, Lord Dalmeny, for helpfully answering my queries.

I am also most grateful to The Waddesdon Archive at Windmill Hill for allowing me to have access to the letters and papers that they hold relating to Neil, and to the Head Archivist Catherine Taylor for being so helpful during my visit. The same applies to The Rothschild Archive London and in particular my thanks are due to Melanie Aspey who supplied scans and transcripts of the letters Neil's cousins Evelyn and Anthony de Rothschild wrote to their parents while on active service with the Royal Bucks Hussars at Gallipoli in 1915 and in Egypt during the Senussi campaign of 1915-16. I am also grateful to The Rothschild Archive London for permission to reproduce two photographs from their collection.

I am similarly grateful to Lord Egremont for permitting access to the Petworth House archive and to the staff of the West Sussex Record Office in Chichester.

My thanks are also due to the following institutions: (a) the British Library (Lord Reading's papers) and to the staff of both the Humanities Reading Rooms and the Asian and African Studies Reading Room; (b) the Parliamentary Archive for allowing me access to the Lloyd George and Bonar Law papers and in particular to Miss Claire Batley, the Senior Archivist, for helpfully answering my subsequent email query; (c) the National Library of Scotland (Rosebery papers) and in particular Dr Amy Tadman, Curator of Political Collections, for answering several catalogue queries; (d) Cambridge University Library and the staff of the Manuscripts Reading Room for access to the Crewe papers; (e) the Bodleian Libraries for access to Herbert Fisher's papers and to Oliver House and the other staff of the Rare Books & Manuscripts Reading Room; (f) the National Archives at Kew for access to a variety of War Office and other files; (g) English Heritage Blue Plaques and in particular to Cathy Power for allowing me to visit and inspect the file relating to Lord Raglan's Blue Plaque erected in 1911 on Neil's London house at 5 Stanhope Gate; (h) the National Trust for permission to reproduce a photograph of Thomas Agar-Robartes and one of

Neil at Eton in 1899; (i) the National Portrait Gallery for permission to reproduce three images; and (j) Wisbech & Fenland Museum for permission to reproduce four of their photographs.

I should also like to record my thanks to the following individuals – His Honour Lord Parmoor for giving me permission to reproduce two photographs from *Life's a Gamble*; Professor Ian Beckett for sending me his file of interviews conducted with the surviving Royal Bucks Hussars veterans in the 1980s; Paul Holden for sending material on Thomas Agar-Robartes and for answering my queries about him; Heidi Egginton of the Churchill Archives Centre in Cambridge; John Preston for supplying me with Peter Bessell's email address; Caroline Usher of the office of David Warburton MP for requesting and then relaying to me information from the House of Commons Library on Neil and Thomas's heraldic shields; Jane Selleck the Eton College Archivist for answering my query about Neil's house and housemaster at Eton; Miles Young, Warden of New College, Oxford, for very kindly looking up and sending me details of Neil's 1903 stay at Sligger Urquhart's Alpine chalet; Jennifer Thorp, Archivist, New College, Oxford, for answering my questions about Neil, Neville Waterfield and Neil's cousin the Hon George Wyndham; John Hyatt for generously inviting me to lunch at Brooks's Club, for showing me the Club war memorial and for permission to reproduce his photograph of Neil's grave in Israel following the wreath-laying to mark the centenary of his death; David Wills for providing me with Neil and Thomas's membership records at Brooks's Club and for sending me images of Neil's entries in the Club's Betting Book; Sean Naidoo for his generous hospitality in Buckinghamshire while I laboured at Waddesdon, for showing me the Reform Club war memorial, and for supplying me with details of Neil's Reform Club membership; and Nicholas Townend, bibliophile and school friend, for sending a long list of suggested sources and reading.

Finally I must add two especial thanks: first, again, to Dr Cameron Hazlehurst for his invaluable help, advice, editing and constant encouragement; and second, to my partner Rupert, not only for tolerantly sharing our life with Neil Primrose over these past years, but also for assisting with my research and writing in ways too innumerable to detail.

PROLOGUE

"May she come to her appointed place in peace," the rabbi of the London Central Synagogue intoned as the dark oak coffin was gently lowered into the grave. It was a cold crisp late November day and at the graveside the seven-year-old Neil and his brother Harry were identically dressed. Their Scottish Stewart tartan kilts and Glengarry caps were strikingly different from the sombre black dress of everyone else, including their father, who stood between them and held each of the boys' hands.

The words of the Hebrew prayers were quite unknown to both boys and the cemetery of the United Synagogue at Willesden was not a place they had been to before. The day before their father had explained to them that it was the place of burial of their Rothschild grandparents and that it had been their mother's wish that she was buried here in accordance with her family's faith.

As the coffin reached the base of the grave and the rabbi ceased speaking Rosebery released his elder son's hand, while clasping Neil's still tighter, and stooped for some freshly dug earth. As he rose and dropped it onto the coffin it caused a drum-like noise that echoed in the absolute stillness.[1] Neil and Harry also threw earth on the coffin; then Rosebery turned and gently steered his two young sons away from the grave, past those of their Rothschild grandparents, and towards his waiting carriage. In silence they passed the leading male members of Hannah Rosebery's family – Lord Rothschild, Baron Ferdinand de Rothschild, Mr Leopold de Rothschild and Baron Edmond de Rothschild. Beyond them stood Mr Gladstone and Sir Henry Ponsonby, Queen Victoria's private secretary, to whom Rosebery bowed. Ponsonby had brought a large laurel wreath with white Cape Everlasting entwined with a white card covered in black ink in the Queen's handwriting: 'A mark of sincere regard from Victoria R.I.'[2]

1

Earlier that morning at 10.30am both boys had emerged with Rosebery from 38 Berkeley Square, behind the coffin. As they had watched their mother's coffin being carried down the wide central staircase of their London home there had been tears, but they had formed a pact with their father that all three of them would try their hardest to show no emotion once outside. There was a vast crowd, and as the coffin was placed in the hearse drawn by four black horses, Rosebery led his sons into the first carriage. Behind it a line of seventy carriages stretched round and beyond the great London square.

As the London *Evening Standard*[3] subsequently reported, "as the hearse started, all of the very large number of standing spectators respectfully uncovered their heads and the blinds of every house in Berkeley Square were drawn as a mark of respect towards Lady Rosebery."

The funeral procession turned out of the Square into Mount Street and then up Park Lane and the Edgware Road to Willesden, where it arrived over an hour later. As the press noted, in accordance with Jewish tradition, no ladies witnessed Hannah's interment and her two daughters, with Rosebery's sister Constance, Lady Leconfield, and Mrs Gladstone, remained throughout behind closed blinds at 38 Berkeley Square.

Hannah had died at Rosebery's Scottish seat, Dalmeny House just outside Edinburgh, six days earlier on November 19th 1890. Following her death the family remained at Dalmeny and only the day before the funeral did they accompany Hannah's body south to London in a special train. For that final night before the burial, four ladies from the Jewish community kept an overnight vigil over the coffin in the upstairs drawing room at Berkeley Square.

Hannah's cousin Lady Battersea wrote the following account of the morning of the funeral in her diary entry for November 25th:

Crowds were already collecting in the street. I went upstairs and in the large front room, on a bier, stood a large oak coffin, which enclosed two other coffins, the inner one containing the mortal remains of dear Hannah. Flowers abounded everywhere; they lined and carpeted the floor, covered the coffin and stood like sentinels at its head.[4]

Gladstone later recorded that he found Jewish obsequies "dignified and touching" although he felt the absence "of our Lord's name". Sir Henry

Ponsonby subsequently assured the Queen of Rosebery's self-control that day in public: "He wishes to show in public that he is able to put aside his sorrow, but in private he breaks down." Three days after the funeral Rosebery himself confessed to the Queen: "at the moment of death the difference in creed makes itself felt and another religion steps in to claim the corpse. It was inevitable and I do not complain: and my wife's family have been more than kind. But none the less is it exquisitely painful."[5]

Religious differences had plagued the couple's relationship from when they first became engaged in January 1878. Rosebery's stepfather the Duke of Cleveland sniffily recorded: "I do not know the young lady personally but I am told the family is well-to-do in the City."[6] Far worse was the severely caustic reaction of Rosebery's mother who spared her son none of her disapproval:

> You can easily suppose how unhappy I must feel in finding that you have chosen as your wife and the mother of your children one who has not the faith and hope of Christ ... I myself do honestly and from the bottom of my heart disapprove of such marriages and could not say otherwise without acting against my conscientious convictions.[7]

Rosebery's younger brother Everard Primrose wrote of the news as follows:

> Archie is to marry Miss Hannah Rothschild and her millions! I really believe the young woman has some 80,000£ worth of hard cash! I think that is enough to buy the consent of a whole tribe – were it even of Levi ... this marriage will be a great blow to my mother – whose house hitherto has alone stood out against an infusion of Jewish society.[8]

Rosebery's eldest sister Lady Mary Primrose[9], who did not marry until October 1885, was at the time of her brother's engagement still firmly tied to her mother and her domineering influence, and so was in no position to take an independent view. However of far more importance to Rosebery was having the approbation of "the person he had always loved most" his sister Constance, and to her he confided that: "the Rothschilds appear pleased."[10]

The engagement was not entered into rashly, as the couple had first met at Newmarket ten years earlier when Hannah was just seventeen and formed a lasting crush on her future husband. The waspishly acidic, and not entirely reliable, Lewis Harcourt subsequently wrote in his journal that on the day of the engagement, Hannah had served Rosebery "very good claret … to inflame him up to the point of proposing."[11]

Hannah herself though was so troubled by her future mother-in-law's reaction, that she suggested Rosebery call off the engagement in a letter to him of January 25th:

> A great dread has come over me about religion. You remember my first words to you? I cannot become a Christian because though respecting Jesus I cannot believe in him. You said that you would not wish me to change and now I am frightened. If my religion is in your way, don't marry me. It would break my heart but I could not face to be a hindrance.

The marriage went ahead two months later on March 20th 1878, first in a civil ceremony held at 9.45am in the registrar's room within the Mayfair Poor Law Board, in Mount Street, and then far more lavishly at Christ Church in Down Street.[12] The Duchess of Cleveland relented sufficiently to attend the Church ceremony and was doubtless pleased to see the Prime Minister, Lord Beaconsfield, a convert to Anglicanism, give the orphaned Hannah away at the altar. She was also at the reception, held at Hannah's London house, 107 Piccadilly, to hear the Prince of Wales propose the first toast to the couple.[13] Whether due to their disquiet over Hannah marrying outside of the faith, or because of the Duchess of Cleveland's hostility, with the sole exception of Baron Ferdinand de Rothschild, no male members of the Rothschild family attended.

Given these complexities Rosebery's understandably terse diary entry for the day reads: "Married. 1. At the Workhouse in Mount Street and 2. At Church in Down Street. To Petworth [his sister's Sussex home] for honeymoon."[14] After a week of marriage Hannah wrote from Petworth to her sister-in-law Lady Leconfield, who had vacated the great house for the newly-weds:

> We two old bachelors agree & are becoming accustomed to married life though I may own that he usually gets his own way; you see we

4

are both (as he said if you remember) spoilt children & I, being the laziest, am the more amenable.[15]

Hannah's acknowledgement that her own childhood had been a spoilt one was quite accurate. Four years younger than Rosebery she had been born in London on 27 July 1851 the first and only child of Baron Meyer de Rothschild[16] and his wife Juliana (nee Cohen)[17]. Her highly educated and rather judgmental cousin Lady Battersea subsequently wrote of Hannah's childhood:

An only child, petted and spoilt by her parents, with no serious bringing up, whose education was woefully neglected but who at a very early age was brought into contact with some of England's greatest men. She never was allowed to enter a cottage, to go where sickness and sorrow dwelt, she was never brought face to face with want or sickness. The poor was merely a phraseology for her. She had but few redeeming qualities as a child.[18]

Her father was the first of the sons of Nathan Meyer de Rothschild to purchase land in the Vale of Aylesbury[19]: in 1842 he first bought land located in the parishes of Mentmore and Wing and then in 1850 he bought the remainder of his 5,500 acre estate together the manorial rights and the advowson of Mentmore. Work began immediately on building a new great mansion at Mentmore to the design of Sir Joseph Paxton: it took five years to complete. The building of Mentmore Towers and the model village was Meyer's great legacy as Lord Crewe has written:

An amazing creation of a wide park, and noble gardens, transmuted, as by the hands of a genie, from its first state of rolling pastures sloping up to the crest of a foothill of the Chilterns, and dotted with fattening bullocks.[20]

The interior of Mentmore was described by the novelist Henry James who was a guest of the Roseberys in 1880:

Everything is magnificent. The house is a huge modern palace, filled with wonderful objects accumulated by the late Baron Meyer de

Rothschild, Lady Rosebery's father. All of them are precious and many exquisite and their general Rothschildish splendour is only equalled by their profusion. [21]

Baron Meyer was a devotee of the turf and built a stud farm at Crafton near Mentmore that led to huge racing success. He won the One Thousand Guineas three times and he was so successful in 1871 that it became known as 'the Baron's year' on account of his success in the Derby, the One Thousand Guineas, the Oaks, the St Leger and the Cesarewitch (three of his victories were with his famous filly *Hannah*).[22] He also served as Liberal MP for Hythe from 1859 until his death in 1874, although it was racing and not politics that brought Rosebery into Meyer's orbit.

Just over three years later in March 1877 his widow Baroness Juliana de Rothschild died aged 46 leaving Hannah orphaned aged 25. Juliana, who had been a hypochondriac with a great fear of draughts, died quite suddenly at Nice while on her yacht *Czarina*. As *The Times*[23] reported the Baroness had sailed from Southampton the previous September "in the hope of benefitting her health which had been delicate since the death of her husband."

Hannah, who had been with her mother at her death, now accompanied her body back to London, where she was buried next to her husband at Willesden on March 16th.

Following her mother's death Hannah was said to be the wealthiest woman in England with assets of £2 million and an annual income of £80,000[24] but great wealth did not bring her happiness and she was terribly isolated and lonely in her gilded cages at Mentmore and at 107 Piccadilly.

It has been written that Hannah's mother had favoured Rosebery as her future son-in-law[25] and so, given Hannah's long held crush on him, it is perhaps unsurprising that within nine months of her death, they were engaged at Mentmore on January 3rd. Just days later Hannah was reminding Rosebery:

Remember, darling I have no one on earth but you. I don't think you know much about my ideas of happiness. I am afraid of seeing little of you in the future. I can be very quiet when you want and work only to help you. If you are Prime Minister, let me imitate Montagu Corry[26].

Lady Beaconsfield used to say he was useful because he was so devoted to his master; I shall be devoted to you.

Later that month Hannah effusively told her fiancé that he had saved her from a terrible life of loneliness.[27]
Rosebery was emphatically not lonely before becoming engaged and had spent 1877 like every other since he inherited his grandfather's title and estates in 1868; as a leading member of fashionable society, fully indulging his passion for the turf, extensive foreign travel, and when in the country, attending and speaking in the House of Lords. This difference in feelings was not concealed by Rosebery's first biographer, his son-in-law Lord Crewe, who characterised Rosebery's feelings for Hannah as "admiration and warm affection" and Hannah's for him as "admiration and adoring devotion".[28]
But who was this 30-year-old man that Hannah had the very highest political ambitions for, and whom she so adored, notwithstanding his intimidating persona?
He was born at 20 Charles Street, in Mayfair, on 7 May 1847. His birthplace, which since 1962 has had a blue plaque recording as much, was actually then the house of his maternal grandfather the 4th Earl of Stanhope. Lord Stanhope's only daughter, Rosebery's mother, who had married Lord Dalmeny in 1843 was said to have been the most beautiful and intelligent young woman at Court and served both as a maid of honour at Queen Victoria's 1838 coronation and as a bridesmaid in 1840 when the Queen married Prince Albert. At the final Court Ball of the 1843 season, held at Buckingham Palace, Lady Wilhelmina met Lord Dalmeny and noted in her diary that he was the 'cleverest and most agreeable of all my partners'.[29] The relationship, formed while dancing in July, progressed rapidly and the couple were married before September was out. The following year Lady Dalmeny gave birth to a daughter Mary, and Constance followed in 1846.
On the birth of his first son Lord Dalmeny wrote to Lord Stanhope "You will rejoice to learn that this morning at ten minutes before 3, Wilhelmina was brought to bed of a son."[30] Forty days later their son was baptised at St. George's Hanover Square, the place of their marriage, and was given the names Archibald Philip and within the family was known as Archie.
Lord Dalmeny had been the Whig MP for Stirling Burghs since 1832, although he did not stand in the 1847 General Election that followed his

son's birth – perhaps wisely as the electors returned a Radical. Dalmeny was heir to his father the 4th Earl of Rosebery who was also a Whig in politics and who had supported the passing of the 1832 Great Reform Bill in the House of Lords. It was the 4th Earl who had in 1817 abandoned the family's historic medieval seat of Barnbougle Castle on the shore of the Firth of Forth for the newly built Dalmeny House located nearby but in a more sheltered position away from the shoreline.

Soon after Archie turned three Lady Dalmeny confided to her journal that she found him "a terribly dull little boy – Conny is a genius in comparison"[31] and in an earlier entry she adversely contrasted Archie with his younger brother Everard (born 1848) "Everard is very different … He is much cleverer, we think."

Later that year, after Christmas, Lord Dalmeny became seriously ill with pleurisy and died quite suddenly of a heart attack aged 40 in January 1851. Perhaps unsurprisingly this tragedy left the young Archie traumatised and he was apparently unwell for several weeks after.[32] Before he was four years old, Archie became Lord Dalmeny, and his grandfather's heir.

The widowed Lady Dalmeny now retreated to her father's seat at Chevening in Kent and there she and her four children remained, until her re-marriage in Chevening Church on 2 August 1854. The young Lord Dalmeny loved these years spent at Chevening House. Already of a solitary disposition he could wander alone in its great parkland and further avoid his mother in its library. He always referred to Chevening as Paradise and in 1924 would tell Lady Stanhope "I hope you realize that as Jerusalem is to a Jew and Mecca to a Mohammedan, so Chevening is to me."[33] It was also during this happy interlude that the precociously bright Lord Dalmeny first became aware that two great Prime Ministers, the elder and younger Pitts, were part of his Stanhope ancestry.

His new stepfather, previously unmarried and destined to remain childless, was Lord Harry Vane, the 51-year-old-younger son of the 1st Duke of Cleveland. All four children followed their mother into Chevening Church on her wedding day, the two boys dressed in Stewart tartan kilts. However there are indications that her elder son was not happy with the marriage: in 1916 he wrote that his stepfather "had been in love with my mother before her first marriage."[34]

Following the wedding, the couple and all four children travelled in Europe for six months. On their return the eight-year-old Lord Dalmeny went to his first boarding school, Bayford House in Hertfordshire. Bayford House was the home of the Rev. and Mrs George Renaud[35] where they ran a small private school accommodating 24 pupils. Years later Rosebery recalled his disquiet at "the coarse sheets of the bed, the being expected to undress without assistance, and the conversation about myself between my room-mates, when I was believed to be asleep, all these are indelible memories of that lonely evening half a century ago."[36]

Lady Harry seems to have been indifferent to her son's absence at school; she neglected to write to him to the extent that in October 1855 Dalmeny wrote to his grandmother Lady Rosebery to enquire about his mother's whereabouts. The young Lord Dalmeny not only suffered from parental neglect. At one point he was severely concussed during a Bayford House game of blind man's buff. Then at Christmas 1858 he was badly burnt while successfully saving the life of the young daughter of the Rector of Chevening after her muslin dress caught fire.[37]

In 1857 following a succession of rented houses, Lord Harry purchased Battle Abbey in Sussex and this, coupled with Bayford's closure (occasioned by the Renauds moving to Somerset), prompted Dalmeny and Everard's transfer "to Mr Lee's well known school at Brighton."[38] The school which had 50 pupils was located in Norfolk Terrace and had been established in 1843 by William Randall Lee. In 1886 it moved to Ashdown House, in rural Sussex, where it still exists.[39]

In 1860 Dalmeny entered Eton College where he was placed in the Lower Remove alongside the cleverest Oppidan new boys. An Eton contemporary later reported that while he was not a great wet bob (rower) or dry bob (cricketer):

He read a good deal by himself – books of history and memoirs and newspapers and parliamentary reports in them … His patrician hauteur was unmistakable. Not an offensive hauteur but that calm pride by which a man seems to ascend in a balloon out of earshot every time he is addressed by one not socially his equal.[40]

His tutor was the academically brilliant but sexually flawed William Johnson[41] who was soon obsessed with his youthful aristocratic pupil. At the end of his first term at Eton Johnson reported to Lady Harry:

9

I find him endowed with heart as well as mind, very sociable, friendly and gay. I find he likes nearly everyone in his house, and is liked, apparently by all, certainly those whom I know and like best. [42]

By the summer of 1862 Johnson was writing inappropriately to Dalmeny during his long summer holiday away from Eton: "I met some excellent Scottish people who talked to me with the greatest affection of your sweet self. I made them quite happy by giving them a glowing account of you" and a year later "take care of your precious limbs. We miss you sadly and wish you to get back."[43]

During the Christmas holiday of 1863 the manipulative and pederastic Johnson visited his pupil at home at Battle Abbey, and in the summer of 1864 the pair went to Rome together. While there the 41-year-old tutor told a friend that Dalmeny, now aged seventeen, was "the wisest boy that ever lived and full of fun too".[44]

Soon after they returned to England on September 6th Lord Harry's brother died and he succeeded to the dukedom and a seat in the House of Lords. He also inherited Cleveland House in London, the magnificent fifteenth-century fortress of Raby Castle in County Durham and a huge landholding that provided an annual income of almost £100,000.[45]

In October 1864 at the start of his final year at Eton, Dalmeny was elected to Pop (The Eton Society); apparently receiving four black balls out of the 23 who voted. In addressing his fellow members he spoke "in his usual vein of sarcastic and cutting wit, making several of the members look very small."[46]

Although not universally popular, he had formed many devoted friendships and was capable of individual acts of kindness; a friend's mother wrote to his grandmother Lady Rosebery to say that her son, upset by leaving Eton, was consoled by Dalmeny, who asked him "to go to the early Communion with him and Wood[47] on Sunday morning; was it not thoughtful of him?"[48]

Eton had certainly made him pious and he was deeply moved by his last Chapel service there. On his confirmation he had told his mother that his unfitness caused him to dread the ceremony, which he regarded as "a high and holy privilege."[49] Even in the 1860s such sentiments were not common in teenage boys but they did not impress his mother who continued to regard him as both indolent and frivolous. The Duchess's views may have been

10

coloured by William Johnson's rather two-faced correspondence with her, in which he frequently condemned her son's lack of application, while praising his intelligence.

Matters came to a head between mother and son during his final year at school when the Duchess announced that he must leave Eton at Easter and miss his final summer half. Worse still she envisaged him being prepared for Oxford by a country rector at Revesby in Lincolnshire.[50] Her reasoning remains unclear but Dalmeny was so furious that over thirty years later he told his own eldest son that he never forgave his mother for attempting to curtail his Eton life. He enlisted the support of his Rosebery grandparents and naturally Johnson backed him in his struggle to stay; ridiculing the idea that a country clergyman could do better than a great public school. Seemingly the mother/son correspondence over this extraordinary incident has not survived but from a letter of the Duke of Cleveland's that has, it is clear that it was not the teaching at Eton but Dalmeny's dissipated life with his friends outside class:

Archie's case is peculiar ... if it had been my own son I should have taken him away, as it is clear to me that the passion for remaining ... arises from it not being a place of study as it ought to be, but of freedom, enjoyment and independence[51]

In this great battle of wills, the son triumphed, probably because of the intervention of his Rosebery grandfather, but the Duchess conceded both with bad grace and only on the condition that he went to Revesby Rectory for three months in the autumn. She also penned an extraordinary letter to her son on his eighteenth birthday that coldly stated:

I trust you will not let this last half at Eton be an idle one, with Mr Johnson or without him, & not let the golden days slip unimproved through your fingers.[52]

The Duchess's reference to Johnson's absence is explained by a line in the *Eton College Chronicle* for May 13 1865:

We are sorry to hear that Mr Johnson has been seriously indisposed, and will not be able to resume his duties as Master for some time.

It seems rather a curious coincidence that at the exact point Dalmeny won his victory by being allowed to return to the school, one of the chief protagonists quit the scene through illness.

In any event Dalmeny enjoyed one last glorious summer half in the school he would always remain devoted to. Following his final day he wrote in his diary for August 4th 1865: "I cannot take in that I am no longer an Etonian."[53] His younger brother Everard left Eton at the same time, although the Duchess would subsequently assert that her compliant younger son did so willingly[54] and was henceforth quite happy to be educated in isolation by a private tutor.

From Eton Dalmeny travelled to Raby Castle where a large house party soon took place. Most of the guests were of no interest to an eighteen year old but two previously unknown to him, Mr and Mrs Disraeli, aroused considerable interest. In the Castle guest book Disraeli gave his profession as 'patriotism' (his first Premiership was still over two years away) and he spent much time with his hostess's elder son later recording: "Dalmeny seemed to me very intelligent and formed for his time of life (not yet of age) and not a prig, which might be feared."[55] Mrs Disraeli flattered him at dinner by saying how sorry she was to hear, from her husband, that he was a Whig; a secret allegiance that he didn't wish his Tory mother to hear. At the conclusion of the visit Disraeli gave Dalmeny an inscribed copy of his 1852 biography of Lord George Bentinck. Many decades later he would tell Neil that Disraeli's Raby visit had started his political awakening.[56]

In late September Dalmeny left Raby for the obligatory stint at Revesby Rectory. On arrival he found other Old Etonians studying there and sarcastically told his mother "It is wonderful how they have improved since they left Eton."[57]

He arrived at Christ Church, Oxford in January 1866 and was there re-united with several of his Eton friends who had been resident at The House since October, the conventional matriculation date. Among them was his great Eton intimate Frederick Vyner who matriculated on October 13th 1865 alongside the Old Harrovian 3rd Marquess of Bute, who became a new friend of Dalmeny's.

During his first term he had his first brush with the Dean[58] for missing morning service in the Cathedral, then compulsory: "told him the morning was too cold. Very amiable," he later recorded.[59] This spirit of grand independence was probably aided by his annual allowance at Oxford of

£600. This figure his Rosebery grandfather set at the same amount he had given his eldest son when at Cambridge in the late 1820s. However it was still apparently considered excessive by the Duchess of Cleveland.[60] Spending heavily on entertaining his Oxford friends to the finest wine and food obtainable would cause him to quip "everything comes to an end, except an Irish grievance and an Oxford bill."[61]

Living as he was at the centre of the wealthy aristocratic set it unsurprisingly was not long before he was invited to join the Bullingdon Club with its culture of heavy drinking and raucous behaviour. The Bullingdon brought him into contact with future prominent politicians across the university: for instance Lord Randolph Churchill at Merton, and Lord Lansdowne at Balliol. However for all of his high living he continued to shine academically in the Modern History Honours School, passing his first University degree exam, Moderations, in November 1867 with plaudits.

Just prior to this exam an unusually long and warm letter arrived from his mother at Raby Castle inviting him to stand as the Conservative candidate at nearby Darlington. His firm and swift reply was that he was "not at all prepared to come forward as a Conservative". In continuing he attempted to soften the blow by raising the probable objection of his paternal grandfather, on both party grounds, and the expense of campaigning for a seat in the Commons which he would automatically lose when he succeeded to the Rosebery peerage.[62]

His words were prescient as Lord Rosebery died on March 4th 1868 leaving his young grandson his estates and title. Those estates comprised a profitable shale mining enterprise, over 21,000 acres of Midlothian and Linlithgow, Dalmeny House and a shooting lodge near Gorebridge, plus a 2,000 acre Norfolk estate at Postwick. It has been estimated that this legacy gave the undergraduate 5th Earl an annual income of £30,000.[63]

In May 1868 Rosebery turned twenty-one and took his seat in the House of Lords but his mother could not be gracious and wrote caustically days later: "I hold there is no perfect character without a grain of ambition and I cannot but regret its absence in you."[64] However her son was now completely independent of her and absented himself from her company. For the Easter vacation following his inheritance he took himself to Italy and found Florence "swamped with Cook's Tourists".[65] During the long vacation he visited Russia with his even richer Christ Church friend Lord Bute. He was back at Dalmeny House before his final year at Oxford began and entertained his Eton tutor William Johnson there. Johnson read one of his Oxford essays and after doing so reported; "He is very clever, and has a peculiar variety of the *haut ton*."[66]

At Oxford in November 1868 he witnessed the General Election that ended Disraeli's first ministry and first brought Gladstone the premiership on December 3rd. The election also put his future political rival William Harcourt into the Commons for the first time, as Liberal MP for Oxford; but as a peer, Rosebery was not eligible to vote for him. Rosebery's party allegiance was still not publicly declared and so when he received a letter at Christ Church from Lord Granville[67] in late January, asking him to second the Address in the Lords, after the State Opening, it was couched with the caveat "if you feel sufficient confidence in Gladstone's Government?"

In his reply, Rosebery disclosed that his private sympathies had been:

wholly enlisted in the Liberal cause for some years … I can never hope to be of the slightest use to the party, though I should be proud of any opportunity of showing my attachment to its principles.

However as to his performing the task requested, he declined on the ground that:

I am only a resident undergraduate of Oxford … and it might damage the Government if … the Peer who seconded the Address was a lad *in statu pupillari*.[68]

A further consequence of Rosebery's inheritance was a growing interest in the turf. In the summer of 1868 he first registered colours with the Jockey Club – primrose and rose hoops and a rose cap. Later that year he bought his first colt *Ladas*. His boast, that he intended to run him in the 1869 Derby and win, soon became the talk of Christ Church. When it reached the ears of the Dean he saw Rosebery and told him that such conduct would be in breach of Christ Church's statutes and unless he abandoned the plan, he would be sent down. As Rosebery was predicted to gain a First in Schools, both Dean Liddell and his tutor Mr Owen attempted to persuade him to postpone his plan until after his final exams, when he would be free to do as he liked, but this Rosebery resolutely refused to do. Therefore to the cheers of the

Bullingdon, the wails of his tutor, and the great regret of the Dean, he left Oxford degreeless at the end of the Lent term of 1869.

In time Rosebery came to regret his actions over *Ladas* but he doubtless enjoyed writing this to the Duchess of Cleveland:

> Dear Mother,
> I have left Oxford. I have secured a house in Berkeley Square; and I have bought a horse to win the Derby.
> Your affectionate Archie[69]

At the Derby, *Ladas*, in a field of 22 runners, trailed in last; perhaps unsurprisingly given his starting odds of 60/1.[70] After his Derby disappointment, Rosebery started to regularly attend the Lords and support the Liberal Government in votes. His sister Constance (now married to Lord Leconfield[71]) reported to the Duchess in July that:

> Archie seems to have taken a very strong Radical turn, which I am very sorry for. Henry has seen a great deal of him in the House of Lords, & tells me that he seems very cold indeed about racing.[72]

His disillusionment with racing did not last and in November 1870 he was elected to the Jockey Club. Racing also led him to purchase what became his favourite house, The Durdans, adjacent to Epsom Downs and close by the Derby course. He bought the house in May 1874 from the Heathcote family, paying £25,000[73], with the intention of starting a stud there. The place already had a racing pedigree, the 1838 Derby winner *Amato* being buried in the grounds[74], but Rosebery enlarged what he acquired and in 1881 built a spectacular indoor riding school. These improvements, following his marriage, were done as part of the consolidation of the Mentmore stud with The Durdans. In consequence breeding was confined to Mentmore but once the foals were weaned they went to Epsom to take advantage of the warmer and drier ground that the chalk sub-soil provided.

The house that Rosebery told his shocked mother that he had secured in Berkeley Square was No.2 and it remained his bachelor residence until his marriage nine years later. It was on the east side and overlooked Lansdowne House, which in time Rosebery and Hannah would rent before purchasing their own house on the west side of the Square. According to Robert Rhodes

James, Rosebery was troubled in 1873 by the Prince of Wales's Private Secretary asking if the married Prince could use his house to entertain his 'actress friends'. Rosebery, who was never intimidated by royalty, apparently replied that it was too small and he trusted the matter would not be raised again.[75] In 1874 he upset the Prince again with his choice of words in the House of Lords when attacking the principle of 'hereditary legislators'.[76]

Rosebery was first invited to dine with the Queen in May 1870 and after she noted "Lord Rosebery is pleasing and gentleman-like and wonderfully young-looking."[77] She probably felt differently in 1875 on reading his speech in the Lords attacking the proposal to give the Queen the additional title of Empress of India. Rosebery had ridiculed the idea that the title was only intended for use outside the British Isles and compared that idea to a medicine labelled "Poisonous for outward application only".[78]

In 1871 in a public speech in Edinburgh, Rosebery enraged his mother by using the term 'an isolated aristocracy' leading her to charge him with being a traitor to his own class. As previously, Rosebery saw no need to climb down to her saying in reply: "I maintain and no Liberal can say otherwise, that the House of Lords is isolated in sympathies from the country."[79]

In 1873 Rosebery crossed the Atlantic for the first time and after visiting Canada, travelled from New York as far west as Salt Lake City. In November 1874 he returned to New York and this time travelled south to New Orleans and spent Christmas in Cuba. Then in 1876 he went again for two more months. There are some indications that the visits fed his youthful radicalism and in one diary entry he wrote: "I am back in England. Miserably smoky and narrow as ever. Is it a dream that I have been in a country where all are born equal before the law?"[80]

One Lords speech in which he avoided controversy was when he spoke to second the Address at the opening of Parliament in 1871, two years after he was first asked. In a moving and much praised speech he spoke with great feeling about the recent siege of Paris. He had himself been in the city only months before the Franco-Prussian war began[81] and knew only too well that what he termed the centre of "luxury and deified pleasure" had since endured "bombardment and famine and death" and "had fed her population of epicures, on husks and rats". Turning then to the victorious new German Empire he expressed the prayer that "when this disastrous war is concluded she may use her great power in the interests of peace and civilisation."[82]

On 20 February 1874 Disraeli returned to office, following the general election, but his close relationship with Rosebery was unchanged by his being in or out of office: in 1870 the two had walked arm in arm up and down the gallery at Stratfield Saye and then in 1876 at a Marlborough House dinner the Prime Minister called Rosebery "dear child" and "pressed my hand against his heart".[83] Therefore Hannah's choice that he, by now 1st Earl of Beaconsfield, should walk her down the aisle before her marriage at Christ Church in Down Street, was an inspired one, and in no way unwelcome in her new husband's eyes.

1

FAMILY REASONS OBLIGE ME TO HURRY TO SCOTLAND

1882 was an eventful year for the Earl and Countess of Rosebery for it saw the birth of both of their sons and the perhaps unusually rapid completion of their family of four children. Two girls came first: Sybil in September 1879, and Margaret (always known as Peggy) in January 1881. Both boys were born at Dalmeny House – Harry on January 8th and Neil just over eleven months later on December 14th. The second birth inconveniently came in the midst of a crisis in his father's relations with the Prime Minister, marked by a flurry of letters between the two concerning Rosebery's threat to resign from office.[1] The sequence of letters also demonstrates Neil's protracted and difficult delivery: on December 6th Rosebery wrote to Gladstone from the Home Office, where he was serving unhappily under Sir William Harcourt as Under-Secretary, to tell him that "family reasons oblige me to hurry to Scotland tonight." Ten days later on December 16th, Rosebery, still in Edinburgh, took up his pen to Gladstone to offer the explanation that his "domestic anxieties" lay behind the interruption of their correspondence.

However geographically inconvenient and prolonged, Neil's arrival was not unwelcome; in March 1910 Rosebery would publicly confess in a speech to Neil's Wisbech constituents that he had loved Neil "ever since first seeing him in the arms of his mother".[2] His feelings for Neil were in great contrast to those he first felt for Harry, to whom it is said he took an immediate dislike on account of what he perceived to be pronounced Jewish looks.[3] Of course dislike of eldest sons and heirs was not then uncommon; Rosebery, who had himself suffered from his mother's great preference for his younger brother Everard[4], was merely following his mother's lead in always maintaining a preference for his second son.

The entire family remained in Scotland until after Neil was baptised on Sunday January 21st 1883.[5] He was given the additional names James and Archibald.[6] The christening ceremony took place privately in the newly restored great hall of Barnbougle Castle and was performed in accordance with the Book of Common Prayer by a former domestic chaplain to the 4th Earl.[7] In his choice of venue, rite, and celebrant, Rosebery neatly sidestepped the difficult dilemma of his being a practising Anglican when in England, while usually attending the Presbyterian Kirk in Scotland. Neil's three godparents were his great-uncle Bouverie Primrose, the Countess of Aberdeen, and the Earl of Northbrook, a former Viceroy of India, then serving in Gladstone's Cabinet as First Lord of the Admiralty.

In June 1883, Rosebery found he could endure being in the Home Office under Sir William Harcourt no longer and so he resigned. After enjoying a summer free of ministerial duties he and Hannah left in September for a seven-month tour of America and Australia. In their absence their young children were left in the care of Rosebery's sister, Constance Leconfield, and so spent most of the period of separation along with their nursemaids at Petworth House in Sussex. Rosebery seems to have taken the arrangement with his ever-adoring sister for granted, but Hannah sensitively wrote to her sister-in-law from San Francisco on October 20th to express the hope that Lord Leconfield was not "annoyed at having the children."[8] Rosebery considered this point to be the ideal moment to travel, while the children were too young to miss their parents or to require parental guidance.

The children were reunited with their parents at The Durdans on March 3rd 1884. Later that day Hannah wrote gratefully to Lady Leconfield that "the girls are very well and the boys enormously grown."[9] At Easter the family, still at Epsom, were joined by the Prime Minister and his wife. This visit was made notwithstanding Gladstone's distress at being informed by Rosebery the previous summer that he would only re-enter his government as a Cabinet minister. Gladstone had earlier confessed to his son that the only people who bothered him more "than all England are the Queen and Lord Rosebery".[10]

However, just as Gladstone when Prime Minister could not ignore his troublesome sovereign, he also could not neglect Rosebery. The die had been cast in 1878 when Gladstone, written off and nominally in retirement, had accepted Rosebery's invitation to stand for Midlothian (or Edinburghshire as it was sometimes called) and had then in his Midlothian election campaign of 1879-80 used Rosebery as his campaign organiser and Dalmeny House as his campaign headquarters. The triumphant outcome saw Gladstone returned not only to Parliament as MP for Midlothian but also to Downing Street as Prime Minister for the second time. The key role Rosebery had played in Gladstone's sensational return to power was known and acknowledged not only across the Liberal Party but the entire country and as such Rosebery was thenceforth literally indispensable to Gladstone.

In September 1884 Gladstone was again a guest of Rosebery's at Dalmeny House when his host suffered a bad fall while riding, that broke his collar bone and led to internal bleeding. The Prime Minister writing to Sir William Harcourt reported "Lord Rosebery suffers a good deal and is I grieve to say, though not alarmingly, seriously ill."[11]

Given the frequency of these Prime Ministerial visits, the Primrose children grew up almost lackadaisical about having Gladstone staying in whichever house they happened to be in. In December 1909, when he was Liberal candidate for Wisbech, Neil confessed in a speech[12] that his earliest memory was of being seated in a chair beside his father and Gladstone as they hotly debated Irish Home Rule over several hours; and, for so patiently and quietly enduring when he was not yet three years old, being rewarded with a photographic portrait of Gladstone that he still treasured.

Neil's infancy not only required him to sit still for long periods, for as soon as he was able to walk, he was expected to appear standing, in public, as part of the Rosebery family tableau. The first such occasion, reported by the *Leighton Buzzard Observer* on July 8th 1884, concerned the annual school fete of the Countess of Rosebery's School at Mentmore. The Wing town band played and tea was served at outdoor tables between games of croquet and cricket. The report continued "prolonged and hearty cheers were given by all upon the appearance of Lord and Lady Rosebery, with the young ladies, Lord Dalmeny and the Hon. Neil Primrose."

In January 1886 the same newspaper reported[13] the presentation of New Year's gifts by the four Rosebery children to both the Mentmore School children and elderly tenants on the Mentmore estate. Each child received a bun and an orange; and the old people "warm clothing, tea, and sugar from the same fair little hands."

In late July 1889 before reaching the age of seven, Neil and his brother Harry aged seven, in their father's absence but supervised by the Vicar of Mentmore, undertook the distribution of prizes at the annual Mentmore

Flower Show. The newspaper report records both boys' "unaffected manner and boyish high spirits appeared to enjoy the scene as much as anyone present."[14]

2

TOO HAPPY AMONG CHILDREN, BOOKS AND HOUSES

In the spring of 1885, almost five years after Gladstone's Midlothian triumph, Rosebery entered his Cabinet as Lord Privy Seal, with responsibility for the Office of Works tagged on. After attending his first Cabinet Rosebery quipped to Lord Northbrook that he found it "more numerous than the House of Lords and not quite so united."[1] This conclusion was prophetic as Gladstone's second ministry, which had been severely shaken by the news of General Gordon's death in Khartoum, was rapidly running out of steam. Rosebery had a strong personal interest in the Sudan as his brother Colonel Everard Primrose was serving with the ill-fated Gordon Relief Expedition. In March 1885 word reached Rosebery that his brother had fallen ill while camped in the desert with his battalion at Korti.[2] General Wolseley subsequently telegraphed that he hoped Everard would recover, but on April 8th he died of typhoid fever at Abu Fatmeh.[3] His adoring mother was distraught, but ironically it was a Rothschild connection in Egypt, and not the British Army, who ensured Everard's personal possessions were brought back to London and delivered to his grieving mother.[4]

Following a Commons defeat, Gladstone resigned on June 24th leading to Lord Salisbury becoming Prime Minister for the first time, albeit in a caretaker role pending the General Election in November. As in 1880 the Gladstones made Dalmeny House their home for the election campaign. Although Gladstone's constituency result massively increased his majority, the national outcome was indecisive and left the Irish Nationalists holding the balance of power. Parnell, the Irish Nationalist leader, was initially set to support the Conservatives but following the deliberate leaking of Gladstone's conversion to Home Rule for Ireland that situation changed.

Following a defeat in the Commons Lord Salisbury resigned and Gladstone became Prime Minister for the third time on February 1st. On the following day Gladstone offered Rosebery the post of Foreign Secretary. The offer represented a spectacular promotion and in accepting Rosebery was not undaunted, telling the Queen it was "too much" and his diary that he was like "a fly on a cartwheel".[5]

Rosebery's tenure at the Foreign Office was brief – a mere six months – although both the Queen and Rosebery's Conservative friend Lord Randolph Churchill thought he left with a much-enhanced reputation.[6] The same could not be said for Gladstone whose Home Rule policy had split his party – 93 Liberal MPs helped defeat their own government on the second reading of the Government of Ireland Bill, and the resulting 1886 General Election decimated the Gladstonian wing of the party: the Liberals were out of office for the next six years.

Rosebery took advantage of being out of office by travelling with Hannah to India. They left in late October and returned in time for Easter 1887.[7] As in 1883-4 the children were left under the care of Rosebery's ever-accommodating sister Lady Leconfield. In December 1886 Rosebery wrote to his sister from Agra saying: "We are enjoying ourselves greatly. The Taj Mahal is on the whole the most perfectly beautiful thing I have seen in the world and the remains of the Mogul Emperors are amazing."[8]

Following his return Rosebery confided in the editor of the *Scotsman* that far from longing to return to office, he was "too happy among children, books and houses to make public life anything but a sacrifice for me."[9]

That summer saw the celebration of the Queen's Golden Jubilee and the especially glittering London social season that surrounded it. This the Roseberys participated in from their palatial, if rented, London home Lansdowne House located in the south-west corner of Berkeley Square. Prior to its almost complete demolition in the 1930s to create Fitzmaurice Place and open the Square to Curzon Street, Lansdowne House was a detached 'country house in town' and easily the grandest residence of the Square.[10] The Roseberys had first rented it from Lord Lansdowne following his appointment as Governor General of Canada in 1883 but this was always a temporary arrangement pending the purchase of their own London home.[11] The latter was achieved in July 1887 with the purchase of 38 Berkeley Square, also on the Square's west side but further north between Hill and Mount Streets. Although without the architectural and historic distinction of

Lansdowne House, No.38 was as Lord Crewe later wrote "a fine and commodious *hôtel.*"[12] It was far more substantial than its single number implied, as it had recently been formed by the re-building of three previous houses (Nos. 36-38) to form a single five-story mansion. Although the house is no longer in existence, the 1950s office block Berger House, built on the same footprint, demonstrates its scale.[13]

Rosebery took a back seat in the process of selecting a new London home; in October 1887 he wrote "I left the matter absolutely to Hannah's decision for, as I hate London, it cannot matter much where I live in it."[14] Contrary to those words the location was perfect and it would continue to be Rosebery's London residence for the rest of his life. Neil too would grow most attached to the house and even after inheriting his own nearby Mayfair mansion he continued to live in Berkeley Square.

For all of Rosebery's professed dislike for the great city of his birth (he was born in Charles Street, Mayfair) he was soon to become very involved with London's governance. The Local Government Act of 1888 created the new County of London (carved out of Middlesex, Kent and Surrey) and the first London-wide authority to govern it. That authority was the London County Council (LCC) and Rosebery was elected as an LCC member in January and then on February 12th 1889 as the Council's first Chairman.

The role had a very heavy workload and on March 17th 1889 Rosebery told Herbert Bismarck: "London leaves me hardly a moment, except a Sunday at The Durdans. I have become a sort of beadle and never write a word except on drainage and street crossings."[15] While acting as Chairman, Rosebery was careful not to entirely neglect his children and was with them at Mentmore for his eldest son Harry's eighth birthday on January 8th 1890. However as the *Leighton Buzzard Observer*[16] subsequently reported the day was far from one of unalloyed frivolity:

Lord Dalmeny on his birthday distributed to all persons on the estate over 60 years, gifts of tea, sugar and clothing. To those residing at Mentmore, Lord Dalmeny, with his brother the Hon. Neil Primrose, carried the gifts to their cottages. With the young gentlemen were Lord Rosebery and Lady Sybil Primrose. Over 100lbs of tea, 200lbs of sugar, 60 guernseys and 50 flannel petticoats, formed this most liberal gift.

Although Harry had now reached the conventional age to go away to school, all of the Rosebery children continued to be educated at home. The boys' tutor, Francis Wylie[17] joined the Roseberys' household in 1888 after graduating from Oxford with a double first in Classics (Wylie came on the recommendation of the Master of Balliol, Benjamin Jowett, who had first cultivated Rosebery as a friend in 1885).[18] The girls were taught by their governess, Miss Vibert. Rosebery, who was always haunted by his first experience of school (fifty years after he first did so he wrote of "the joy and exultation of going to school – so quickly evaporated"[19]), was in no hurry to inflict it on his sons. So far as his daughters were concerned he would always disapprove of girls' boarding schools. An advantage of his reasoning was that the children could remain with their parents whichever of their houses they were living in. It also meant that Rosebery, notwithstanding his busy life, could supervise and monitor their tuition. A further advantage was that it gave Rosebery the freedom to take one or other of his sons with him on LCC business. In this way Neil was favoured with attending the opening of the new Manchester Square Fire Station, located in what is now Chiltern Street.[20] The new building could accommodate three engines and nineteen officers and firemen and was to serve as the principal station for the west of London. As the next day's *Morning Post*[21] reported, on the opening ceremony:

> three calls were made to test the alertness of the brigade. Within 30 to 40 seconds of the call, two engines, horsed and equipped left the station and made a round of the block. On the third call the youthful younger son of Lord Rosebery occupied a seat at the centre of the engine and evidently enjoyed the excursion.

Hannah also ensured that all of her children were included when they all attended Queen Victoria's visit to Waddesdon Manor (the recently completed Buckinghamshire house of Hannah's cousin Ferdy) in May 1890.[22] The visit was not entirely a private one as the Queen also visited Aylesbury. As a result she came in an escorted procession of carriages, containing a huge entourage, including two of her daughters, courtiers and both her Highland and Indian attendants. As well as being a very great honour conferred on the house of Rothschild, the spectacle in young minds would have been one that was hard to forget.

25

That autumn the family went north, as usual, for the shooting and stalking on the Dalmeny estate and it was there on October 7th Hannah became unwell with what was soon diagnosed as typhoid fever. The condition was then untreatable and often fatal and, as it was not understood exactly how it was transmitted, Rosebery swiftly evacuated his children from the main house to Barnbougle Castle. There they remained while the fever took its lengthy course, with the tragic outcome that they never saw their mother again.

On October 18th Rosebery informed his sister Constance: "Hannah's temperature is 104 and it has been high for 24 hrs. But I do not think she is worse."[23] Gladstone's anticipated visit was cancelled and he and his wife stayed in Edinburgh instead. On October 25th Rosebery was told to prepare for her death that night and in a note he sent to the Gladstones in Edinburgh he asked them to "pray for me and the bairns" and Hannah, knowing how ill she was, charged Rosebery with never neglecting the children.[24] The next day she improved but then relapsed into delirium on November 13th. On the following day the Queen wrote from Balmoral to express her anxiety for both the patient and Lord Rosebery; she added "I know this terrible illness so well that it enables me to understand all the fluctuations of hope and fear that are dealt."[25]

Hannah died on November 19th and although Rosebery's sister Constance had by now been at Dalmeny for many weeks, helping to nurse Hannah, Rosebery was at first too distraught to communicate with her directly; and so while sitting with his wife's corpse wrote: "I cannot tell you now, or perhaps ever what you have been to me in this long agony. And now I ask you – by Hannah's deathbed – to be a mother to her motherless bairns."[26]

In his diary Rosebery described Hannah's last breath, following 50 days of fever, as "a gentle sigh of rest, almost pleasant to hear." He continued with what happened next:

I went down to the Castle and watched a beautiful dawn of melting fog until it was time to see the children. I first told the boys when I heard chattering. Neil cried bitterly but Harry was quiet. With the girls, Peggy sobbed painfully, Sybil whispered into my ear at once, 'I must be a mother to them'.[27]

3

I AM HERE WITH NOBODY AND NOTHING BUT THE CHILDREN

On the first evening following Hannah's funeral, Rosebery and the children left London for Mentmore[1] and there they remained for many weeks. Rosebery shared his pain in returning to the place with Hannah's old nurse: "We must go to Mentmore at once, or I shall never go there again; for every inch of it will be painful; so the plunge must be taken without delay."[2]

For Christmas Rosebery sent his favourite sister Hannah's locket which contained two photos, one of Harry and one of Neil, and expressed the hope that "you will sometimes wear it in memory of my darling."[3]

In the interval between Christmas and New Year, Rosebery wrote an unusually warm letter to Sir William Harcourt, who had just before Christmas sent a letter of sympathy: "At first, one was dazed by the hundreds of letters one received ... now the sympathy of one's friends comes with double healing power, for the senses are clear and the loneliness infinitely greater. I am here with nobody and nothing but the children."[4]

In mid-December Rosebery had written to his close friend Reginald Brett: "I should greatly like to see you, if anybody. But the fact is I am antigregarious just now, and perhaps morose."[5] However grief stricken and lonely Rosebery was, he remained punctilious about observing the traditional festive custom of giving gifts to his elderly Mentmore tenants. Accordingly on New Year's Day 1891 the elderly assembled in front of the house to receive the usual gifts of food and clothing from Rosebery's four children. The *Leighton Buzzard Observer*[6] records that Rosebery "remained out of sight" but speculated that he "doubtless observed the scene from an upper window."

In mid January 1891 Rosebery left for Italy travelling alone and semi-incognito as 'Mr Rose'; while he was away he sent his sons, accompanied by Francis Wylie, to Brighton, while the girls and Miss Vibert went to The Durdans. On the eve of his departure he explained to his sister "I am going off tomorrow ... the train should take me to Milan & leave me there with the world before me ... The Boys are at Brighton ... Neil was assuming the appearance of a stale crumpet, so I thought I would try the chain pier."[7] From Italy he went to Greece and at Marathon visited the place where his Eton and Christ Church intimate, and probably his first love, Frederick Vyner, had been murdered in 1870.[8]

He returned to England in time for his wedding anniversary, which he marked by taking his daughters on a visit to Hannah's grave. On a lighter note he returned with facial hair, prompting his eldest daughter to compose a letter to Aunt Constance which all four children signed, asking her to use her influence to get him to "remove his whiskers."[9]

Rosebery's restlessness was not over and in April he went to Portugal and Spain and then to Austria and the health spa at Gastein. From there on July 16th Rosebery wrote a letter to Gladstone in which he gloried in his isolation: "3,500 feet above the sea and 3,500 miles from public life."[10] While abroad Rosebery received the unwelcome news that Francis Wylie had accepted the offer of a lectureship at Balliol and so would be leaving his post as Harry and Neil's tutor at the end of August. Rosebery, who remained unwilling to send his sons to school, once again enlisted the help of Benjamin Jowett to find a successor, and informed his sister on July 11th: "It was a terrible relief to hear that Jowett thinks he knows of a suitable successor to Wylie for I attach immense importance to that appointment."[11]

Although much deprived of his company, Rosebery's children were not entirely deprived of treats as the *Daily Telegraph* noted on June 26th "the Rosebery children have been staying at the Granville Hotel, Thanet, for the past fortnight." While in Thanet the children were principally under the supervision of Wylie and Miss Vibert, but for several days they were joined by Aunt Constance who reported on her visit to Rosebery, now in Vienna. From there on July 26th he responded: "I was delighted to receive your letter of the 20th. It was very good of you to go to Ramsgate and your visit must have been an incalculable joy to the children."[12]

Aside from the boys' tutor and the girls' governess, the other person standing in loco parentis in his absence was Rosebery's private secretary Neville Waterfield[13]. Waterfield had joined the Rosebery household in the summer of 1890 and so had shared with the entire family the traumatic tragedy of Hannah's illness and death. Thereafter he was a long and friendly fixture in their young lives, and much relied upon by Rosebery who would appoint him his Assistant Private Secretary at the Foreign Office in August 1892[14] and then to the same role at 10 Downing Street in 1894. In 1898 Raymond Asquith recorded his view that Waterfield's good looks had first got him the job and that "inclines one to believe the worst of his illustrious master."[15] Waterfield certainly had no great academic credentials. From the *Eton Chronicle* it seems his success at Eton was confined to the playing fields (running and football). At Oxford he failed his Honours Moderations in 1885, and so only obtained a Pass degree in 1887. He left Rosebery's employ in 1903 and subsequently became Secretary to the Oxford University Appointments Committee. He would remain a bachelor until he married in February 1922 at the age of 57 – he died childless and a widower in August 1940.

Benjamin Jowett's correspondence sheds further light upon Rosebery's 1890 quest for a private secretary[16], and may perhaps explain the University gossip that Raymond Asquith was aware of. It discloses that Jowett had proposed Speaker Peel's eldest son whom he considered "very able" and who had attended Balliol and obtained a second-class classics degree in 1889. For unexplained reasons Rosebery rebuffed the proposal and went on to appoint Waterfield. The unsuccessful Peel would go on to enter Parliament in 1900, the Cabinet in 1922, and in 1929 be created Earl Peel.[17]

The final illness of his elderly step-father brought Rosebery back to London in August, so as to be with his mother.[18] Following the Duke's funeral at Raby Castle, Rosebery wrote to the Duchess at Battle Abbey (now her dower house) to say that their grief and common widowhood had at last brought them closer together.[19]

In September the boys' new tutor Hyla Holden[20] arrived at Mentmore from Balliol College where he had just graduated. He passed Rosebery's initial assessment and after a few weeks he reported to his sister Constance: "I think him a success but it is difficult to shine in the wake of the incomparable Wylie."[21]

In the final months of 1891 Rosebery's public seclusion gradually reduced; in October he stayed along with Harry and Neil, with the Gladstones at Hawarden Castle.[22] In November he, with Harry, Neil and Peggy, attended a lecture on Dickens's characters held in the schoolroom at Mentmore.[23] After Christmas he took the children to Petworth House on a visit to his sister; a surviving letter demonstrates that four of his servants accompanied them – his valet, a footman to look after both boys, and a maid each for the girls.[24] Although Neville Waterfield was spending Christmas with them, Rosebery reluctantly left him behind at Mentmore as he explained to his ever-obliging sister: "I hardly like to propose a tenth guest, but I know you like him … and we are all extremely devoted to him – but I cannot come like a horde of locusts."

They were back at Mentmore for January 8th when he was present on the terrace at Mentmore for the usual presentation of gifts and to hear Neil publicly express his thanks to the school children for the kind wishes they had sent him on his ninth birthday (December 14th 1891).[25]

In January 1892, as in the previous year, Rosebery departed for Italy where he spent a month between Rome and Naples. On his return to Mentmore he found a local outbreak of flu: "I found the children remarkably well. In a month they have been entirely under Mr Holden. He is now down with influenza and they will now be entirely under Miss Vibert! Who is now better."[26]

Not until the spring of 1892 did Rosebery tentatively resume public life by agreeing to be an entirely passive candidate for East Finsbury in the LCC election. Only after being elected by a substantial majority did he first address and thank his electors at a public meeting held in the Clerkenwell Road on March 14th.[27]

At the end of June the General Election came and Gladstone arrived in Edinburgh for what was to be his final Midlothian election campaign. Rosebery brought Neil, attired in a kilt, with him to the station platform to welcome the Gladstones to Edinburgh, and then conveyed them to Dalmeny House in his carriage.[28]

This was the Gladstones' first visit to Dalmeny since Hannah's death and Rosebery showed them her bedroom which had been left untouched, in an echo of Queen Victoria's treatment of the Prince Consort's. Having got through the ordeal of doing so, Rosebery allowed his children to first enter the hallowed shrine as he subsequently told his sister: "I took the children to Hannah's bedroom today as I wanted to get it over. Sybil cried a good deal."[29]

The fortnight's campaign suffered from both bad weather and an ailing[30] 82-year-old candidate. The result was a massive fall in his majority from 4,361 to 690.

Rosebery, who had told his sister on July 10th "If you could only guess what I am enduring here"[31], now recuperated from the strains of Gladstone's re-election campaign by taking a cruise of Scotland's western isles, and for the second part of it Harry and Neil accompanied him.[32] They were back at Dalmeny on August 1st and three days later the Liberal politician John Morley noted the happy domestic scene in his diary:

Dined at seven with the children at the table. They were delightfully merry. To see Rosebery with them is to blot out his singular flaws and leave him wholly loveable.[33]

The national outcome of the 1892 General Election was that the Liberals had done far worse than had been expected and, as a result, Lord Salisbury clung on as Prime Minister until defeated in the Commons on August 13th. Two days later the Queen reluctantly sent for Gladstone, who with Irish Nationalist support would form his fourth and final ministry. After much pressure and prevarication Rosebery agreed to serve as Foreign Secretary and travelled to Osborne with the rest of the new Cabinet to accept the seals of office. After Rosebery had kissed the Queen's hand she said "It is so long since I have seen you and you have gone through so much" before adding "I hope the work will be good for you."[34]

The Queen's hopes were rapidly fulfilled; the demanding workload seemed to both improve his geniality and eradicate his self-centred morbidity. Rosebery's children as well as his colleagues were the beneficiaries. Almost two years had passed since Hannah's death and Rosebery's insistence on the children only being dressed in black mourning clothes started to attract criticism[35] and was relaxed.

However, in the case of his sons, Rosebery made a far more important change to their former regime by deciding, with some reluctance, that the time was now right for them to go to school. Although not completely clear, it is possible that Rosebery was driven to the decision by Hyla Holden's resignation – at this time he returned to Balliol to study for his Bachelor of Divinity degree, pending his ordination.

Rosebery selected a private preparatory school in Farnborough which was then a small town. The headmaster was the Rev. George Carter[36] MA who had been head since 1887 and would remain in post until 1906, when he ended his teaching career and took on the easier life of a country vicar.

Rosebery enrolled both of his sons together to start in the January term of 1893. One attraction of Farnborough was not very far or inaccessible from The Durdans which now became his only regular place of escape from London.

Although Harry was now aged 11 and Neil 10, Rosebery still regarded them as little boys as he recorded in his diary entry:

January 20th – The little boys rather low. Neil got me to read The Sick Stockrider to him, – a poor consolation, as he had wept the last time I had read it [a melancholy Australian poem by Adam Lindsay Gordon]. We dined all five together, – not cheerfully.

January 21st – We all spent a miserable makeshift morning, but boys very brave. I made all the children write their name in my bible, (Harry for the first time as Dalmeny) and read John chapter xiv. Then I went and bought the boys bibles, and frames to hold their parents' portraits. At last at 3.25 they went off. Shall I ever forget the cab with the precise initialled new luggage on the top?

In January 1893, Rosebery and Gladstone were in the midst of a crisis over the government of Egypt as this further diary entry for Saturday January 21st discloses:

Before the Cabinet yesterday I sent the boys to Mr Gladstone to ask for his blessing before going to school. It was a touching and beautiful sight. They, and I think he, deeply moved. Alas – five minutes afterwards he and I were hammer and tongs over Egypt.

Rosebery also recorded in a letter to his sister that "the Boys were spendidly brave and so was Peggy, who has some latent heroism, but poor Syb sobbed on their necks."[37] However, her tears may not only have been over parting; she and Peggy were never permitted to escape their governesses for school.[38] They were also allowed very little female or indeed any society – a month after Harry and Neil went away, Sir William Harcourt stayed at The Durdans and noted his was the first entry in the visitors' book since the previous November, four months earlier.[39]

At Farnborough, just as later at Eton, Harry distinguished himself on the sports field. According to his biographer, while at his prep school Lord

Dalmeny "won the half-mile and the Man-at-Arms trophy and was Captain of Cricket and Football."[40] Neil, more sensitive, intellectual and of a weaker and smaller frame, did not shine at games. That he did not do so, is confirmed by a line in his *Eton Chronicle* obituary: "never very strong, he won no great success in athletics at Eton".

During the holidays the boys were re-united with their sisters and, subject to his onerous workload, their father. Their school year was ended early in July 1893 by an outbreak of diphtheria at Farnborough and they started the summer holiday quarantined at The Durdans. On account of this Rosebery vacated the Foreign Office and based himself at Epsom, for, as he explained to his sister, they "have no one but me to look after them."[41]

Once their period of quarantine was over Rosebery left his children at Mentmore where the annual flower show[42] was taking place, while he took a rest-cure at Bad Homburg. While there Rosebery narrowly escaped being horse-whipped by the Marquess of Queensberry. Queensberry had convinced himself that the Foreign Secretary was engaged in a homosexual relationship with his 26-year-old son Viscount Drumlanrig, and since July had been writing repeated and threatening letters to Rosebery. Two weeks after Rosebery arrived in Bad Homburg, Queensberry followed him there and wrote again, threatening the whip. While this confrontation never came to pass, the episode could scarcely have had greater potential to become a scandal: the Prince of Wales was staying in the same resort and involved himself by persuading Queensberry to calm down and leave for Paris. Nothing was reported in the British press and Rosebery attempted to joke about it in a subsequent letter to the Queen: "It is a material and unpleasant addition to the labours of Your Majesty's service to be pursued by a pugilist of unsound mind."[43]

Rosebery did not share with the Queen the full detail of the charge of homosexuality, although from his own memorandum of the incident it is clear that he was aware that the deranged marquess had told all and sundry in Bad Homburg that Rosebery was a "boy pimp and boy lover."[44] Rosebery could also not deny that the entire embarrassing episode, and the far worse events that were to follow, stemmed from his own foolish promotion of the young and pretty Francis Drumlanrig – known to his intimates as 'Francy' or 'Drummy'. There was a family link in that Francy's maternal grandmother was Lord Leconfield's older sister, but it was her estranged husband Alfred Montgomery[45] who doted on his eldest grandson and first introduced him to

Rosebery at his house in Hertford Street, Mayfair. Alfred Montgomery was a notable wit and gossip and, notwithstanding his marriage, was always considered a 'confirmed bachelor' by Victorian society; and the muscular Lord Queensberry would always attribute his sons' effeminacy to their Montgomery blood.

Montgomery's claim to fame was his appointment in 1830, when aged just 16, as private secretary to the Marquess of Wellesley (elder brother of the Duke of Wellington) - a position he retained for twelve years until Wellesley's death.[46] Now an old man, he apparently wanted Francy to replicate his own career by serving as Rosebery's private secretary. The plan came to fruition in November 1892 when Rosebery appointed him to join Neville Waterfield as an additional assistant private secretary at the Foreign Office.[47] On appointment, Drumlanrig was a junior officer in the Coldstream Guards, without civil service or diplomatic experience. Educated at Harrow and Sandhurst he was described as "very good looking, with fair hair and blue eyes. It was quite pretty to hear him … the sort of dear little fellow you could not help loving."[48] In addition to both Waterfield and Drumlanrig, Rosebery had the services of the career diplomat Francis Villiers[49] who the Foreign Office assigned to him as his Private Secretary in both 1886 and 1892-4. Quite why the Foreign Secretary required two assistant Private Secretaries as well during 1892-4 remains unclear.

Unsurprisingly, eyebrows were raised, but when within six months, and at the extraordinarily young age of 26, Drummy was raised to the peerage as Baron Kelhead[50], and then a month later given a place in the Government as a Lord in Waiting to the Queen[51], the rumour mill was set spinning. This is reflected in the London newspapers: the editor of the *St James's Gazette* wrote on June 9th: "For a week the world has been wondering why Lord Drumlanrig was made a peer. He is young, inexperienced and – Lord Rosebery's private secretary." The following day the *Graphic* was reporting that Rosebery "desires to have a secretary in the House of Lords for his own convenience. This is one explanation of the circumstances which is current."

Of course - as the newspapers also reflected - it was Gladstone, suffering from a serious shortage of Liberal peers, who was ultimately responsible for the further promotion of Drumlanrig; but as they wrote at the time, in the absence of Rosebery's favour, it was inconceivable that the young army officer would have risen so far and so fast. Far more serious than society and newspaper gossip was the reaction of Drumlanrig's father, who had long nursed the grievance of being excluded from the House of Lords by his fellow Scottish peers[52] – they had declined to elect him as one of the sixteen of their number to sit in the House of Lords. At first Queensberry merely felt snubbed at being overtaken by his son, but then convinced himself that Rosebery had both seduced, and then rewarded his son for sexual favours.[53]

Gladstone's Home Rule Bill passed the Commons in September 1893 but within days suffered a massive defeat in the Lords on its second reading. Rosebery had led for the Government in the Upper House and it was felt he had performed poorly. Perhaps it was clear that his heart was not in it: he had earlier told the Queen that he did not consider the measure "a panacea for the secular ills of Ireland" but given the margin of defeat 419 votes to 41, however Rosebery had spoken would not have changed the result.[54]

As Rosebery's sons returned to school for their second year at Farnborough, it was becoming clear that Gladstone could not long continue in Downing Street. At the year's end he turned 84 and was barely able to read. In contrast Rosebery was only 46 and *The Times* had recently called him 'an over-worked Atlas'.[55] Rosebery's relative youth was a sensitive matter as his only serious rival to succeed Gladstone was Sir William Harcourt, the Chancellor of the Exchequer. Harcourt was twenty years older and had been elected MP for Oxford when Rosebery was an undergraduate there. In Liberal Party terms Harcourt was Gladstone's natural successor, but on account of his rude and bullying manner was unacceptable to the rest of the Liberal Cabinet, and more importantly to the Queen.

Gladstone presided over his final Cabinet on March 1st 1894 and two days later the Queen asked Rosebery by letter to become her Prime Minister, informing him: "he is the only one of the Liberal Government in whom she has any real confidence and she earnestly presses him to undertake this task for a time, at least for her sake and for the good of the country."[56] Sir William Harcourt – and perhaps more so his highly ambitious and scheming only son Lewis (always known as Loulou, and then acting as his father's private secretary) – did not take well to being overlooked. These feelings worsened on March 3rd when by a Privy Council mix up, Sir William was led into the Queen's presence alone, and so assumed he was to be asked to form a government.[57] By this mistake the Queen was, perhaps un-characteristically, most amused; but it only served to add to the rancour between Rosebery and both of the Harcourts, and made for a bad start to his premiership.

The official ceremony of kissing hands that formally made Rosebery Prime Minister took place in the afternoon of March 5th at Buckingham Palace. Rosebery entered into his new role with solemnity and mindful of Hannah's absence: earlier in the day attending the 8.30am Communion service at Christ Church in Down Street, the church where they had been married.[58] The days of Prime Ministerial children attending the initial and final Palace audience were then very far off and Neil and Harry were away at school. Later that month on coming home for the Easter holiday they saw their father for the first time as Prime Minister, but as Rosebery did not initially move from Berkeley Square to live in Downing Street, the change in his status probably had little impact upon their lives. The Premiership also made no difference to Rosebery's lack of sociability, as is confirmed by his Easter Day 1894 letter to his sister at Petworth in which he confirms being alone with the children.[59]

Towards the end of the Easter holiday, Rosebery took Neil on a visit to Gladstone at his house at Dollis Hill, and recorded in his diary: "April 18th – Drove with Neil to see Mr G. at Dollis Hill. Mr G. in bed ... Neil asked for his blessing and received it."[60]

4

I HAVE TRIED EVERY OPIATE

Rosebery's premiership rapidly went awry and many of the reasons it did were foreseeable. Firstly he was handicapped in Parliament because he was stuck in the overwhelmingly hostile House of Lords. Had he had a loyal lieutenant acting for him in the Commons this may have been mitigated; but acting in his place as Commons Leader, as well as Chancellor, was his difficult rival Sir William Harcourt. His already poor relationship with Harcourt worsened over the budget. They clashed over the introduction of inheritance tax and Harcourt, who won the tussle, was both rude and patronising over Rosebery's lack of financial knowledge and understanding. Less predictably Rosebery had trouble adopting the right tone in his speeches; and then there were Foreign Office issues, which his chosen successor Lord Kimberley struggled to deal with. More damagingly the rest of his Cabinet colleagues sensed that he was not comfortable in, still less enjoying, the role.

The sole significant ray of sunshine came on June 6th 1894 when he became the first Prime Minister in history to win the Derby with his horse *Ladas II*, although even that success annoyed the nonconformist puritan wing of the Liberal Party. Rosebery was even condemned from the pulpit by a Congregational Minister in Blackburn and Neville Waterfield was given the task of brushing off such criticism in a terse letter in response that was released to the press.[1]

Curious as it may now seem, Rosebery found that he had more free time than when he was Foreign Secretary (because he was less prone to receiving a steady stream of despatches from all around the globe) and Harry and Neil were not neglected during that summer's school holidays. He took both of them with him to Dunrobin Castle to stay as guests of the Duke of

Sutherland; en route there, they paused at Culloden Station to view the battlefield.[2] He also took both boys with him to the Doncaster Races, where they witnessed their first Classic, the St. Leger, and stayed as guests of Viscount Halifax at Hickleton Hall.[3]

However, even a year after the unpleasantness at Bad Homburg, it appears that the Marquess of Queensberry was still causing trouble over Rosebery's relationship with Viscount Drumlanrig. Edmund Backhouse (admittedly dismissed by one of Rosebery's biographers as a "pathological sexual fantasist and fraudster"[4]) asserts in his memoirs[5] that, after leaving Bad Homburg, Queensberry was determined to find proof that Rosebery and his son's relationship was sexual; that during the summer of 1894 his private detectives had obtained the evidence of two maids who had changed the sheets of the bed that Rosebery and Drumlanrig had shared in Bourne End, Buckinghamshire; and that he was now threatening to publicly expose the Prime Minister. That Queensberry's detectives were capable of dredging up such sordid details is demonstrated by the subsequent Oscar Wilde trials, when evidence relating to the state of Wilde's bed at the Savoy Hotel was given in court.

The idea of this threat is corroborated by a letter in Rosebery's surviving correspondence with his sister[6], which indicates that Rosebery was being threatened, or blackmailed, in early October 1894. The context of the letter was that Rosebery had been compelled to leave Dalmeny House, where his sister was staying, on account of the First Sino-Japanese War and the need to be in London to see Foreign Office telegrams from China and Japan concerning the same. The letter is dated October 10th 1894 and uniquely his location is merely given as 'London'; it reads:

I am in a bad way. I have slept my first nights out of London, at Durdans and Newmarket, as I am afraid of the knocking here – I have some hopes of getting away tomorrow night.[7]

Exactly what he meant by the "the knocking" is not explained but surely it refers to an unwelcome and persistent nocturnal caller at his house in Berkeley Square.

The effectiveness of any threat of exposure would obviously be diminished if Drumlanrig married, and in fairness Drumlanrig had spent the summer season of 1894 attempting to find a wife. (He also absolutely refused during that summer to dine in public with his younger brother Lord Alfred Douglas and Oscar Wilde, despite his younger brother imploring him to do so.)[8]

He first pursued Pamela Wyndham but she had apparently heard the rumours surrounding his sexuality, and turned him down.[9] Within a couple of weeks he proposed to and was accepted by Alix Ellis, daughter of Major-General Arthur Ellis, equerry to the Prince of Wales.[10] Although un-provable, the engagement bears all of the hallmarks of a hastily hatched plan by the Prince and Rosebery, to avert a sensational national scandal. Loulou Harcourt wrote in his diary: "Drumlanrig is going to marry General Ellis's daughter, it makes the institution of marriage ridiculous".[11]

News of the match led to more society gossip as General Ellis had no money to provide his daughter with a marriage settlement.[12] On the day of his engagement Drumlanrig wrote to Rosebery saying: "I hope that you will not consider that marriage is likely to impair the efficiency of a private secretary or that it is a crime to be visited with as heavy a penalty as lack of moustache on a military attaché".[13]

Perhaps in a sign of just how precipitate the engagement was, Edward Stanley, Conservative MP for Bridgewater and the uncle of Alix Ellis, agreed to host a shooting party at Quantock Lodge, his Somerset estate, so that Alix's family, including General Ellis and her brother Gerald, could get to know her new fiancé.[14] None of them could have anticipated what happened next.

In the afternoon of October 18th, following the shoot's luncheon break, Drumlanrig (who had gone off alone, as he had explained, to look for a winged bird shot before the break) was found dead beside a hedge with his head covered in blood. His shotgun lay across his stomach and he had died from a single gunshot through the roof of his mouth.

According to General Ellis who wrote to Rosebery on October 22nd there was no issue over the engagement prior to Drumlanrig's death: "Drummy was devoted to you – as well you know – and so proud to serve you and to earn your good opinion." Ellis continued that Drummy was: "The most loveable youth I ever met. No wonder my poor child was fond of him. They would indeed have been a bright and happy couple and quite devoted to each other. She is just now stunned by the news and turned into stone by the sudden shock."[15]

Certainly the conspiracy theories and gossip were further fuelled by the absurd verdict of accidental death that was reached by the Coroner's jury. The inquest took place within days and was held in the same house where the shooting party had taken place. The local doctor who had attended the scene gave the clear evidence that the shot had passed through the roof of the mouth and that Drumlanrig's mouth was open at the time. That it was, was also consistent with the evidence of the other guns who testified that the sound of the single shot had been strangely muffled and 'deadened'.[16] Of course the suicide of any house-guest of the local MP would amount to a considerable scandal; but when that guest was a young aristocrat with a place at Court, and closely connected to the Prime Minister, it was far easier for the local jurors to find the death a tragic accident. Few were taken in, and even Queen Victoria, who over the past year had got to know her young and attractive Lord in Waiting, immediately raised the validity of the verdict with Rosebery.[17]

It is also material that two days after Drumlanrig's death Rosebery was the victim of a hoax telegram that implied his resignation, and which was leaked to the press. The telegram purporting to come from Rosebery was sent to the Hôtel des Anglais in Nice and sought to reserve eight rooms for his use and announcing his arrival for the following day. The telegram was first reported in *Reynolds's Newspaper* (then a Sunday scandal sheet) in a small report and without comment as to its astonishing implications. On the following day the *Pall Mall Gazette* informed its readers: "The hotel manager was regretfully compelled to the belief last evening that he had been made the victim of a practical joke. Lord Rosebery is currently the guest of Lord and Lady Tweedmouth at Ninewells, Berwickshire." Any normal father whose son had just shot himself would not busy themselves with writing hoax telegrams, but Lord Queensberry was not a normal father, and even at his son's funeral was described as being jaunty, clown-like and full of bravado.[18]

On the same day as the hoax telegram was sent, Queensberry sent Rosebery an abusive and threatening letter, in which he threw the blame on him, that father and son "have parted without reconciliation" and that "this bad blood between us was made by you."[19]

Having lost his eldest son, Queensberry's obsessive focus turned to preventing what he viewed as another impending tragedy, involving the relationship between his third son, Lord Alfred 'Bosie' Douglas, and the author Oscar Wilde. The consequent sequence of events would lead to Wilde's conviction and public disgrace.

Given Queensberry's behaviour, it was impossible for Rosebery to attend Drumlanrig's funeral and burial in the family vault at Cummertrees near their Kinmount estate. He did though send a wreath[20] and Neville Waterfield to represent him. Rosebery was not the only reluctant absentee at Drummy's obsequies; Oscar Wilde sent flowers with Bosie to lay on his brother's grave.[21]

Following the funeral a group of Drumlanrig's friends organised a memorial subscription but Rosebery, seemingly now anxious to distance himself from the affair, asked his sister to "inform privately who ever is responsible for the Drumlanrig memorial that I will not subscribe ... I have send 50£ in memory of the poor boy to the Evelina Hospital for sick children which I thought the best thing to do."[22]

Whatever his private feelings over Drumlanrig's death, as Prime Minister Rosebery had no option but to carry on as normal, and as if nothing very untoward had happened. His sudden resignation was of course unthinkable; it would have ruined his reputation, the Queen would probably have refused to accept it, and what possible pretext could the nation and Empire be given for it? Mercifully when he first heard news of the shooting he was in the remote seclusion of the private country house of the Lord Privy Seal[23]. However on October 25th he re-appeared in public at the annual Cutlers' Feast in Sheffield. Next, on the day following the funeral, Rosebery made a major speech in Bradford that was intended to re-launch his wobbly ministry. Its subject was the reform of the House of Lords and the pressing need for a Commons resolution against the Lords. However the speech was not a success and *The Times* recorded of it: "Lord Rosebery has no plan. He does not even have a resolution." The Queen was enraged by what she termed "that violent speech".[24] More seriously for Rosebery, his own Cabinet were divided, with some favouring abolition, and within a month the whole idea of an anti-Lords resolution was shelved. The Government's lack of direction began to be reflected in by-election results that cheered the opposition and led Chamberlain to say to Balfour "what a pricked bubble Rosebery is".[25]

As usual, Rosebery spent Christmas 1894 with his children at Mentmore.[26] As soon as the New Year dawned he was separated from them by a visit to Sandringham where the shooting continued despite deep snow.

In the following week he was summoned to Osborne by the Queen, leading him to complain to his sister: "these Royal commands intended kindly, fall very cruelly".[27] After two nights at Osborne he returned to find a telegram from Petworth announcing that his favourite nephew, George Wyndham, was gravely ill with typhoid fever. Rosebery telegraphed back "I am grieved beyond measure please keep me constantly informed" but there were to be no more bulletins as George died two days later on January 13th.

George Wyndham was 26 and Lord and Lady Leconfield's eldest son. Educated at Eton and New College, Oxford, he had gained a second class honours degree in Modern History in 1890. At his death he was serving as a Lieutenant in the Grenadier Guards and the newspapers recorded that the Prime Minister "had a high estimation of his talents and prospects."[28]

On hearing of his death Rosebery confessed to his sister that he and his children felt "stunned and stupefied"[29] and all four children wrote separate letters of condolence to their favourite aunt. Harry wrote of "the terrible news which Papa told us last night. It was so awful that I could hardly understand it at first." Sybil in her letter looked back to her mother's death in 1890: "I earnestly wish we could be with you now and try to be to you what you were to us nearly 5 years ago." Neil's is perhaps the most emotionally buttoned up and written in the same precise and tiny hand that he retained as an adult:

> My darling Aunt Connie,
>
> I am sure you know how hard it is to express one's grief into words, but I know you will understand what I feel without my expressing it.
>
> Your loving nephew,
> Neil

Rosebery now cleared his diary and hurried to Petworth to comfort his distraught sister and in consequence missed that week's meeting of the Cabinet.[30] However as the funeral clashed with the National Liberal Federation annual meeting at Cardiff, that Rosebery was due to address, he was reluctantly compelled to miss the funeral and left Neville Waterfield to represent him.[31] En route to Cardiff, Rosebery's train stopped at Swindon from where a telegram was despatched to Petworth saying: "You know how my sympathy is with you all on this terribly trying day."[32]

As Ossa piled upon Pelion, Lord Randolph Churchill died the following week aged 45, and four days later Rosebery led the political elite at his Westminster Abbey memorial service.[33]

Amid all this tragic loss and grief, there was no improvement in his political fortunes and on February 19th, Rosebery was so exasperated by his divided and unsupportive Cabinet that he threatened it with his own resignation. This ultimatum led to a flood of letters of support and two days later Rosebery withdrew his threat, but any revival of his authority over the Cabinet was, within days, negated by his own illness.

Following a Royal dinner party at Windsor Rosebery became seriously ill with flu and by February 25th he was bed-ridden at The Durdans. Although he rapidly recovered from the flu-like symptoms he then started to suffer chronic insomnia, followed by depression and anxiety - even admitting to suicidal thoughts. The Cabinet met without him on March 11th and on March 21st his friend Reginald Brett found him worse than he had been the previous week. Brett recorded that Rosebery complained of loneliness and they discussed his re-marriage as a solution, but Rosebery feared being the victim of a fortune hunter.[34]

News of Rosebery's illness now got into the press and *The Times* predicted his resignation was imminent. Loulou Harcourt was jubilant and wrote in his journal: "What a purgatory he is suffering! I would like to be one of his nurses watching him pass through it."[35] By early April he was somewhat better but there were setbacks of sleeplessness. His anxiety was probably not helped when, on the second day of the claim for criminal libel that Oscar Wilde had mounted against Lord Queensberry following his "posing as somdomite" [sic] card, Rosebery's name came up in open court. His name was in a letter Queensberry had written referring to Wilde as a "damned cur and coward of the Roscbery type" that was read out.

Perhaps fortunately, Easter 1895 fell in the middle of the month of April, meaning that Neil and Harry on returning from school were spared from seeing their father at his worst. It remains unclear how aware Sybil and Peggy were of their father's condition, although for part of the illness his sister took them away to Petworth.[36] Even his devoted sister Constance was not permitted to remain at his side; his physician Sir William Broadbent took charge and two nurses were engaged to look after him.[37] This may have been to ensure that neither his family nor the regular servants fully witnessed his condition. Neville Waterfield also acted throughout his illness as the Prime

Minister's loyal gatekeeper, ensuring that his Cabinet colleagues were kept away and so remained unaware of the full extent of his incapacity.

A few days after Easter he was well enough to be catching up with neglected despatch boxes and to contemplate returning to London, writing: "One of the drawbacks of my indisposition is the chronic chaos of papers" before joking "I have tried every opiate but the House of Lords and that experiment must soon be undertaken."[38] When he did return to Downing Street, he lived there as, at the time he became ill, he had already arranged to close up his Berkeley Square house for repairs.[39]

In May Rosebery completed his convalescence with a week's cruise on the Admiralty yacht, going along the south coast to the Scilly Isles. On his return he was found to be in good spirits and they were raised still further when his horse *Sir Visto* gave him a second Derby win on May 29th. Loulou Harcourt who Rosebery had by now correctly characterised as a "serpent" wrote: "Damn the fellow! He is invincible - on the turf."

His Government, however, was not invincible, and in the Commons on June 21st it was defeated on a vote of censure of the Secretary of State for War, which arose from the allegedly inadequate supply of cordite to the army. The next day the Cabinet, almost with relief, agreed to resign and Rosebery went to Windsor to inform the Queen. In his final days, while Lord Salisbury was given time to form the replacement government, Gladstone came to a dinner in Downing Street. On June 28th Rosebery was back at Windsor for his farewell audience. The Queen made him a Knight of the Thistle, a rare honour as he already had the Garter. She also gave him a large marble bust of herself for, whatever their political differences, the Queen regarded him personally with great fondness.[40] That evening he visited Hannah's grave but he was not unhappy, and prompted by his sons' return from school, told his sister on July 7th, that he felt "like Harry or Neil on the sudden proclamation of a whole holiday."[41]

5

ETON

At the unusually young age of 48, Rosebery had joined the small and exclusive club of ex-Prime Ministers. However he remained leader of the Liberal Party and as the Queen acceded to Lord Salisbury's request for a General Election and Parliament was dissolved for it on July 6th, his party leadership could be expected to matter. Rosebery saw things differently and after a spat with Lord Salisbury in the Lords on the day of dissolution, left London with his children, for Scotland. As his house in Berkeley Square was still filled with builders and workmen, he had been attending the Lords as a commuter from Epsom. On July 11th he wrote to his mother from Dalmeny House, to say how pleased he was to be among the 'London homeless': "It is a rapture to feel that one has no pied-a-terre in London, and so a valid excuse for remaining in the country."[1]

In earlier General Elections Rosebery had had the task of entertaining the Gladstones, but in 1895 there was a new Liberal candidate for the local Midlothian constituency and it seems Rosebery thought this an opportune moment to leave his elected colleagues to their fate, and flee the scene. In consequence he chartered a large yacht, the *Santa Cecilia,* and made himself entirely unavailable by taking a cruise of the Western Isles. He, both boys, and his secretary Neville Waterfield boarded the yacht on the Clyde and sailed first for Arran. They then took in Ailsa Craig and Jura.[2] On docking at Oban, Rosebery received the, to him, joyous news that Sir William Harcourt had been defeated in his re-election campaign at Derby, and that Loulou had been seen "looking like a piece of blotting paper that had been rained upon for a week."[3] In a letter from Orkney to his sister, he informed her that he had "slept like a hibernating animal since embarking ... and the night after I wrote to Sir W. Broadbent from Portree I slept 7 and a half hrs without waking."[4]

Rosebery considered the overall election result, which left the Unionists with a majority of 152, not only inevitable, but cathartic; as in his view it was positive that his party had been "purged as by fire".

The all-male cruise party returned to Dalmeny Park on August 12th and were re-united with Sybil and Peggy[5]; Rosebery apparently considering that yachts were no place for his motherless daughters. Perhaps to make up for the neglect of his elder daughter her sixteenth birthday was celebrated with considerable ceremony at Dalmeny on Saturday September 14th. All of the estate workers, their wives and children were given dinner in the riding school, which had been specially converted into a dining hall with the Rosebery family seated on a raised dais. Toasts were drunk to the Queen, Lord Rosebery and each of his four children separately. As the *Linlithgowshire Gazette* noted "all of the toasts were drunk with enthusiasm."[6] Afterwards athletic sports were held in the grounds and Lady Sybil presented the prizes.

Following this celebratory weekend, Rosebery and his sons travelled south. Their destination was Eton. That Rosebery had chosen his old school for his sons is unsurprising; his son-in-law Lord Crewe later wrote that for all of his honours, being an Old Etonian was what mattered most to him.[7] In Liberal Party terms the choice was not controversial as Gladstone had attended the school, and Rosebery in his first summer as Prime Minister had attended the Fourth of June celebration as a guest of the Provost.

As in the case of their prep school, Rosebery insisted that Harry and Neil were kept together in the same Eton house. That house was Cotton Hall, only built fifteen years earlier and set in spacious grounds on the north side of Eton Wick Road. Its well-established House Master was Walter Durnford.[8] Durnford's background and own education would have been most acceptable to Rosebery. His father was an Eton contemporary of Gladstone's who had married the daughter of a famous Eton headmaster, Dr Keate, and who was then Bishop of Chichester. His uncle F.E. Durnford (universally known to the boys as "Judy") had been Lower Master or deputy head throughout the time Rosebery was in the school.[9] Walter Durnford himself was a schoolboy at Eton at the same time as Rosebery, although unlike Rosebery was a King's Scholar and so in College; he had then gone up to King's College, Cambridge and after a brilliant result in the Classics

Tripos had been elected a College fellow. However in 1870 he chose to return to Eton as an assistant master. Despite this brilliant academic record, Durnford was not intimidating and according to *The Times* "treated the boys as equals and recognised their independence".[10] The same newspaper also recorded that "his house was one of the best known and best managed in the place" and given that assessment it is unsurprising that Rosebery was content to entrust his young sons (Neil not yet 13) into his care. The arrangement doubtless also suited Durnford by bringing him firmly into Rosebery's elevated orbit – it was to be posthumously written of Durnford that: "the obscure perhaps attracted him less."[11]

After leaving his sons at Eton, Rosebery only perfunctorily re-engaged with politics, before making a lengthy trip to Spain that lasted until the boys' term at Eton ended. Christmas was as usual spent at Mentmore and after it some of his former cabinet members tried to persuade him into political activity, but the response that came back was 'Mentmore is unyielding'. His disillusionment with politics was deep rooted and the wounds he felt he had suffered at the Harcourts' hands very slow to heal.

As Rosebery later confessed, ideally he would have resigned the Liberal Party leadership after the 1895 General Election but that was not possible "without incurring the reproach of deserting the party at a period of unusual depression." As his sons returned to Eton for their second year Rosebery decided that he could endure the Liberal leadership no longer and in a dramatic press release on October 7th 1896 informed the nation that "the leadership of the party, so far as I am concerned is vacant, and that I resume my liberty of action."[12]

Gladstone, who had almost been a surrogate grandfather to Rosebery's children, died in May 1898. They had last seen him the previous September when Rosebery took all of his children to visit him while he and Mrs Gladstone were holidaying in Perthshire.[13] As his children's relationship with Gladstone meant much to Rosebery, he ensured that Neil and Harry came up from Eton to attend his Westminster Abbey funeral.[14] At it, sitting alongside their sisters, they witnessed their father act as one of the ten pallbearers. Also serving in the same capacity was Sir William Harcourt; and the two leading Liberals were mirrored by the two leading Conservatives, the Prime Minister, Lord Salisbury and the Commons Leader, Arthur Balfour. In a very singular tribute leading the coffin carriers was the Prince of Wales together with his son the Duke of York.

The same year saw the death of Baron Ferdinand de Rothschild and again Rosebery ensured that his sons attended his memorial service held at the Central Synagogue in Great Portland Street.[15] Ferdy, as he was referred to in the family, had continued to take an affectionately avuncular interest in the Rosebery children after Hannah's death, and had had the four of them to stay at Waddesdon in April 1894.[16] In his will, Ferdy left Neil (and Harry) £5,000 to which they gained access on their coming of age.[17]

Even after Rosebery ceased to have a prominent role in party politics, his and his children's peregrinations between his houses remained fixed: Christmas at Mentmore, Easter at The Durdans and late summer to autumn in Scotland, so as to shoot and stalk on his Scottish estates. Outside these fixtures and once free from political office, Rosebery spent weeks at a time away in southern Europe. In 1896 he even missed the Derby (and the Prince of Wales's victory with the horse *Persimmon*) by being in Spain.[18]

In the following year, Rosebery's frequent wandering, and indecisiveness as to whether he preferred Spain to Italy, were stilled by his purchase of the Villa Delahante, at Posillipo on the Bay of Naples. Rosebery had known and loved the area since his youth and had visited the Villa Delahante with his wife in 1882, recording in a letter: "Hannah was amazed and stupefied by the beauty of the place".[19] Fifteen years later the Villa, which had two guest annexes, a small pavilion at the water's edge, and its own small harbour, was his for £16,000. His Eton friend Eustace Neville-Rolfe was Consul General at Naples and not only smoothed the purchase but also supervised the place in Rosebery's absence.

An early problem that co-incided with the purchase was the arrival of Oscar Wilde and Bosie at a nearby villa. Rosebery had been tipped off by the Prince of Wales that Wilde was living at a nearby villa; and in a panic wrote to Neville-Rolfe: "A letter I received from the Prince this morning makes me fear that the villa will be uninhabitable. I am told that Oscar Wilde himself is next door".[20] In early March 1898 Rosebery received word from Rolfe that Wilde had left Naples for Paris (Bosie had left some months earlier), and that he was now 'safe' to make his first visit to the Villa as its owner. Thereafter Rosebery would spend a significant part of each year at Naples, and once Neil left Eton, he would frequently accompany him.

At Eton on the final Saturday of the 1899 Lent half, Neil and Harry were confirmed, in the chapel, by the Bishop of Oxford. Although they were just two among 170 school confirmation candidates, their two names were uniquely reported in the national press.[21] By being singled out their celebrity status, even in the rarefied precincts of Eton, was confirmed.

At the end of the Easter holidays the boys' names were again prominently reported in relation to their sister Peggy's marriage to the Earl of Crewe. The marriage was opposed by the bride's grandmother on the ground that Peggy was much too young;[22] but, as with his own marriage in 1878, Rosebery ignored his mother's objection, and the wedding took place in Westminster Abbey in front of 600 invited guests on April 20th. Neil and Harry's role was to escort the Prince of Wales to his stall on the south side of the choir.[23] Outside the Abbey, Rosebery's continued popularity with the London populace was highlighted by the huge and cheering outdoor crowd. The street vendors made a killing by selling them real, or cheaper artificial, primroses, and that day's *London Evening News* was even printed on primrose-yellow paper.[24]

Following the wedding the boys returned to Eton and what for Neil was to be his final term there. That unexpected turn of events came about due to the sudden early retirement of his housemaster Walter Durnford. Durnford had for long been "sorely chastened by his enemy the gout"[25] but in the summer of 1899 he decided that he could, given the persistency of his attacks, no longer continue at Eton. Because he remained unmarried, and still held his Cambridge fellowship, he retired to live at King's, and there he would eventually become Provost.

As the 1899 summer half at Eton ended, Neil was 16 and ordinarily would have expected to spend two more years at the school, but in an extraordinarily indulgent move Rosebery permitted him to leave; having determined that a private tutor would now prepare him for university and the career in diplomacy that had apparently already been decided upon.[26] Rosebery's decision about Neil is still more surprising because he was content to leave Lord Dalmeny in the school, by switching to a new house[27] for his final year. This was a real break between the brothers who had hitherto been raised and educated like twins, but in Rosebery's defence, the outcomes justified the decisions. Dalmeny had recently been elected a member of the Eton Society[28] and in his final year would rise to become its President.[29] He would also gain entry to Sandhurst from Eton's army form[30], and would gain considerable sporting accolades by playing both in the 1900 Eton v Harrow cricket match and by captaining the winning Collegers v Oppidans Wall Game.[31] Neil on the other hand was not sporting and if he was to be prepared for university at home, this was probably the best point to make the break from school. Given Rosebery's love of Eton and his great fury when his mother tried unsuccessfully to remove him from there in 1865, it seems certain that Neil wished to leave the school. Neil had grown fond of Durnford, and his humorous pose "that made coercive discipline un-necessary".[32] That he had is demonstrated by his subsequent attendance of re-union dinners for members of Durnford's Eton house in both 1910 and 1911; and perhaps starting over in a new house held no appeal. For Rosebery, removing Neil from Eton risked embarrassment, as it implied that he did not trust another housemaster to care for his younger son. However the significant attraction of having Neil back at home and as his close companion eclipsed all other concerns.

The person Rosebery selected to tutor Neil privately was Francis Wylie who had last had the role eight years earlier, in 1891, when he had departed for Balliol College as a lecturer. In the interim Wylie had become a fellow of Brasenose, and so the role was perhaps somewhat beneath him, but the 33-year-old bachelor don was generously rewarded by Rosebery for his teaching services. The arrangement also enabled him to travel abroad in considerable style at Rosebery's expense, and enabled him to share in the princely comforts that those staying in Rosebery's houses enjoyed. It also gave him favourable exposure to Rosebery, and their connection would soon lead, via the Cecil Rhodes Trust, to the transformation of Wylie's life and his legacy.[33]

For almost two years Wylie would supervise Neil's tuition, alongside his own College teaching, and would travel abroad with him in University vacations[34], so as to improve Neil's modern languages.

One obvious drawback of Neil's private tutoring was that it very largely removed him from the society of boys of his own age. It also put him in close daily contact with his father, then most unusual in upper class society. In fact the only significant relief Neil had from his father's society was when out hunting, an activity Rosebery disliked. Neil's enthusiasm for hunting, which he shared with his brother, started young. By the age of sixteen Neil had become a dedicated and regular participant in the Whaddon Chase Hunt, which was the closest to Mentmore.[35] In consequence, after leaving Eton, Neil would now spend more of the hunting season at Mentmore, pacifying his father with the excuse that there he was not inaccessible to his Oxford tutor.

Given that Rosebery had already determined that Neil's future lay in international diplomacy he exposed him as much as possible to the international elite. This process had started in 1898 when Neil had accompanied his father to the Queen of Holland's coronation.[36] During Neil's final summer before going to university, Rosebery and Neil entertained the German Crown Prince at Dalmeny House and took him sightseeing in Edinburgh.[37] Prince Wilhelm, who would be the last German Crown Prince, was just a few months older than Neil, and when the War came would be given command of the German 5th Army in France.

Rosebery's privileged position also exposed Neil to life in British embassies, such as Rome in March 1901.[38] From Rome father and son went south to Naples, where they spent Easter, before travelling in the British battleship *Caesar* to Malta to stay with the Island's Governor, Sir Francis Grenfell.[39] The centrepiece of the visit was a Review of the Mediterranean Fleet in which over 11,000 sailors took part.[40] After the Royal Navy had returned them to Naples, Neil went to Geneva where, on the ending of the Oxford term, Francis Wylie joined him. Neil was in Geneva when his grandmother the Duchess of Cleveland died in Wiesbaden on May 18th.[41] The Duchess was in Germany to undergo eye surgery and died quite suddenly of heart failure a few days after the successful operation.[42] Rosebery repatriated her body and she was buried next to her second husband at Staindrop in County Durham. Poignantly fate decreed that she died in the same year as her lifelong friend Queen Victoria, whose birth year (1819) the two women also shared. A few years earlier Raymond Asquith met her at Dalmeny House; exaggerating her age, described her as "a painted relic of the first Empire in a marvellous state of preservation: face like a well bred parrot and not a single grey hair on her head."[43]

Earlier in 1901, in January, Lord Leconfield died at his London home, 9 Chesterfield Gardens, and three days later a special train carried his body to Petworth where he was buried on January 10th. Rosebery and all four of his children joined Lady Leconfield on the train and stayed at Petworth for the funeral.[44] That they did so was unsurprising; Lady Leconfield was their favourite aunt and Rosebery's children were also fond of their numerous Wyndham cousins, including Charles[45] who now inherited the Leconfield title and estates.

In the early months of 1901 Rosebery and Neil needed to decide upon and then apply to the Oxford college that Neil was to take up residence in that October. It seems that Rosebery specifically ruled out Christ Church on account of his own 1869 defenestration when an undergraduate there; but two of Neil's Wyndham cousins George and Hugh[46] had each attended New College and obtained BA Honours degrees in Modern History. George had tragically died of typhoid fever in 1895 but Hugh, who was far closer to Neil in age, had obtained his Oxford degree in the summer of 1899. It was probably his influence (and also possibly that of Neville Waterfield who had studied at New College 1883-87) that persuaded Neil and Rosebery that New College was the college to apply to.

The first step was to apply to the Warden who in 1901 was the nonagenarian James Sewell. He had obtained his fellowship in 1827 and had headed the college since 1860. In January 1903 Sewell died in the Warden's Lodgings and was buried in the Cloister.[47] Despite Sewell's long tenure and age, he was apparently not a bar to progress and by the end of the nineteenth century the college had been transformed from a 'Wykhamist backwater' into one of the University's top four colleges. The man usually credited for this transformation was the energetic former Dean and soon to be Warden, William Spooner.[48]

Neil's application to the elderly Warden was approved and he was invited to attend the college in order to sit the college's own entrance exam. He was successful in the exam, held in late May 1901, having travelled from Geneva to Oxford with his tutor Francis Wylie to take it.

6

OXFORD FRESHMAN

In September 1901 Rosebery and both of his sons were re-united in Scotland for their annual autumn shooting holiday. In early October, Harry returned to Sandhurst for his final session there, while Neil went up to Oxford and into residence at New College. Before he did so Rosebery needed to decide upon the amount of Neil's annual allowance. To help decide he wrote to his sister Constance Leconfield and asked her to "tell me confidentially what allowance Hughie had at Oxford."[1]

Neil's matriculation before the Vice-Chancellor was reported in the press, alongside the rather misleading words: "The Hon. Neil Primrose who has studied abroad for the last two years is expected to enter the diplomatic service."[2]

In his first term Neil was required to and did pass Responsions (the University's entrance exam) but otherwise the indications are that Neil did not settle quickly and happily into Oxford[3]; he struggled socially, and also intellectually with the new and unfamiliar subject of law that he had opted to study. Perhaps given his previous cossetted life, returning to an academic institution after two years out of school was a shock. Neil, who was always prone to shyness, was also for the first time very much on his own: unlike at Eton and prep school, Harry was not there with him; neither was his father, with whom he had spent the bulk of the last two years. Neil also no longer had a known and trusted personal servant at the end of a bell-pull. So far as his Eton contemporaries were concerned, they had not seen him for over two years and may have resented the heavily gilded and much reported life that Neil had enjoyed, while they completed conventional schooling. Further negative factors were probably that the standard of college accommodation, and the food and drink, could not compare to those his father had provided.

Neil did have Wylie nearby at Brasenose but he was not a law tutor and could now only offer Neil moral support, plus perhaps a quiet word to his new tutors.

As Neil gladly returned to his father after his first term, Rosebery was using the Government's Boer War problems, and the Liberal Party split that the War had provoked[4], to attempt a remarkable political comeback. He did so in a much anticipated speech at Chesterfield on 16 December. Neil was at his side and had accompanied him there in a special train from St Pancras.[5] Rosebery's speech provided a patriotic beacon of hope to a war-weary nation, unsettled by military failure and government ineptitude. He also provided an alternative to the perceived unpatriotic, even anti-imperialist, Liberal leadership of Henry Campbell-Bannerman. As a result the *Daily Telegraph* wrote: "there is nothing remaining for Liberalism but complete submission" to Lord Rosebery's leadership.

In January 1902, prior to returning to Oxford, Neil and his father stayed with the Duke and Duchess of Sutherland at their Staffordshire seat, Trentham Hall. During the visit Henry Asquith, also staying with the Duke, made a major speech to 5,000 pottery workers at Hanley. Rosebery, not wanting to upstage his former Home Secretary, stayed put at Trentham, but Neil attended, and was discreetly seated with the rest of the Duke's party in a balcony seat overlooking the main audience.[6] Early in his speech Asquith, trying to bask in the warm-afterglow of Rosebery's speech at Chesterfield, told the audience that Neil was present among them. He probably rapidly regretted doing so, as the audience started to shout "put him up" and "come to the front" and only when Neil moved down and sat next to him on the platform could Asquith continue.[7]

The extraordinary enthusiasm for Rosebery's younger son in the Potteries probably encouraged Rosebery to take Neil with him for a major speech he made in Liverpool on February 14th when he called for a clean slate in Liberal domestic policy and the abandonment of Irish Home Rule. However for Neil the far more important speech of the day was the one he made after lunch at the Junior Reform Club. His exact words were not reported but his delivery was praised in the *Pall Mall Gazette*[8] as being "with an ease and readiness which recalled to many Lord Rosebery's feats of oratory in his younger days." Henceforth the press dropped their prediction of a diplomatic career for Neil, in favour of one in politics.[9]

What Neil's Oxford tutors made of his much publicised Liverpool trip, made during term time, is not known, but it certainly raised the profile of the nineteen-year-old undergraduate within the University. Because of it, Neil was sought out by another aristocratic undergraduate at Christ Church, Thomas Agar-Robartes. Thomas was the eldest son and heir of another Liberal peer, Viscount Clifden. Although Lord Clifden's wealth was modest in comparison to Rosebery's, his Cornish estate at Lanhydrock included lucrative mineral rights that cushioned him from the prevailing decline in agricultural rents. In fact Lord Clifden's mineral wealth had enabled him to purchase a second great landed estate, that of Wimpole Hall, Cambridgeshire in 1894.

In several respects Neil and Thomas's rapidly-formed, and soon devoted, undergraduate friendship was unusual. Thomas was over two and a half years older than Neil[10] and was two years ahead of him within the University.[11] By the early months of 1902, Thomas was both a popular and prominent undergraduate, and unlike Neil, highly socially confident, to the point of ebullience. They had overlapped at Eton but given their age gap and difference in Houses[12] there is, unsurprisingly, no evidence that they knew each other there.

It is though clear that Thomas knew Lord Dalmeny at Eton as both first became members of Pop in May 1899.[13] Given this coincidence it may be the case that Rosebery prompted Harry to write to Thomas in Oxford and ask him to take his unhappy younger brother under his wing. Equally Thomas may have approached Neil unprompted, after initially seeing him as a bridge to his famous father.

The weeks of that year's Oxford Lent term were highly eventful ones in terms of Liberal Party politics: on February 24th, Rosebery at a meeting in his Berkeley Square home launched the Liberal League, with himself as President, to promote his own sectional, right wing form of Liberalism. Neil was an early member and Thomas, who was never converted to Irish Home Rule and always shared Rosebery's Whig-tinged strand of Liberalism, soon joined.

Amid the rather frenzied politics of the spring of 1902, Neil was expected to pass his first year Law Prelims (Honours Moderations) in May. The Easter vacation was meant for revision but Neil accompanied Rosebery and his sister Peggy to Paris where they stayed at the Hotel Bristol[14] then located in the Place Vendôme and a firm favourite of both Rosebery and of King

Edward VII. Paris though was only a staging post for Cannes, where they embarked on Rosebery's new steam yacht *Zaida*. Prior to his purchase of the yacht in November 1901, Rosebery, who found cruising helped his insomnia, had periodically chartered boats, but from now on he (and Neil) would spend far more time cruising on his yacht. The *RYS Zaida* was a twin-screwed schooner of 350 tons that had been built in Cowes a year earlier by Messrs. J S White.[15] At 150 feet long and 23 feet wide, with a captain and crew of seven, she easily held her own among the era's super-yachts and Rosebery would cruise her extensively across the Mediterranean.

On this maiden voyage with Rosebery on board, the *Zaida* went from Cannes to Corsica, and then on to Naples, which the party found too sweltering to stop at, and so proceeded via Capri to Sicily. From there they returned to a more clement Naples, before going on to Marseilles and then by train via Paris to London.[16] Neil was just back in time to return to Oxford and sit his exams. Unsurprisingly given his spring schedule, Neil scraped a pass but before he had his results, and before the term was out, he left Oxford to accompany his father to Leeds where he was to make a major speech at the Coliseum. A week ahead of the speech the *Evening Standard*[17] carried the rather pompous announcement that "Mr Neil Primrose has intimated from Oxford that he will attend his father's speech in Leeds".

By this point Neil evidently confided to his father that he feared he may have failed his law exams and as a result it was agreed that Neil would effectively start again the following year, studying Modern History as Rosebery had done almost forty years earlier. Sanction for this switch was obtained from Herbert Fisher, who had been a fellow of New College since 1888 and who would now supervise Neil's study of English and European history from the fall of Rome into the 19th century.[18] Fisher, who in 1925 would be elected Warden of the College, was seemingly a sympathetic tutor to academically undistinguished, but socially prominent undergraduates. He had in the summer of 1902 just finished teaching Waldorf Astor who would be awarded a fourth class degree in that year's Modern History Final Honours School.

However Fisher was no pushover and Neil was given a long reading list for the vacation and possibly a warning that he would not be given another chance. On hearing this news Rosebery wrote from The Durdans: "I want you to get a coach for part of the Long Vacation. Get someone you like. I will pay."[19] Rosebery also stamped upon Neil's idea that he would rather live in shared Oxford lodgings with Thomas: "I want you to go back into College at any rate for a year. I think it is half the battle at Oxford."

Neil's term ended with the usual festivities including a New College Ball attended by 600 in a vast marquee erected in Holywell Quad and at which Neil and Waldorf Astor acted as stewards.[20] Just before the College ball, Neil also attended his first meeting of the Bullingdon Club, to which Thomas had recruited him and of which Thomas would be the following year's president. Rosebery had also been a member in his own undergraduate days, and at Thomas's prompting, Neil tried to get his father to come – seemingly but for it clashing with the Court ball at Windsor he would have done.[21] A year later, in June 1903 Neil and Thomas had more success, as Rosebery's diary entry discloses: "We dined at the Bullingdon dinner in the barn. I sat next Agar-Robartes the president, with Neil next to me."[22]

7

HE HAS NO IDEA WHAT WORK IS

For the first part of the long vacation, Neil was mainly in London with his private tutor at Rosebery's house in Berkeley Square. London did not entail a complete separation from Thomas, as Viscount Clifden's London house was also in Mayfair, just a few minutes walk away at 1 Great Stanhope Street (since re-named Stanhope Gate). Once Rosebery was no longer detained in London by attendance in the House of Lords, he and Neil again joined the *Zaida* in the south of France and visited Tunis, before spending reading time in the Alps, at Courmayeur.[1] As usual September was spent in Scotland and father and son visited the King at Balmoral[2], where, following Queen Victoria's death, smoking was permitted in the drawing room. Another guest at the Castle was Winston Churchill, Conservative MP for Oldham and then flirting with Rosebery's dream of forming a new centre party. Churchill left Balmoral with Rosebery and Neil, and then stayed on with them at Dalmeny House.[3]

In October Neil returned to Oxford and started his history degree course under Herbert Fisher's tutelage. During this repeat first year of Neil's, Rosebery clearly involved himself and took care to cultivate Fisher, by entertaining him at both Berkeley Square and The Durdans, and by frequently corresponding with him.[4] However the evidence is that it made little difference to Neil's lack of application to study. Thomas was now in his fourth and final year at Christ Church, and a poor role model as is confirmed by Lord Clifden being told by his son's despairing tutor: "I have done my utmost for him."[5]

That year Thomas not only served as Bullingdon Club chairman but was also Master of the University drag hounds and spent much of term time out hunting. He was also reported in the press as being with Neil at term time race meetings far from Oxford, such as Warwick[6] and Bath. Perhaps Thomas had concluded that even attempting to obtain a degree in that year's Finals was hopeless following his tutor's verdict that: "he rushes wildly at a paper without thinking of what he is putting down."[7]

At the end of term the pair were separated when Neil went to Mentmore for that year's Christmas festivities. These included the Christmas Fat Stock Show in Leighton Buzzard at which Rosebery exhibited his beef cattle. Following the show a dinner was held and Neil was given the job of proposing the health of the ladies. In his brief pre-toast speech Neil joked that: "he could not understand why his name was coupled with this toast for he was an undergraduate at Oxford, where he was pursuing that purity in high life to which so many strove after but did not succeed in attaining."[8]

For the New Year, Rosebery and his three unmarried children went north to Edinburgh and there over several days Harry Dalmeny's coming of age was lavishly celebrated. The first event was a birthday ball for 400 in Edinburgh at the Assembly Rooms.[9] The following night Rosebery held a Tenantry Dinner and then, the night after that, the shale miners employed by Rosebery's Dalmeny Oil Company were entertained in the estate's riding school.[10] Amid the evening celebrations the 21-year-old subaltern in the Grenadier Guards[11] received deputations from Queensferry town and the local parish councils. Rosebery gave them all lunch and both Harry and Neil made speeches. Neil's was in response to a toast to the Rosebery family and the press did not hide the common assessment that Rosebery's younger son was far the better public speaker.[12]

Back in Oxford, Neil continued to hunt in term time; even returning to Mentmore during the week for a meeting of Lord Rothschild's Staghounds, and a ball there.[13] When the hunting season ended, there were point-to-point races. First came the Oxford University races and then a fortnight later the Oxford and Cambridge Steeplechase was held at Ledburn, to the north of Mentmore. Both Neil and Thomas were present and rode in some races.[14] Rosebery, on seeing the press reports, was rather sniffy about what he termed "these hunt races" but had "no serious objection so long as they do not take too much of your time and you do not particularly disgrace yourself or break your neck."[15] During the Easter vacation Lady Sybil married Charles Grant, an officer in the Coldstream Guards then serving as regimental adjutant. Grant had recently served in the Boer War and married in uniform, wearing his South Africa medals. It was a far more modest affair

59

than Peggy's and took place at Epsom, with a special train from Waterloo bringing the London guests. The *Daily Telegraph*[16] noted that both Neil and Harry, who received the guests at Christ Church, wore ties in their father's racing colours and buttonholes of wild primroses.

At the end of May, Rosebery had the rare pleasure of reading in *The Times*[17] that Neil and Thomas had done something he did approve of – attending an Oxford University Liberal League meeting, addressed by Sir Edward Grey. Both Neil's current tutor Herbert Fisher and his previous tutor Francis Wylie also attended.

Thomas's final term at Christ Church was one of particular exam-free hedonism. In June he was the centre of the traditional Bullingdon Club photo taken in Christ Church's Canterbury Quad. Neil is shown in Bullingdon dress next to Thomas, with Thomas's younger brother Francis also present.[18] Later that month Thomas played in the Varsity polo match: Cambridge were trounced by 14 goals to 1. So while Thomas left Christ Church without a degree he had at least gained an Oxford polo blue.

Neil's term ended with Herbert Fisher's lengthy vacation reading list, and the suggestion that he did the reading in a quiet but pleasant town in Burgundy. When Rosebery learnt this, knowing well of Neil's inability to apply himself alone and un-supervised, sent off the following deceptively light hearted letter to Fisher:

> Neil tells me that you recommend him Chatillon as a good place for a spell of reading. But would it not be well for a tutor – some pleasant going fellow who has just taken honours – to be with him and guide his studies?[19]

The person selected to guide Neil's studies was Noel Skelton, who had just left Christ Church with a second in Modern History in that year's Final Honours School.[20] Skelton was a college contemporary of Thomas's and this, as well as being a Scot[21], may have helped with his recruitment. Although Skelton was not in the high-living Bullingdon set, he had some profile in the University and evidently had come to the attention of the controversial Balliol junior dean and tutor in Modern History, F.F. 'Sligger' Urquhart. This is apparent because instead of Chatillon, Neil and Skelton spent a month together as guests of Urquhart's at his Alpine chalet that became known as the Chalet des Anglais. Exactly how this invitation was extended is unclear but Urquhart was a terrible snob, who thought Balliol would be improved by admitting more men from the leading public schools[22]; and so Neil was probably considered something of a catch for that year's reading party. It has also been written of Urquhart that "he liked handsome young men, and photographing them, but was probably celibate"[23] and Neil and Skelton were indeed photographed with five other male guests during their stay.[24]

While Neil was in the French Alps enduring the Chalet's quite spartan conditions, Rosebery was also in high altitude, at Gastein, taking his annual health cure. The previous months had not been easy ones for Rosebery in terms of Liberal Party politics. First the conclusion of a peace treaty with the Boers removed the main issue that had precipitated Rosebery's return to politics at Chesterfield and prompted the formation of the Liberal League. Second the Unionist turmoil over Joseph Chamberlain's call for the abandonment of free trade had revived overall Liberal fortunes; but Liberal opposition to the proposed imperial *zollverein* sat ill in many Liberal minds with Rosebery's imperialistic Liberal League. Third Rosebery had been under pressure to put up one of his sons as Liberal candidate for Midlothian ever since the Master of Elibank, elected as MP there in 1900, had announced that he would not be re-standing there for election.[25] His dilemma was that Harry, while of age, was a poor public speaker and quite happy as a young Guards officer, while Neil, although far more fitted to be candidate, was not yet 21.

Neil left the Chalet on September 5th and went as usual to Scotland to shoot on his father's estates. While Neil had been away in France, Thomas had been adopted as the Liberal candidate for Bodmin[26] – the seat took in his father's Cornish estate at Lanhydrock – and Harry had resigned his commission[27] as a necessary prelude to his own adoption for Midlothian. Neil remained at Dalmeny House until he returned to Oxford and helped his father entertain the usual stream of male politicians, including Sir Edward Grey and Winston Churchill.[28] Early in October Harry made his first speech to the Midlothian Liberal Executive and as the *Daily Telegraph* reported next day[29], it was not a great debut: "Lord Dalmeny was obviously nervous and not trusting himself not to read his speech, read it with nervous rapidity."

Back in Oxford Neil was now without Thomas's close companionship although press reports indicate that they continued to attend race meetings together during term time.[30] Unsurprisingly Thomas's departure from Oxford left a void in Neil's university life and made him once more a somewhat needy and demanding son. At this time Rosebery was also in demand by the King and their competing demands led to an unusually terse note to Neil in early November 1903: "If I can get away from Sandringham on Saturday I will try to get to Oxford from Saturday to Monday. But it is very doubtful."[31]

The Oxford term ended just before Neil's 21st birthday on December 14th and unlike his brother, Neil was permitted to celebrate it in private at Mentmore with a group of family and friends of his own age group. From the Mentmore tenantry Neil received a Georgian silver inkstand and a gold penholder and pen.[32] The *Sporting Life* congratulated him on attaining his majority.[33] Rosebery spent Neil's birthday in Scotland where he entertained the officers and men of the Black Watch at Dalmeny House[34] but on the previous day he despatched the following effusive letter to Neil at Mentmore:

My darling Neil I send you all my love and all my hopes on this 21st birthday. It is a pity that I cannot spend it with you. The watch you wanted should be with you tomorrow. Another gift will follow in due time.[35]

Although Rosebery spared Neil of the fact on his birthday, he had recently received a disappointing end of term report on his son's progress from Herbert Fisher that Rosebery answered, quite candidly, on 15 December:

I am very grateful for your letter. The words you use of Neil I have often used to him – but he has no idea of what work is. He considers term time a period of vacation, and vacation a holiday. Please find a coach.[36]

Unsurprisingly given his previous service, and Edinburgh home, Noel Skelton was given the job of attempting to get Neil to make up for his neglect of term-time study. In consequence Neil and Skelton re-met at Dalmeny House and remained together there, alongside Rosebery, until the Oxford term resumed.

Rosebery was delighted by Skelton, and by what he did for Neil during that vacation, as the following letter marked 'confidential' that Rosebery sent to Fisher makes clear:

Do tell me what I owe Skelton, and fix your award on the liberal scale, for I like him extremely, and am grateful for the heart and interest he has shown in his task. He is a fine and manly young fellow, and I thank you for having sent him. He will see you and explain his ideas as to Neil.[37]

For all of Skelton's efforts, the problem remained that when in Oxford Neil was free from close supervision and thus was able to take on things that seriously interrupted his historical studies. This took place almost straight away when Neil agreed to help out his cousin Lionel de Rothschild by agreeing to become acting Master of Lord Rothschild's Staghounds. News of this role necessitating his presence at numerous hunts across 'Rothschildshire', and at the Ascott kennels, was soon reported in the *Daily Telegraph*.[38] Neil also absented himself from Oxford for London meetings of the Liberal League and so was at Rosebery's side for a significant speech in which he attacked protectionism; stating "it was no less than criminal to set people balancing between the price of food and the maintenance of the Empire."[39]

Within days of this speech and his seeing Neil in London, Rosebery told Fisher that he had shared his concerns about Neil with Francis Wylie, during a Rhodes Trust meeting, "and he said he would have a talk to you on Neil."[40] Rosebery was not only forgetful of his own undergraduate excesses, but was also inconsistent; wavering between indulging and criticising Neil. He also continued to demand Neil's uninterrupted company during University vacations and that Easter the two, with Rosebery's friend Evan Charteris[41], took a Royal Mail steamer to Gibraltar where they joined the *Zaida* and sailed for Naples, via Seville, Algiers and Biserta.[42]

In the summer term of 1904 Neil followed Thomas into the Oxford University polo team. The team captain was Harold Pearson, son of the 1st Viscount Cowdray, who had played alongside Thomas a year earlier and who would enter the Commons in 1906 as Liberal MP for Eye. Another team member was Ralph Brassey, son of the Liberal MP for Banbury and also a resident of Berkeley Square. As a warm up for the Varsity polo

Match, the Oxford team played and drew against the Queen's Own Oxfordshire Hussars in a match played on Port Meadow.[43] Winston Churchill played against Neil in his regiment's polo team; just days earlier he had crossed the floor of the House of Commons to take his seat amid the Liberal members on the opposition benches.

After the end of term the Varsity Match was played in London at the Hurlingham Club, with Rosebery, Harry and Thomas watching in the stands, as Cambridge secured a narrow 4-3 victory.[44]

For that year's long vacation Neil declined all invitations to attend Alpine reading parties, and to join his father on his yacht, and for the first time arranged how he spent his vacation time himself. This new-found independence probably sprang from his being of age and having access to the money bequeathed by his mother's cousin, Ferdinand de Rothschild. In July he spent time with Thomas and Harry in Brighton.[45] In August, from an undisclosed location, he attempted to reassure his father than he had at least opened his books – drawing this sarcastic response from the *RYS Zaida* on August 22nd:

You will not I think get much reading in the month of August, as reading (I don't mean simply sitting with a book) requires to be pursued with system and almost with passion and without interruption to be of any real use.

In September Neil was back with his father in Scotland, from where it was announced that both Neil and Harry were to be made JPs for the County of Midlothian.[46] On October 1st they attended the Edinburgh Sheriff Court and took the oath of office.[47] Later that day Neil left Edinburgh for London and then Paris, for a final bout of hedonism before commencing his final year at Oxford. He evidently returned, with friends in tow, to Berkeley Square, and leaving an unwelcome mess that upset the servants, received the following rare parental rebuke:

I never doubted that you would enjoy yourself in Paris or at the various race-courses where you love to spend your golden hours. But I did not like to be treated like an hotel-keeper. I am much more anxious about your work. It is now or never with you. You must not fail in your degree after 4 years of residence: it would be a discredit.

Let me know your plans of reading and study both for term and vacation during the 8 months that remain. I suggest that you do not hunt more than once a week at any rate.[48]

8

BULLINGDON NIGHTS

Neil's final year began with his election as president of the Bullingdon Club[1]; he succeeded Viscount Lewisham, who had succeeded Thomas as president in 1903. The aristocratic members of Bullingdon were drawn from supporters of both major parties in the early years of the twentieth century and in 1904 this produced open political rivalry when the 21-year-old Viscount Turnour, then in his third year at New College, was selected as Conservative candidate for the Horsham by-election. Evidently Lord Turnour had previously flirted with joining the Liberal League and Neil, Thomas and Harold Pearson were happy to set aside Bullingdon Club loyalties and attempt to impede his election by speaking in the constituency in favour of the Liberal candidate. The press were quickly briefed and engrossed; with the *Daily News*[2] carefully explaining the background to this immature rivalry:

> Lord Turnour and Mr Pearson made a bargain some time ago that if either became a candidate the other would take the chair at a meeting against him. In fulfilment of the challenge Mr Pearson will take the chair at a Liberal meeting in Crawley on Thursday and Mr Primrose and Mr Agar-Robartes will support him. The meeting of Sussex labourers and Oxford undergraduates ought to be a lively affair.

The *Evening Standard*[3] also assured its readers that despite their political differences, social relations with Lord Turnour remained quite unaffected:

Before the meeting Viscount Turnour let it be known to his supporters that they should listen carefully to what was said at the meeting and that he bore his friends no animus at all.

The meeting took place the day before voting in the George Hotel at Crawley and although ostensibly a Liberal meeting the room held many Conservative supporters as well as London reporters. The *Daily News*[4] subsequently reported that:

> Mr Pearson, wearing an immaculate white waistcoat, told the assembly that a mere six months earlier Lord Turnour was about to become a Liberal but now, he noted that the Conservative candidate declared himself an enthusiastic supporter of Mr Balfour ...
>
> Mr Agar-Robartes who wore a large pink flower in his buttonhole set the meeting in a roar when he characterised the present Government as being one of inefficiency, incompetence, muddle and mess ...
>
> Mr Primrose who was greeted with a loud cheer said that Lord Turnour had had the immodesty to compare himself to the younger Pitt. At this point there were cries made in the audience of "speak up schoolboy". Mr Primrose continued by saying that Protectionism caused national corruption and increased the cost of living ... in spite of cries of "Horseflesh" Mr Primrose went on, not the least disconcerted.

When the result was declared, Lord Turnour was elected by 784 votes and so became the youngest member of the Commons. He would then hold the seat continuously until 1951.

No doubt Neil thought the Horsham outing an amusingly jolly excursion into what was then rural Sussex; but whether it was wise, especially for Thomas, is another matter. Fortunately the press did not make the distinction that he, unlike the others, was no longer in residence at Oxford; but those in the know must surely have wondered why the 24-year-old who had left Christ Church over a year earlier was still getting involved in Junior Common Room spats. The episode certainly generated much publicity and the following week's *Bystander*[5] carried large portrait photos of Neil and Thomas side by side under its 'People of Interest' column. While the underlying text referred to both Harold Pearson and Viscount Turnour, was there perhaps a knowing editorial innuendo in the prominent connection of the two men's photographs?

During Neil's final year at Oxford he did form one important apolitical friendship that was to count for much during the final months of his life. It was with Fred Cripps who first came to New College in October 1903 and shared Neil's love of hunting, racing and polo. He would also follow Neil as Chairman of the Bullingdon Club and has written[6] of Warden Spooner's ability to see the best in everybody: that meant he was tolerant of both undergraduate idleness and unsanctioned absence from the college in term time.

Rosebery's written communications with Neil during his final months in Oxford are particularly mercurial. In early March he curtly dismissed the idea of his coming up to Oxford that term[7] and then as the end of term approached, demanded a clear answer from Neil as to his Easter vacation plans: "I did not understand your plans and I am not sure that I do now. Are you going to live here while coaching or with the coach?"[8]

In May, Rosebery wrote from Naples to dismiss Neil's proposal that he speak to the University Liberal League: "As to the League, I should do it no service in its present condition by coming to speak. Oxford as they say is always in extremes – high Tory or Socialist."[9]

Rosebery's ill temper may have been as much caused by his growing political isolation and realisation that the Liberal Party did not want or need him, as it was by Neil's continued dissipation. His mood and relations with Neil improved when he won the Derby for the third time with *Cicero*. Neil had missed the race and subsequent Epsom celebrations due to exam purdah, and this prompted an unusual fatherly confession of guilt: "I am almost ashamed to tell you how touched I was by your spending a sleepless night before the Derby without a bet."[10]

Neil's Finals were spread over the week leading up to the end of term and his celebration of their completion neatly coincided with his final Bullingdon dinner as President. As Rosebery had attended Thomas's final dinner it was perhaps natural that Neil wanted his father to attend his own; but Rosebery was uncertain about coming as he wrote on June 13th:

It strikes me that I might be rather in the way at the Bullingdon dinner, as the presence of an aged chump is apt to be a cloud and a restraint –

and my only pleasure would be seeing you as President. So perhaps I had better give it up. I am thinking of you and your examination.[11]

In the event Neil and his father agreed a compromise that Rosebery would meet Neil alone before the dinner, but would attend the following morning's breakfast that Neil was to give in his rooms, that his tutor Herbert Fisher was also invited to. Fortuitously, for some unexplained reason, Fisher failed to attend, leading to the following noteworthy letter that Rosebery wrote to Fisher from Mentmore later that day:

I was sorry that you could not breakfast with Neil this morning because I wanted to thank you for your letter which was warming to my heart and which I shall always preserve ...

I shall be satisfied and relieved if Neil gets a degree at all; for as you say he has no idea of continuous work. Probably he never will have unless political action stirs him deeply. But I am no longer interested in that fact. I have become philosophical, we cannot shape these boys beyond a very limited extent. If they grow up healthy English gentlemen in the best sense, and not without intellect or intellectual tastes, we should thank God, and not ask for more. Indeed I comfort myself selfishly by thinking that if Neil were a Japanese in industry, efficiency and public spirit, he would not be so delightful a son to me.

You say truly that he has got much out of Oxford. He did not, I remember, like going there and he hankered at first after Christ Church where I had been. Yet last night he spontaneously assured me that the four years he had spent at Oxford were the happiest of his life, and I think he added, ever expected to spend. This is all to the good, for they have not been years of folly, though there has been enough of that.

9

YOUR FRIEND IS EVEN MORE DELIGHTFUL

Neil's final interaction with Oxford University came when he played in the University team on the polo grounds of west London: on June 24th he played and won 7-4 against the House of Commons polo team at Roehampton.[1] Two of the four players from the Commons team were well known to him – Winston Churchill and his recently elected New College friend Viscount Turnour. Two days later Neil played in the Varsity polo match at the Hurlingham for the second time and was again defeated, this time by 9 goals to 4. However there was some consolation in that *The Times* report of the match described Neil as "a good clean hitter".[2]

In July Neil received his degree result – he was placed in the Third Class[3] which given everything was not a disappointment and in June 1906 he returned to Oxford to receive his degree.[4] Neil's reward for achieving this degree result was a four-month tour of the United States and Canada, while he and his father pondered what he should do next.

At this time Balfour's Unionist government was tottering and the General Election was eagerly anticipated by Liberal candidates such as Thomas and Harry. Neil spent time with both of them in Brighton in August, and in September he was reported as staying at Lanhydrock as the guest of Thomas's father.[5] During his stay an enormous, and ultimately fateful, Liberal garden party was held in the grounds. Over 5,000 Liberal supporters attended and speeches were made by Thomas and by his Bodmin Liberal Association Chairman, Arthur Quiller-Couch.

Later that month Neil left Liverpool for Canada and Rosebery interrupted his Scottish holiday to see him off at Euston. Rosebery, who had himself first crossed the Atlantic at a similar age in 1873, found the parting from his younger son highly emotional as is plain from his first letter marked '1' and written at Mentmore on the day following Neil's departure:

> Twenty minutes after you rolled out of the station, carrying so large a part of my heart with you, my darling, I came down here.
>
> Number your letters as I mean to do, so as to see if they all arrive.
>
> Your letter has just come with the postmark London! Harry suspects you have never left and are hidden in some purlieu – having got out at Willesden and returned.[6]

In his next letter Rosebery sent Neil news of his racehorses, what and how many birds he'd shot, and his significant house guests, such as the Archbishop of Canterbury.[7] By mid-October he was fretting that Neil "had vanished into space" and then a few days later "a joyful day for I received your letter of the 6th posted at Rimouski".[8]

Rimouski, near the mouth of the St. Lawrence river, was where Neil disembarked before continuing by rail to Quebec and Montreal. At Montreal Neil went to Laval University and addressed the law students in French. His visit was widely reported and news of it soon reached Rosebery in Scotland: "There is a paragraph in the *Scotsman* today that you have delivered an address in French to the students of Laval University. Harry will be green with envy."[9] From Montreal Neil went west to Ottawa and then on to Winnipeg, Calgary and finally Victoria in British Columbia.

In November Rosebery stayed with the King at Sandringham for four days of shooting; informing Neil from there that they had had "clouds of partridges – I never saw so many" before complaining that his son's letters were insufficiently detailed about the Canadian climate, hotels and way of living.[10] Later the same month he went to Cornwall where he stayed with Thomas at Lanhydrock for a week of Liberal League speeches across Cornwall. In a letter of November 27th Rosebery described to Neil his first impressions of the house and Lord and Lady Clifden. On Thomas he wrote:

> Your friend is even more delightful here than elsewhere. He is charming to his family who adore him. When he speaks there is a roar of welcome and he looking very bright and peaceful delivers a short speech containing generally the unexpected. The other day at Truro

speaking to 5,000 people about Chinese labour he said the mines were worked by 'methods of barbarism' we all shuddered and chuckled.[11]

Rosebery's final speech was in Bodmin, in support of Thomas's candidature and made in front of 15,000. In part of the speech, which caused a national sensation, he attacked Campbell-Bannerman's stance on Home Rule with the words:

> I object to it mainly for this reason: that it impairs the unity of the Free Trade party, and that it indefinitely postpones legislation on social and educational reform … I will then add no more on this subject, except to say emphatically and explicitly and once and for all that I cannot serve under that banner.[12]

To Neil, Rosebery gave the bland explanation that "I had in the last speech to repudiate Campbell-Bannerman on a declaration he had recently made on Irish Home Rule"[13] but as many thought he was speaking for the entire League and not just for himself, his words caused trouble between him and his Liberal League Vice-Presidents, Asquith and Grey, who thought the speech a disaster, and only of help to the Unionists.

Once Rosebery's speaking tour of Cornwall was over, Thomas returned to London and while dining alone at Brooks's Club wrote Neil a lengthy account of Rosebery's visit and how he had charmed everybody, including his sixteen-year-old sister Violet.[14] As he explained: "everybody fell in love with him … I do wish you had been there." Commenting on Rosebery's controversial speech at Bodmin he continued: "the speech has to my mind cleared the air and done good for the genuine Liberal League candidates." On Campbell-Bannerman, Thomas quite freely expressed his hatred of him and predicted he would split the Liberal Party: "there is sure to be a big split in a few years' time … if there isn't I don't think there will be much room for Harry, you, & me to pose as Liberal candidates."

From British Columbia, Neil crossed the border into the United States and visited Seattle and San Francisco before proceeding on to Denver and Colorado Springs. By now it was clear that the General Election was imminent and Rosebery accurately predicted to Neil on November 29th: "The Government may probably resign next week. CB will hasten to form a Government and the election will be in January"[15] but Rosebery, perhaps blinded by his disdain for CB (Campbell-Bannerman) kept insisting to Neil that he should not bother to return. "I doubt it will be worth seeing," he wrote on November 27th and then again two days later: "I should not hasten home for the election if I were you". Whereas in fact it would result in an unprecedented Liberal landslide, in which the Party gained 216 seats, and CB was given the largest anti-Conservative majority in over 80 years.

On December 5th Rosebery wrote with the sad news that one of Neil's New College friends had died in a racing fall and that the effects of his Home Rule speech in Bodmin continued to ripple out and was now impacting on Lord Dalmeny's campaign in Midlothian:

Ralph Brassey[16] is dead – he had a fall at the Varsity steeplechase at Huntingdon … I last saw the boy at that breakfast in your rooms after the Bullingdon dinner.

Harry has gone off to the last two meetings insufficiently prepared I think.

I am afraid the poor boy will have trouble caused by me … I am most unpopular … because of my repudiation of CB's Home Rule speech which they think un-necessary and calculated to divide the Party. Of course I do not care for that except for Harry. They can only strike at me through him, which I hate. Anyhow I am glad you are out of this Election. [17]

Perhaps Rosebery was in denial about the seriousness of the situation; for in reality the formation of the Campbell-Bannerman premiership in December 1905 destroyed the influence of Rosebery's Liberal League. One of Rosebery's biographers Robert Rhodes James has written that Rosebery's Bodmin speech on Irish Home Rule "effectively killed" the League[18]. Rosebery, while perhaps not appreciating that the situation was terminal, apprised Neil of the League's political toxicity on December 7th:

Tonight I got a telegram from the Secretaries of the League to say that all of the Vice Presidents of the League (Asquith, Grey, Fowler and Haldane) had accepted office and that 'formalities' prevented them attending the Council meeting on Monday. Should the meeting be held? I suppose there is a general denial of attendance among those who hope for office.[19]

On December 14th Neil turned 23 and Rosebery who had now abandoned the unpalatable political scene in London, wrote to him from the Hotel Bristol in Paris that day:

> One line of congratulation on your birthday my dearest Neil. Jimmy [de Rothschild] and I are going to celebrate it tonight by a dinner at the Café Anglais[20] of the most sumptuous character.[21]

Waspishly commenting on his son-in-law Lord Crewe's joining the new Liberal Cabinet, Rosebery continued: "Crewe is pleased, I think, at being Lord President of the Council, I am not sure that the more ambitious Peggy is satisfied."

On December 20th Rosebery was back in London and sent his son his Christmas best wishes:

> I have received your two letters from Denver and Colorado Springs. Your mother and I stayed at Denver.
> Harry has made a speech saying that he will vote for any Irish measure that CB may propose ... I suppose he was forced into it. I fear his prospects are gloomy. A happy Christmas for you my darling.[22]

By now Neil had spent time in Chicago and he reached New York in time to spend Christmas there. On New Year's Eve Rosebery wrote to Neil in New York and made clear to him that the following was 'Secret'':

> I send my loving wishes for the new year but after all you have them always. I am a little pre-occupied about your immediate future. Frankly I would rather you went into business than politics – it is the cheaper of the two. Nor should I care to bring you in just now even if there was a vacancy. Nor just now would a Liberal constituency be much attracted by your name!
> I had thought of asking E. Grey to take you as an extra private secretary. But I am not very keen that you should enter into relations with the present Government – even with him.[23]

Neil remained in New York throughout January 1906 and so missed the General Election in which Thomas was elected MP for Bodmin, and Harry MP for Midlothian. Harry, for all of his father's gloomy predictions had achieved a very respectable majority of 3,217 votes. Following the declaration, *The Times*[24] commented:

> We congratulate [Lord Rosebery] the more heartily because he must regard the general result of the election with mixed feelings. He is the most conspicuous and interesting figure upon the Liberal side: yet he is entirely outside of this Liberal victory.

As if to emphasise his agreement with this, Rosebery would henceforth sit in the Lords on the cross benches.

Neil returned in February as his father was recovering from a severe cold: "so that I cannot meet you at Southampton, as I wanted to, but am going up to London to welcome you there. Harry says you will return with an accent and spitting a good deal."[25] Neil was back when the King opened the new Parliament on February 19th. Days earlier the Prime Minister, possibly in an attempt to repair relations with Rosebery, asked Lord Dalmeny to second the Address. This Rosebery apparently forbade Harry to do[26] and for this he has subsequently been condemned.[27] However it may be that Rosebery reasonably feared that his eldest son was not up to doing what was a daunting task for even the most able backbencher, and so wisely spared him the embarrassment. What is plain is that a few weeks later[28] Harry made a nondescript maiden speech on the army estimates and then never spoke to the House again. Rosebery was seriously perturbed by Harry's poor record of attendance in the Commons as he told Neil later that year: "I am seriously worried about Harry's non-attendance and fear that may affect your chance of a seat. But I am not sure that I weep over your not being in Parliament at this period, which is one of transition."[29]

It seems most unlikely that Neil felt like his father about his absence from the 1906 Parliament and his sense of exclusion may have grown in April 1906 when his Oxford friend Harold Pearson was elected as Liberal MP for Eye in a by-election. This meant, as the papers pointed out, that Neil was the only one of the juvenile Oxford quartet involved in the 1904 Horsham by-election who was not now in the Commons.[30]

In order to occupy his younger son and lessen his political frustration, Rosebery made a significant investment in the All British Car Company Ltd. The company was first registered on March 15th 1906 with Neil listed as a director and eight days later he attended his first board meeting in Edinburgh.[31] The background to the Company's formation was an agreement (concluded on March 10th) to purchase the business, property and assets of Johnston & Company Engineers and Motor Car Manufacturers of McPhail Street in Glasgow for £44,500 in cash and £30,000 in All British shares. The total share capital of All British was £250,000 of which Rosebery subscribed £3,000 in his own name, and £750 in Neil's. Details of the share prospectus, in which it was implied that the prime mover behind the venture was Lord Rosebery, were reported in the *Daily Telegraph*[32] and the *Morning Post*[33]. Another director was Andrew Drysdale who had been employed as factor on the Dalmeny estate since 1890. By the time of the August 1906 board meeting that Neil attended in Edinburgh, the share subscription was complete and the All British had signed a contract to build and supply 100 motor omnibuses for service on the streets of London. Although all seemed rosy, within 15 months the company was in liquidation and Neil and the other directors were being called upon to repay the company's £28,000 overdraft that they had guaranteed.[34] In the interim it is apparent that the Glasgow works had been seriously mismanaged, resulting in terrible delays in completion of the bus chassis. How much personal responsibility Neil bore is impossible to say but plainly the persons with day-to-day supervision of the factory were seriously at fault, leading to an expensive and embarrassing business failure that impaired both Neil and Rosebery's reputations.

It is not clear if or how often Neil visited the Glasgow works but Andrew Drysdale acted as company chairman and Rosebery seemingly blamed him for the disaster.[35] As well as the loss of the original investment and the settlement of the overdraft, Neil also had to pay legal fees associated with the threatened action by the company's trade creditors to establish personal liability on the part of the directors; only in the autumn of 1909 was that aspect quietly settled by Neil's lawyers.[36] In settling when he did, Neil removed any anxiety that the All British affair would affect his then imminent Commons election campaign.

When not engaged in the duties of his company directorship, Neil went hunting in Ireland and then made sure that he attended all of that summer's significant race meetings including the Derby and Royal Ascot. During Ascot week came the surprising news that Thomas had been un-seated at Bodmin by an electoral court, following the hearing of an election petition brought by his Unionist opponent. The petition's main ground was that the great garden party held at Lanhydrock in September 1905 had amounted to "deliberate, skilful and effective treating" of the Bodmin electorate.[37] The petition noted that up to 5,000 had attended the free garden party "and refreshments though non alcoholic were provided on a lavish scale" and "musical bands and other amusements were provided."

Two High Court judges heard the petition in the Bodmin Court House. Mr Justice Grantham in the leading judgment noted that Thomas (the respondent) "had just left college when he became the accepted candidate" and the judge accepted "that he did not know that he was doing wrong and that he had no corrupt intention" but that his Liberal agent, Ralph Millman "must have known and yet allowed him to do it". The judge continued: "how any sane person could give advice to the father or mother of the candidate to hold such an entertainment … passed his comprehension" although he did add that Lord and Lady Clifden "had not been guilty of anything disreputable or disgraceful."

In the far shorter second judgment, Mr Justice Lawrence merely said: "Millman knew he was doing a corrupt thing and he was guilty. The seat would be declared vacant."[38] Thomas, who had not taken the risk of being deprived of the seat at all seriously, now (despite the judge's words) took the verdict as a matter of family honour. A few weeks later he publicly attacked Mr Justice Grantham for humiliating his mother by making "cheap jokes" to counsel as she was giving her evidence in the witness box.[39]

The verdict caused a national sensation and necessitated a by-election and a fresh Liberal candidate. The press quickly noted that after the conclusion of events in court, Thomas had left Cornwall to consult Lord Rosebery; doubtless he was also consoled by Neil. Within days the London newspapers were speculating that Neil would be the by-election candidate, with the *Globe*[40] reporting: "it is understood that Neil Primrose will be invited to be Liberal Candidate" and the *Daily News*: "the principal name before the Bodmin Liberal Executive is Neil Primrose's."[41] Elsewhere the press noted that "the fact that the un-seated member has been staying with Lord Rosebery adds to the speculation that his younger son will stand."[42]

Within a week the speculation was ended by a brief press release saying that Neil "did not feel in a position to entertain the proposal" made to him by the Bodmin Liberal Executive.[43] As this decision was reached when Neil and Rosebery were together, there is, alas, no correspondence to explain the reasoning behind it. Perhaps the explanation was no more complicated than that Rosebery stuck to his previously expressed wish that Neil was best out of the 1906 Parliament and Neil went along with this. However another explanation may have been that Neil's candidature might attract unwelcome scrutiny of his relationship with Thomas, which was the only thing that connected Neil to the remote constituency. Also given the centrality of the Lanhydrock estate within the constituency, Thomas (who Rosebery now knew, from his Cornish speaking tour, to be a loose cannon) could not be kept entirely out of the by-election campaign.

If this did form part of Rosebery's reasoning, he was vindicated by actual events. Thomas made an ill-considered speech in Bodmin on July 19th in which he characterised the by-election "as a personal matter" and asked the electors to preserve "the honour" of Robartes by returning the Liberal candidate.[44] The prompt response of the Unionist candidate was election placards worded "Are you a bondsman or are you free? Remember the ballot and let Thomas see!"[45] while the *Daily Mail*[46] sneered that: "the appeal to feudalism is regarded as quaint coming from a once Liberal member." For all of this, when the result came the Liberal candidate Freeman Freeman-Thomas won by 1,093 votes, which was an almost identical majority to that Thomas had achieved six months earlier.

Thomas was further consoled in late September when Rosebery lent Neil his yacht and sent them both off on a six-week cruise of the eastern Mediterranean, with Rosebery planning to join them later in Venice. As the following letter Rosebery sent to Neil on board on October 2nd makes clear[47], it had already been decided that Neil would stand in the 1907 London County Council election:

I have a great idea of going to Rio and Buenos Aires on Nov 30. It will take 48 days altogether. Would you like to come if the LCC permit?

Give my love to Thomas. I hope you are both mastering the Near Eastern Question.

On October 18th Rosebery wrote again from Scotland to inform Neil that his maternal great aunt Lucy Cohen was dangerously ill in London and so he was changing his plans:

> Great aunt Lucy is very ill. Last Sunday she seemed as bad as possible but now Peggy thinks she may last some time.
> But I think in view of this, of parliament, and of my absence at Rio, as well as the shortness of time I could spare, I must give up the hope of joining you ... Love to Thomas.[48]

As these letters, and the *Zaida* cruise itself demonstrate, Rosebery had no concern at all about Neil's continuing closeness to Thomas. After his death in 1915 the press wrote quite freely that Thomas was almost a third son to Rosebery and in another letter to Neil he makes no distinction between the three:

> Sometime between Aug 20 and 30 [1907] we ought to take two days shooting at Rosebery if I can get away from the House of Lords. I wonder what days would suit you and Harry and Thomas?[49]

Rosebery's tolerance is perhaps unsurprising as he had also formed passionate male friendships at Eton and at Oxford. Frederick Vyner, whose place of death in Greece he visited in 1891, some 21 years after his murder, is one instance. On the first anniversary of Vyner's death when Rosebery was just weeks away from his 24th birthday, he wrote in his diary as he secretly wept over his photograph:

> I can believe in no future state where we can be divided. I hardly think that death divides us now.[50]

10

HE HAS SUCCEEDED TO A FORTUNE

Neil's great aunt Lucy died aged 67 on November 5th 1906 at her Mayfair house in Great Stanhope Street (now Stanhope Gate). She was the youngest daughter of Isaac Cohen[1] of the wealthy bullion broking family; and her eldest sister Juliana, who had died in 1877, was Neil's maternal grandmother. Lucy and her other sister Anna Louisa never married: the two wealthy sisters lived together and dedicated themselves to helping Jewish and other charitable causes.[2] Once Hannah's mother died in 1877, her two Cohen aunts were her sole link to her maternal family and when Hannah herself died in 1890 her four children became the Cohen sisters' closest relatives. Prior to Hannah's death in August 1889 it is clear that the Rosebery children holidayed with their maiden great aunts at the Birnam Hotel in Perthshire[3] but once Hannah was dead it is unclear quite how much contact there was.

Great aunt Anna died in 1902 leaving Lucy as the sole possessor of their joint fortune that included a large terraced house at Hove, Nevill Court near Tunbridge Wells, and the Mayfair house. Rosebery did not treat aunt Lucy with indifference: in August 1905 he and Neil spent a weekend at Nevill Court.[4] Later that year when Neil was in the United States, Rosebery told Neil that great aunt Lucy "is hurt that you did not write to say that you were going abroad … so please write to her."[5]

Whether Neil did so is unclear but under the terms of her last will dated December 18th 1905, Neil was named as the principal beneficiary. The total value of her estate was an eye-watering £564,000 and Rosebery was named as one of the four executors. Her properties were disposed among three of Rosebery's four children: Sybil receiving the house and contents in Hove, Peggy receiving Nevill Court and contents, and Neil the freehold of 5 Great

Stanhope Street and the separate stabling that she owned nearby in Carrington Mews. Neil knew Great Stanhope Street well as his aunt Constance had lived at No.12 since the death of her husband, and Thomas's parents' London house was in the same exclusive street of fifteen houses, adjacent to Hyde Park.

Neil also inherited all of the house's valuable contents that were later described as "objets d'art, beautiful old furniture, tapestries and valuable china."[6] In addition to her properties, Lucy Cohen left very substantial liquid assets and these devolved to several charities and more significantly to Rosebery's children as follows: Lady Sybil Grant £40,000, Countess of Crewe £40,000, Lord Dalmeny £5,000 and the Hon. Neil Primrose £150,000. In terms of 2019 values, Neil's monetary legacy alone equates to around £15 million and as the press were not slow to highlight, at the tender age of 23 he had inherited a vast fortune, that put him way ahead of both Thomas and his older brother Harry in the 1906 wealth stakes.

Probate of the will was granted rapidly on November 28th and within a fortnight Rosebery sent the following birthday letter to his highly fortunate younger son:

Tomorrow is your birthday but quite an exceptional birthday. You can start on this new year on an independent basis and on the brink of public life so that my heart is even more than usual with you, if that is possible, and I form new hopes and aspirations for you. I dare say they will not all be realised and for the ambitions part I care the least. But I do care intensely that you should maintain a high standard of honour and usefulness and perhaps selfishly that you should always be to me the son that you have been. God bless you my darling, triumph this and all the coming years.[7]

If Rosebery had any serious fear that from now on Neil would pursue an independent life of idle dissipation he was rapidly reassured. In terms of Neil's lifestyle his new wealth made little obvious change and he did not desert his father and move across Mayfair to his new house in Great Stanhope Street. All that Neil did do to his new property was to give its exterior a fashionable Edwardian makeover by re-facing the brick with Portland stone and adding some expensive decorative neo-Louis-XVI stone details.[8] The property was also heightened, by adding a further floor to provide additional bedroom accommodation for servants. Otherwise the interior was left untouched; and once the external alterations were done in the spring of 1908, the property was profitably let out fully furnished during the London season. Neil's first tenants were Lord and Lady St. Leven and his surviving financial records show that he received an annual rent in 1911 of £1260 and half yearly rent of £735 in 1912.[9] The house had a distinguished former occupant the Crimean War Commander Lord Raglan[10] who lived there between 1834 and 1854 and as a result Neil agreed to the LCC erecting a blue plaque on the house.[11] This probably explains the house's survival today, albeit rebuilt internally when converted into luxury flats.

Equally, in terms of politics, Neil's inheritance made no difference to the previously formed plan that he would stand in the LCC election that spring. Obviously Rosebery had a strong connection with Council as its first Chairman and election to it was by now a well-recognised first step on the path to Parliament. As early as July 1902 the press had noted that Rosebery had taken Neil on a visit to the Council chamber.[12] The Council had 118 members elected together for a three-year term and representing 58 two-member constituencies, plus 2 representing the City of London. A little confusingly Liberal candidates then stood under the 'Progressive' banner and Conservatives as 'Moderates' and then from 1906 'Municipal Reformers'.

In the Lewisham constituency the Progressive member since 1904, Arthur Stanley[13], was standing down and so Neil was adopted there[14] to stand alongside James Cleland[15]. A week after their adoption all of the Progressive candidates were presented to London by the President of the Local Government Board[16] at a huge gathering at the Queen's Hall. In introducing Neil, the Cabinet Minister John Burns did not hide his paternity or his recent inheritance:

I welcome tonight Lord Rosebery's younger son who is going to show what more young rich men ought to show, that so far as he is concerned he does not intend in London affairs to walk or pursue the primrose path of dalliance.[17]

In another column the *Pall Mall Gazette*[18] described Neil as "a coy Progressive debutante" who was given "a very sympathetic reception". The

1. *Hannah, Countess of Rosebery*

2. Lord Rosebery

3. Neil and Harry Dalmeny c1886

4. Neil at Eton, 1899

5. Mentmore

6. Dalmeny House

7. The Durdans

8. 38 Berkeley Square, London

9. Thomas Agar-Robartes, 1902

10. Thomas Agar-Robartes, c1905

11. Neil, Lord Rosebery and Lord
    Dalmeny at Royal Ascot, 1910

12. Neil and Harry with
    James de Rothschild
    at Royal Ascot

A. Caricature of
Mr. Neil Primrose.
(L) M.P. for Wisbech; and youngest son
of Lord Rosebery. Born 1882.

13. Caricature of Neil, c1912

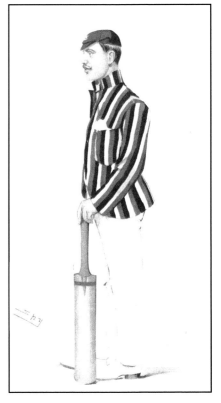

14. Spy cartoon of Harry, 1904

Daily News was as interested in reporting Neil's good looks as his politics: "Mr Primrose is singularly handsome, with an athletic, well-knit figure and a fine face that recalls his father's." The *Evening Standard* of February 12th did report Neil and Cleland's election address; it called for the municipalisation or public sector provision of electricity across the capital, as well as the extension of the constituency's tramway system to Brockley.

Predictably the Municipal Reform candidates for Lewisham called for trams to be a run at a profit to the ratepayer and attacked the electricity scheme as inevitably loss making.[19] Rather more surprisingly in terms of South London politics today, Neil's principal opponent was another hunting obsessed aristocrat who had served as Bullingdon Club Chairman the year before Neil. This resulted in the following profile in the *Bystander*[20]:

Viscount Lewisham[21] – son and heir of the Earl of Dartmouth who bears the name of the borough he seeks to represent was very popular at Oxford where he was President of the Bullingdon and Master of the House [Christ Church] Beagles.

Rosebery kept away from Lewisham but closely monitored the contest from Berkeley Square and in mid-February reported hopefully to Herbert Fisher in Oxford: "Lewisham is doing Neil a world of good. I hope it will be the making of him. He has succeeded to a fortune but is I think quite unspoilt".[22]

Neil though did enlist the help of another family member, his brother-in-law, Lord Crewe, who came to Lewisham and made a speech attacking the opposition's change of name from Moderates to Municipal Reformers: "Everybody knew they were distinctly anti-municipal and as to reform they hated the word."[23] However, he did no good and the Municipal Reformers triumphed across London in a way that mirrored the Progressives' performance in 1904.[24] In Lewisham, the eponymous Viscount topped the poll with 11,028 votes; his running mate closely followed with 10,818. Neil gained 6,893, with Cleland just ahead on 7,004. The sole Labour candidate gained just 118.[25]

The indications are that Neil took his defeat badly, having as Rosebery told Fisher put "all his heart" into it. Rosebery's feelings were rather more mixed: he told the Duke of Devonshire the following month that he welcomed the poor Progressive result as it restrained the over-mighty Liberal government in Westminster[26]; and he snobbishly joked to Fisher[27] that the Lewisham electorate had thought Neil a scion of the Primrose soap making dynasty[28] and as "Lewisham is a great place for laundries" the wrongful association had cost him votes.

Whatever views Rosebery expressed in private about the 1907 London election, when a vacancy arose for an LCC Alderman Rosebery pulled strings to ensure that Neil was elected by the Progressive councillors to fill the vacancy, and he was present in the Council Chamber to see Neil take his seat in March 1909.[29] The role of Alderman was not entirely free of duties and Neil now joined two Council committees, as well as attending some meetings of the full Council[30] and occasionally spoke in debates.[31]

The *Bystander*[32] and other society publications continued to obsess about Neil and his social life, even to the extent of reporting which restaurants he patronised. In March 1907 soon after his LCC election failure they reported that he was often to be found at the fashionably chic Maison Jules restaurant in Jermyn Street with his young and unmarried male friends.

One place where Neil and his friends could dine in greater privacy was Brooks's Club in St James's Street. Rosebery had proposed Neil for membership in 1904, and Thomas had joined two years earlier. Harry Dalmeny was also a member, as was Neil and Harry's cousin Lionel de Rothschild[33], and the Club's Betting Book contains numerous bets that the four young members made.[34] An example is in November 1907 when Neil rashly bet Lionel £10 that there "would be fewer Labour members in the next House of Commons than in the present House of Commons".[35]

In April Neil, with his father and Harry, was reported[36] as staying for the Guineas Newmarket meeting with Thomas and his parents at their other country seat Wimpole Hall in Cambridgeshire.[37] But Neil was not content just to lead the life of a West End and racecourse playboy and continued to yearn for a political life. In May Rosebery joined the *Zaida* at Venice before sailing round Italy to Naples, but Neil declined to join him. His father's letters to him in London indicate that Neil was suffering from lassitude: "I wish you would play polo this summer for it does you so much good. I never see you look so well as when poloing". He also suggested that his son "attend some of the parliamentary debates to give you a sniff of the atmosphere".[38]

Neil's frustration was probably not helped by his elder brother being in the Commons when he did not wish to be there. Harry Dalmeny's true vocation was cricket rather than politics and he continued to hold the Surrey captaincy as an MP during both the 1906 and 1907 cricket seasons.[39] The consequence of his neglect of his duties as MP for Midlothian came to a head in October 1907 when an anonymous letter was printed in the *Scotsman*[40] from a Midlothian Liberal voter who stated that "the electors of the county have been treated with little less than contempt by this young man". The letter was quickly followed by a meeting of Lord Dalmeny's Liberal Association to consider a motion of no confidence in their MP. However, as the *Evening Standard*[41] put it Dalmeny was "a popular sportsman and much liked figure" and the motion against him received only two votes.

Neil did as usual as his father wished and played polo that summer. On July 12th he played at Wembley Park Polo Club[42] alongside Winston Churchill who was then in his first Government role as Under-Secretary of State for the Colonies. Later that month the newspapers carried the first news of Thomas's engagement to Lady Theo Acheson[43]. Lady Theo was the third and youngest daughter of the Earl and Countess of Gosford and she and her two sisters had been immortalised in a John Singer Sargent portrait, exhibited to great acclaim at the 1902 Royal Academy Exhibition. The painting had been commissioned by their maternal grandmother the Duchess of Devonshire, also known as the Double Duchess[44], and a racing companion of Rosebery's since his first days on a racecourse.[45]

When news of the engagement broke, Rosebery was away in Gastein, but always an avid newspaper reader wherever he was, he wrote rather waspishly to Neil on July 31st: "I do hope Thomas's marriage is not true, though she is a very nice girl."[46] Rosebery need not have been concerned as by August 8th the *Cornishman* carried a contradiction issued on Thomas's behalf. But the matter did not end there: Lady Theo was the cover-girl of the *Bystander* of January 15th 1908 when the false rumour of her engagement to Thomas was re-announced, and the story only died out when the *Bystander* of February 26th 1908 carried the following words: "I am requested by her father the Earl of Gosford[47] to give the statement emphatic denial. She has never been engaged to anyone and the announcement has been frequently contradicted."[48]

Exactly what occurred involving Thomas and Lady Theo and how it led to such a severe misunderstanding is unclear. Thomas was destined never to marry and never suffered another even rumoured engagement. Lady Theo would not marry until August 1912 when she married the far less financially eligible diplomat Alexander Cadogan[49].

Quite what Lord and Lady Clifden made of these false rumours of their eldest son's engagement is unclear, but it was their destiny to produce a family of nine who, for whatever reason, had an almost complete aversion to marriage. Their eldest child Mary was the first to marry in her fortieth year, in 1919. A year later their third son Arthur, who subsequently became the 8th and final Viscount Clifden, married; his daughter, born in 1922, was Lord and Lady Clifden's only grandchild. Like Thomas, their other three sons and three daughters never married.

11

NEIL HAS FOUND A CONSTITUENCY

1908 brought welcome developments for both Neil and Thomas. In the first days of January the Liberal MP for St. Austell, William McArthur, announced his resignation. McArthur had held the seat since 1887 and had served as a Whip in Rosebery's Government. The St. Austell constituency neighboured the Bodmin seat and was solidly safe for the Liberals[1], unlike Bodmin, which was then a Liberal/Unionist marginal. Unsurprisingly given this, almost immediately there was speculation in the press that Thomas would be the Liberal candidate and before the month ended he was adopted. Across Cornwall the unfortunate events of 1906 had attracted considerable sympathy for Thomas and in that independent-minded county he was widely regarded as a patriotic Cornishman who had been unjustly deprived of his election by interfering outsiders. Given this sentiment and the seat's deep seated Liberal hue, the Unionists decided not to field a candidate and Thomas was elected unopposed on February 5th.

Just over a month later the *Evening Standard*[2] carried the story that Cecil Beck, MP for Wisbech since 1906 with a majority of just over 1,000 votes, had announced to his association that "he will not contest the seat for private reasons and … Neil Primrose is mentioned as the probable Liberal candidate." Exactly what Beck's reasons were remains unclear for, while he retired from the Wisbech seat, he stood as a Liberal candidate twice elsewhere before being returned to the Commons in December 1910.[3]

What is clear though is that Beck had reached an agreement with Neil to step aside and make the seat available for him. That a deal was done in advance is demonstrated by Rosebery's letter to Herbert Fisher: this was written three days prior to Beck's announcement and states "Neil … has found a constituency … This is secret."[4]

Of course both Neil and Rosebery were in a position to make a financial inducement to Beck to step aside but the fact that Neil and Beck became and remained close friends (and Beck even served as an usher at Neil's wedding seven years later) rather suggests that this was not merely a financial transaction. Beck was a member of Rosebery's Liberal League and so perhaps was motivated to act as he did by devotion to the League's chairman.

Within three weeks of Beck's announcement the Wisbech Liberal Association met to consider Neil's nomination and, after hearing his speech and no other, unanimously adopted him.[5] Neil's speech might have been written by Rosebery. In it Neil stated that "he was in favour of reform of the House of Lords" but that "such reform should come from within that House" and that "he was a free trader" and "was opposed to a separate Parliament for Ireland."[6]

Neil may have thought that following his long wait to secure a Liberal seat his way into Parliament would be straightforward but this was not the case and over the next 20 months until the General Election, Neil's candidature would be severely buffeted by events.

Things did not initially go awry. The resignation of Campbell-Bannerman in April 1908[7] brought to an end Rosebery and Neil's total exclusion from Downing Street. Prime Minister Asquith was, unlike his predecessor, always held in high regard by Rosebery, and although Rosebery did not re-establish any political influence over him, their social relationship continued. In consequence Neil and Rosebery dined with the Prime Minister in April 1909[8] and Neil was asked again, without his father, in July.[9]

In August 1908, Neil holidayed with his father at Vichy where they stayed at the Hotel du Parc. For Rosebery it marked a change from Gastein that he was quite happy with: "Vichy is rather pleasant," he told his sister, "I have an excellent hotel, an easy cure, an appreciable climate and Neil."[10]

Press reports of Neil's elevated social life in London were not unhelpful as he nursed his future constituency. Neil also managed to combine visits to the constituency with stays at Sandringham. In October 1908 he finished off a day spent shooting partridges with the Prince of Wales[11], with a Liberal meeting at Littleport.[12] In December he was again a guest at Sandringham[13] and during his stay rode out with Princess Mary of Wales on her debut outing with the West Norfolk Foxhounds.[14]

Neil was back in London between his Sandringham visits to see his father open the new premises of the Liberal League in Queen Anne's Gate. The opening was followed by an inaugural dinner for several hundred members and among the guests were Thomas, Harry, and Cecil Beck.[15] However congenial the League's new premises were, by 1908 it was little more than a social club where like-minded right wing Liberals could meet. As a political organization of any influence it was now entirely moribund and powerless to stop the leftward march of the Liberal Party.

Quite evidently Lord Dalmeny appreciated as much when he wrote on Boxing Day 1908 to inform his constituency secretary that he would not stand again at the General Election:

It is being forced upon me more and more that my politics are not far enough advanced to meet the views of the Liberal Party as at present constituted, and in some way I have been disappointed by the course of events. While I am a sincere admirer of the Prime Minister and have general confidence in his colleagues, I cannot but feel that the party, as a whole, is bent on forcing the pace and bringing with increasing vehemence, legislation which I should be unable to support.[16]

For just over a month Harry's letter remained private but on January 31st it was read out at a constituency meeting in Edinburgh, causing a press sensation.[17] As it was, Neil was away in Monte Carlo, staying at the Hotel de Paris[18], and as parliament was not then sitting Thomas was with him. However, as the *Daily Telegraph*[19] soon reported, Neil's gambling was interrupted by the pressing need to compose a letter to the Wisbech Liberal Association "to deny the rumour that he intends to follow Lord Dalmeny, and retire as candidate."

Next month Neil had to endure another adverse development and bad publicity arising out of Rosebery's dismissal of the factor of his Dalmeny estate, Andrew Drysdale. As the *Daily Telegraph*[20] reported Drysdale had been in Rosebery's service for 25 years and had been his factor or estate manager since August 1890, without any complaint. However on January 1st 1909 his employment was summarily terminated and he was required to hand over all of the estate's books and records before being escorted out of the estate office. Drysdale reacted by instituting a £10,000 slander suit in the

Court of Session. He alleged that Rosebery's conduct had ruined his career and that his employer was motivated by malice arising from a private grudge relating to the affairs of the All British Car Company Ltd.

More worryingly for Neil in court papers that the *Telegraph* quoted from Drysdale alleged that:

In 1906 Lord Rosebery induced him to become a director of the Company and subsequently he was elected Chairman but he said he was only to hold the position until Neil Primrose was ready to take over. Unfortunately before he did so the Company was forced into liquidation and a guarantee Neil Primrose had given to the Company's bank was called in.

At the preliminary hearing in which Rosebery's counsel asked for further time to prepare a defence, he stated that his instructions were that Neil was never envisaged as a future company chairman. The Lord Ordinary adjourned the matter to a later date.

Unsurprisingly, given its potential to discredit Neil in the run-up to his Wisbech election campaign, the case never returned to court and presumably Drysdale was quietly compensated in return for his silence.

12

THE END OF THE OLD STRUCTURE OF SOCIETY

On April 29th 1909 David Lloyd George introduced his People's Budget, proposing large increases in death duties and income tax, including the introduction of a super tax on incomes over £3,000 p.a. However most revolutionary of all was an unprecedented new capital tax on land ownership. This was to be levied at the rate of ½d in the £ on the current value.

On Budget day 1909 Neil was with his father in Venice living on the *Zaida* and Rosebery, in ignorance of events in London, was entirely content, telling his sister that day: "Neil and I are very happy here together. But he has to leave tomorrow for the LCC which is a desperate wrench."[1] Days later things had changed and Rosebery who was still in Venice wrote to Neil:

> I think we shall go to Ravenna tomorrow for a day and then return here. Then I may come over to England for ten days as the budget seems to necessitate some immediate arrangements. Would you send me the Budget Speech in pamphlet form ... I hate reading it in the newspapers and there is no hurry – I know quite enough! It is nothing less than a revolution the end of the old structure of society as we have known it in Britain. But this about the budget is for your eye alone. I should like to know what people say on the subject.[2]

Rosebery did not revise his initial views or hold back for long on publicly expressing them. On June 21st he wrote to *The Times* saying: "This is not a Budget but a revolution, a social and political revolution of the first magnitude." On September 10th he spoke publicly about the budget in

Glasgow to the Chamber of Commerce. In his speech he categorized it as "inquisitorial, tyrannical and Socialistic ... the end of all, the negation of faith, of family, of property, of monarchy, of Empire."[3]

The following day Prime Minister Asquith wrote to Rosebery: "I read your speech with the most profound regret. It marks the parting of the ways between every one of your old colleagues who have in the past fought under you or by your side."[4] However, Rosebery did not care: he had already resigned as President of the League and as a member of the National Liberal Club; but for all of Rosebery's theatrical severance of his links with the party he had once led, his younger son remained a Liberal candidate and for his political future Rosebery continued to care deeply.

Neil's difficulties in Wisbech had already become acute before his father's Glasgow speech. He faced twin attacks on related grounds. The first was from the radical Liberal and former MP Charles Conybeare[5] who contended that Neil's conservative political opinions made him unfit to represent the constituency's Liberal voters. The second was from the Liberal MP for South-West Norfolk Richard Winfrey[6], who alleged that Neil's 1908 adoption as Liberal candidate was illegitimate and that the selection ought now to be re-opened.

Conybeare's attack on Neil came first, in the form of a letter to a Wisbech newspaper[7] dated August 4th:

Will the electors be satisfied to have as their representative in the next Parliament one who ... though sitting on the Liberal benches will be voting against the party of Freedom and Progress ... and supporting the millionaires of the House of Lords against the toiling millions of the nation?

Under his signature Conybeare described himself as:

A convinced Radical and enthusiastic advocate of Land Reform, a determined enemy of the House of Lords, and a strenuous supporter of the present Government.

Conybeare soon followed up his letter with a speech to a Liberal meeting at Whittlesey in which he denied that his intention was to split the Liberal vote in the constituency but that he wanted to bring home to Liberal supporters "the importance of having a thoroughly sound land reform and democratic candidate."[8] After this speech, Richard Winfrey, MP for a neighbouring seat and reasonably fearing its loss to the Unionists if the Liberal vote fractured, publicly raised the issue of Neil's hasty adoption, made in the absence of a choice, nineteen months earlier:

> Mr Beck announced his own retirement at the next election and at the same time he said he had found a worthy successor. The whole thing was cut and dried before the rank and file of the party were aware of the situation. I am confident that if a choice had been given – I mean if the usual practice had been followed and two or three names of suitable candidates placed before the Liberal Council a wiser choice would have been made.[9]

Unsurprisingly in this situation, Neil was urgently asked to address a special meeting of the Wisbech Liberal Council. This he did at March on September 8th when he explained that he supported the Budget with the sole exception of the proposed capital tax on land values. This he predicted would inexorably rise from ½d to 2d or 3d in the £ and so lead to forced sales, which would decrease land values and the revenue generated.[10] After Neil had addressed the meeting a vote of confidence in him was passed by 61 votes to 1.[11]

This overwhelming vote of confidence seems to have seen off the threat made by Charles Conybeare to stand against him. In early October the *Evening Standard*[12] accurately predicted that he was soon to become the official Liberal candidate in Horncastle, Lincolnshire, where he would fail in January 1910 to unseat the defending Conservative candidate, Lord Willoughby de Eresby.

With Conybeare out of the way and having easily survived the confidence vote, Neil was now safe to turn his fire on his other Liberal opponent, Richard Winfrey. This he did at March, Cambridgeshire on October 6th with the following stirring words:

> I declare absolutely and finally that I will not be drummed out of the Liberal Party by Mr Winfrey or Mr Conybeare, who by trying to sow dissension in our ranks have shown themselves to be traitors to our cause.[13]

Later in the same speech Neil returned to his continued opposition to the proposed land tax, explaining that the cost to the Government of introducing such a tax would be enormous as a valuation of all land would need to be conducted and regularly updated.[14] Furthermore he felt it unfair that the tax would fall unfairly heavily on landowners with holdings close to urban areas; and as the proposal originated with the Labour Party, a Liberal Government should not promote it.

At the close of the meeting Neil's candidature was boosted by words in his support, expressed by the East Anglian Regional Liberal Chairman[15], who told the audience that there had been nothing unusual in the manner of Neil's selection and "rightly or wrongly they intended to carry him as candidate."[16]

Richard Winfrey struck back by pointing out Neil's opposition to the Liberal Government on a range of policies ranging from Home Rule to the abolition of the Lords veto:

This then is the half-baked kind of Liberalism the Wisbech Division is apparently committed to, and because I dare to offer the mildest protest, I am dubbed a traitor by a young man who has been brought up in the purple, and never been called upon to do an honest day's work in his life.[17]

However, after the House of Lords rejected the Budget Finance Bill by 350 votes to 75, Parliament was prorogued for the General Election on December 3rd. From then on, Neil was safe from further attack by his fellow Liberals.

13

YOU ARE ALL THAT IS LEFT OF THE FAMILY NEST

Away from politics 1909 was an eventful one for Neil. February saw his brother's surprise engagement to Dorothy Grosvenor[1], the eighteen-year-old daughter of Lord Henry Grosvenor and a cousin of Bendor the fabulously wealthy 2nd Duke of Westminster. On the day of the announcement[2], Rosebery, at his most candid, commented on the news to the Prince of Wales (later George V):

> The news came on me like a bombshell never having seen or even heard of this young lady or had an idea that anything of the kind was in contemplation, that it took my breath away.[3]

Two days earlier Rosebery wrote in similar gloomy terms to Neil, while attempting to re-assure him that his own relations with Harry would be unimpaired by the unexpected and unwelcome marriage:

> You need not be afraid of this making a difference between brothers. It is much more likely to draw him away from me. That is natural and cannot be helped. He cannot be the same again …
>   You are all that is left of the family nest and you will soon fly away too but in the meantime I hope you will sit sometimes in the lonely hearth till there are grandchildren.[4]

The wedding took place on the Thursday of Easter week at St. Paul's Knightsbridge and Neil performed the duty of best man.[5] The reception took place in a borrowed house, 13 Grosvenor Square, for the bride's parents were far below Rosebery's league of wealth and did not own a London house. This fact may help to explain Rosebery's opposition, but as Harry's biographer subsequently wrote: "It was an ill-starred marriage. Within a few years it was effectively over, and within ten years was officially ended by divorce."[6]

That summer's social season was, as it transpired, King Edward VII's last and, perhaps in order to cloak the looming revolutionary axe that the People's Budget seemed to represent, was particularly brilliant and glittering. Neil as usual spent much of it playing polo and attending the leading race meetings. At the Derby the King's horse *Minoru* won the race, giving him a third victory, following those of 1896 and 1900 when he was Prince of Wales. Then at Royal Ascot Jimmy de Rothschild's horse *Bomba* won the Gold Cup and as the *Bystander*[7] reported following the race, Neil and Harry carried their kinsman "in triumph for a long celebratory drink."

In early July Neil attended the King and Queen's final State Ball at Buckingham Palace for 1,700 guests. By this stage after his frequent visits to Balmoral and Sandringham and theirs to Rosebery's numerous homes, the King knew Neil well, and Queen Alexandra had adopted him as something of a pet; an affection that was to be of life-long duration.

Later that month Rosebery entertained the Prince and Princess of Wales at Mentmore. The Prince had last visited when a bachelor in 1889, when Hannah still reigned over her father's great mansion. But that was not the only thing to have changed in the interim: the Prince and Princess, with their staff, travelled by car from Marlborough House to Mentmore. The Prince recorded with precision in his diary that the 38 mile journey from central London took just under two hours before continuing: "tea in the garden; fine and warm. This is a beautiful house, full of lovely things, I was here just 20 years ago." The family part of Rosebery's house party consisted of "the Dalmenys, Lady Sybil & Charles Grant & Neil Primrose."[8]

In an unprecedented move caused by the Budget, the Commons did not rise for the traditional summer recess in July and continued to sit throughout August and September. In consequence Neil remained in London and the *Evening Standard* reported on August 10th that he and Thomas "have been among those dining at the Savoy Hotel over the past few days." Earlier in the summer the *Daily Telegraph* had noted them together during the King's visit to Sandown Park, and the same newspaper listed them together at Aintree for that year's Grand National.[9]

1909 was also the year when Neil took what would prove the fateful step of joining the Territorial Army, as a Second Lieutenant in the Royal Bucks Hussars.[10] The regiment had been formed in 1794 in the context of the French Revolution, as a volunteer cavalry unit, with the dual purpose of defending the country from invasion, and of subduing internal disorder. Originally styled the Buckinghamshire Yeomanry, the regiment was designated 'Royal' by Queen Victoria and first served overseas in 1900, during the Boer War. Following Haldane's Territorial Army reforms, that brought in central funding and national standards of training and organisation, it was finally renamed as the Buckinghamshire Yeomanry (Royal Bucks Hussars).

Historically the Yeomanry was an adjunct to traditional County society and its officers were drawn from the county's leading families. Therefore, as during the second half on the nineteenth century Buckinghamshire gradually became 'Rothschildshire', members of the Rothschild family were awarded commissions. For instance Nathaniel Mayer de Rothschild (ennobled in 1885 as Baron Rothschild of Tring) was commissioned as a Second Lieutenant in 1863[11] and his son Lionel Walter de Rothschild (who subsequently became the 2nd Lord Rothschild) served as an officer in the regiment between 1890[12] and 1909 reaching the rank of Major[13]. In terms of Neil's own generation his three Rothschild cousins at Ascott, the sons of the 1st Lord Rothschild's younger brother Leopold, all served in the regiment: Neil's contemporary Lionel was first commissioned in 1903 and promoted to Lieutenant in 1908, his younger brother Evelyn joined him in 1907 and the youngest brother Anthony followed Neil into the regiment in 1910.

Aside from these family connections, Neil's New College friend Fred Cripps joined the regiment as a subaltern while still an undergraduate at Oxford University in 1904[14] and many of the other officers and men would have been well known to Neil through his hunting with the Whaddon Chase Hounds and Lord Rothschild's Staghounds. In fact it was often said at the time that members of the county yeomanry were simply playing at soldiers and that their camps and exercises really only served to extend the camaraderie of the hunting season. Certainly Rosebery did not see Neil as a natural soldier and when in September 1915 Neil was first put at serious risk of harm, Rosebery recorded "he is not the least military". However in that militarised era Neil was surrounded by uniformed figures: his brother-in-law Charles Grant was a professional soldier; Harry had been through Sandhurst and although compelled to resign his Guards commission when selected to stand for Parliament, remained on the General Reserve of Officers[15]; and Thomas was then serving as an officer in the Royal 1st Devon Imperial Yeomanry.[16]

The regiment was composed of four squadrons, each centred on a town within the county – Buckingham, Aylesbury, High Wycombe and Chesham. Unsurprisingly given its proximity to Mentmore, Neil was posted to the Aylesbury squadron.[17] His first experience of soldiering under canvas took place in May when the regiment held its annual camp at Ascott Home Farm[18], on the estate of Leopold de Rothschild and only a few miles from Mentmore.

Neil's friend Fred Cripps has left a vivid account of these 'camps' which involved the officers dining in full dress uniform at the adjacent great houses of Ascott and Waddesdon, followed by card playing late into the night.[19]

So far as Neil's officer training was concerned, although the Territorial and Reserve Forces Act of 1907 had tightened things a little, the obligation placed on officers was only to undertake a written and oral examination within the first year of service. As for horsemanship, Neil needed no training and would have brought to camp his best hunters from Mentmore. He would also have supplied his own cavalry sword and officer's revolver.

At brigade level the Royal Bucks Hussars formed part of the South Midland Mounted Brigade, along with the Berkshire Yeomanry and the Queen's Own Oxfordshire Hussars, and every third year a brigade camp assembled. The first of these that Neil attended was held in Blenheim Park at Woodstock. Also present were Winston Churchill and F.E. Smith in their capacity as officers in the Oxfordshire Hussars and they and Neil apparently stayed up until dawn playing chemin de fer for high stakes in F.E.'s tent.[20]

14

TAKE TO HEART LORD ROSEBERY'S ADVICE

The new year and Neil's election campaign did not get off to a promising start; in part because he was not prepared to forsake the pleasures and dangers of the hunting field, notwithstanding his imminent campaign. The result was a New Year's Day dislocated shoulder after a fall near Oakham while hunting with the Cottesmore Hounds. It necessitated an un-planned return to London, and what his father termed 'a horribly painful putting in'. But it also meant that he missed the start of his own campaign, which was launched in his absence by his brother-in-law Lord Crewe at the Public Hall in Wisbech.[1] Neil was fortunate in this (and not only to have a sister married to the Lord Privy Seal and Liberal leader in the Lords) because this was the first General Election in which peers were permitted to speak on public platforms in support of their party's candidates.[2]

Neil arrived in the constituency on Tuesday January 4th, just over three weeks before the poll. On the same day his father wrote to him from Scotland:

I am afraid I must write a letter about the Election as I owe it to my conscience. But I do not think it can hurt you as … there is an English love of fair play which would react against any attempt to strike at you through your Father. I only wish I could keep silence.[3]

When Neil first saw his father's letter, addressed to an elector from Devon who had asked him how he would vote if he were an elector, he must have wished he had. The letter, widely reported in the press a few days later[4], left no room for doubt that if able to vote, Rosebery would support the Unionists: "On 3 out of 4 issues on which the General Election will be fought I am at variance with the Government." In listing them Rosebery was unambiguous in his opposition to the Government's recent conversion to

'Socialism', the Budget (in which 'Socialism' found expression) and an Irish Parliament.

Only in its quest for a reformed and efficient second chamber can I support them ... naturally I write with both natural pain and reluctance but obeying the dictates of both conscience and patriotism.

Rosebery failed to consider that he, a former Liberal Prime Minister, could not provide this national judgment without it impacting upon his son's local campaign; and for Neil's Unionist opponent Rosebery's intervention was manna from heaven. That opponent was Thomas Garfit, a banker from Boston, Lincolnshire, who had stood in 1906 and lost by 1,045 votes. The intervening four years had witnessed a national revival in Unionist fortunes, but in Neil he had a young, glamorous, newspaper idol rival, making it a tough fight to deprive the Liberals of the seat. As such Neil cannot have been surprised that the Wisbech Unionists took advantage of Rosebery's advice, although whether he was prepared for it to be at the centre of their campaign literature is another matter. That literature had emblazoned across it: "Electors of North Cambridgeshire take to heart Lord Rosebery's advice! Vote for GARFIT".

In these circumstances, Rosebery wisely kept away from the contest, but he did send a motor car and his driver Albert to assist in transporting Neil and his supporters around the large and mainly rural constituency. Neither candidate gave an address within the constituency on his nomination papers; Neil gave his as 38 Berkeley Square and described himself as "Alderman, London County Council". His Unionist opponent's address was a little nearer - Kenwick Hall, Louth, Lincs. and his description was "Gentleman, JP, DL."[5]

In Neil's campaign speeches he stuck to the safe issue of Free Trade and "untaxed bread" and the Lords' veto which he characterised as "absolutely indefensible" when exercised "as a right conferred by heredity".[6] On January 15th Rosebery wrote with relief from Scotland:

The sight of my son's handwriting was like water in the desert, for I have been longing to have a word from you ... meanwhile I devour the Wisbech papers.

I am delighted that you are cheerful as to the result. I see that Garfit is checked by the crowd when he attempts to quote me. I am delighted the motor is so useful – Albert is seeing life.[7]

Alone at Dalmeny House, and fretting about the result and his own responsibility for a defeat, Rosebery wrote again on January 23[rd:]

I am languishing for news of you and Wisbech. After the declaration tell Albert to send a telegram simply 'In' or 'Out'. Till then I only half exist. Any news of Thomas?[8] I see Grenfell easily managed to take Bodmin.[9]

As Rosebery's letter indicates both voting and declarations then took place across a number of days. In Thomas's St Austell constituency the poll was held on January 24th while Neil's was two days later. The day itself was marred by the death of an elderly Liberal-supporting voter who suddenly collapsed while being conveyed to vote in a motor car attached to Neil's campaign.[10] Some superstitious local commentators regarded that as a bad omen but when the declaration came Neil was declared elected by the slim majority of 200 votes.[11]

Following the declaration and having been based throughout in a Wisbech hotel, Neil swiftly returned to London to celebrate his narrow victory. His movements were now even more public property and the following Monday's *Times* reported his departure from London for Dalmeny House and a re-union with his father. Rosebery displayed an almost childish delight in adding the letters MP to his son's name:

This note is only to show the pride and pleasure with which I direct to you as MP for the first time, and to thank you for your delightful visit.[12]

Nationally the Unionists had gained 126 seats but with Irish Nationalist support the Liberal Government remained in place when Parliament was opened on February 15th. Just 3 days before the new Parliament met, its new Member for North Cambridgeshire was reported out hunting with the Belvoir.[13]

Soon after the new Parliament opened, and knowing quite how precarious Edward VII's hold on life now was, Rosebery and Neil hosted a dinner for the Prince of Wales at Berkeley Square. The all-male guest list of sixteen included Arthur Conan Doyle and the editors of Punch and The Observer. In terms of politicians there were more Unionist MPs (James Clyde, F.E. Smith and Lionel de Rothschild) than Liberals (Rufus Isaacs); although the recently retired Liberal MP Sir Robert Perks and the Prime Minister's eldest son, the barrister Raymond Asquith, were also present. The Prince evidently enjoyed the evening and recorded in his diary: "At 8.30 I dined with Rosebery, he gave me a very pleasant dinner & I met many interesting people to all of whom I talked."[14]

Later that month a victory dinner for Neil was held in Wisbech at which his father spoke and proposed the health of the new Member. When news of the event first came out there was much press speculation as to how Lord Rosebery would overcome the conundrum that he had advocated the Unionist cause. The following report in the *Luton Times and Advertiser*[15] is not un-typical:

Lord Rosebery advised the electorate of England to vote against the Liberal Party. The Wisbech electors did not follow his advice and now his Lordship is – presumably – to congratulate them on their action.

The dinner, held at the Selwyn Hall in Wisbech, was attended by 240 people; the organisers wanted Rosebery to feel so at home that the Hall was specially decorated with murals showing the Scottish landscape. The proceedings commenced at 7.30pm when Rosebery, Neil and Lord Peckover (with whom they were staying at Bank House) arrived. In his much anticipated and widely reported speech Rosebery dismissed the Unionists' use of his views against Neil as "hitting below the belt"[16] before jokingly declining to say anything about the contemporary political situation because "you are unfortunately familiar with my views because, I understand they adorned every wall in the constituency." Moving onto safer ground Rosebery proceeded to make almost a 'best man's speech' – reciting a succession of jokes at his son's expense; he started by saying Neil had to be the youngest ever Alderman and in reference to his immaturity continued "I believe you in Wisbech are famous for the art of forcing fruit and vegetables to maturity and I have no doubt that a constituency such as this will force my son to maturity."

Rosebery then turned to the even more excruciating (for Neil) topic of his bachelor status:

whether he will undergo that further process marriage I do not know. Those are secrets which sons do not impart to their fathers as a rule, but even if he has no such idea at the present he may be satisfied with the wedded bond which he has entered into with this constituency.[17]

Perhaps unsurprisingly, in replying to the toast Neil made the briefest of remarks and largely confined himself to thanking those present for their support.

His speech-making skills were rather more on display some weeks later when he made his maiden speech on the topical subject of relations between the two Houses of Parliament:

I hope that one day we shall see the House of Lords reconstituted in a manner which will give us a Chamber ... which shall be fair, which shall not forward the aspirations of any political party, and which shall be free from the influences of any class or any particular interest, and which shall perform its functions under the inspiration, so far as human nature can be under that inspiration, of impartiality and common sense.

He then proceeded to report on his constituents' views on the second chamber:

I take it as an average Constituency, though naturally I think it is far above the average. No electors were more infuriated against the Veto of the House of Lords than were my Constituents. They considered that it was founded on a basis of injustice, and that it was exercised in a wanton and unconstitutional way. But throughout the election, on every occasion when the question was raised, they agreed that a Second Chamber was necessary.[18]

Rosebery, who had himself made an important speech on Lords reform just weeks earlier[19] and who very probably had a role in the speech's formation, watched from the Peers' Gallery. Another attendee, there almost without precedent, was Queen Alexandra. The Queen sat in that part of the Ladies' Gallery reserved for the Speaker's wife. As *The Times* reported next day as soon as she had heard "the successful maiden speech" she rose to leave. In so doing, she probably missed the extraordinary compliment paid to Neil by the Irish Nationalist MP Stephen Gwynn, who followed Neil in the debate:

I think the Committee will agree that the speech to which we have just listened, with its distinction and charm, has gone far to convince us that, after all, there is something in the hereditary principle.

The *Daily Telegraph* later praised it as "fluent, well informed and well arranged and marks him out as a young man of promise."

Quite what his fellow newly elected MPs made of such overt royal favouritism and prominent national scrutiny of a maiden speech, is not recorded; but Neil appears to have been untroubled by being set apart (Thomas excepted) from his fellow backbenchers. In fact the duo's exclusive closeness, which they advertised by keeping to the dying habit of wearing their top hats in the chamber, was noticed on both sides of the House, and increasingly in the Press Gallery.

In April 1910 they both rode in the House of Commons point-to-point race, which was open to Commons Members who had been active in the 1909-10 hunting season and was ridden wearing hunting dress. The race was divided into two classes, Light and Heavyweights, but ridden together with the former class in red coats and the latter in black coats.

Amusingly Neil and Thomas were placed in different classes and ended the race with most different outcomes – Neil was placed third in the Heavyweights while Thomas, a Lightweight, was an uninjured faller.[20]

15

THE COUNTRY LOVES A LITTLE INDEPENDENCE

On May 6th 1910 King Edward VII died quite suddenly of heart failure. He had been in poor health since the year began and had spent most of March and April trying to recover at Biarritz. The King arrived in London on April 27th and within ten days he was dead. One of his son's first actions on becoming King was to inform the Prime Minister, Asquith, that he would not open his first Parliament until the Royal Accession Declaration was no longer in the form of a denunciation of Roman Catholic doctrine. This was because the King objected to uttering a form of words that were so offensive to his loyal Catholic subjects.[1]

On the death of Queen Victoria an unsuccessful attempt had been made to make this change; and so Edward VII was obliged, on opening his first Parliament, to take the same anachronistic oath as had been used by every monarch since 1688. Almost a decade on, the political situation was much changed, with the political composition of the Commons being in antithesis to that of the Lords. As a result there was a real threat to the survival of a Parliament just three months old and it was impossible to safely predict when the next State Opening would be. In this uncertain climate the Cabinet felt obliged to rapidly accede to the new King's demand by introducing legislation to revise the Royal Oath. The speed of the Prime Minister's move, when coupled with his Government's reliance upon the support of Irish Nationalist MPs for survival, and the secrecy that the new King's demand was the main reason behind it, undoubtedly led to 'Protestant' disquiet. Perhaps some discontent was inevitable but for it to lead the young pleasure-seeking duo of Neil and Thomas to the very centre of 'Protestant' religious opposition seems extraordinary. It also brought them into a far sharper national focus as perhaps they opportunistically intended.

The Accession Declaration Bill received its first reading in the Commons on June 28th and was passed by 383 votes to 42. Both Neil and Thomas spoke and voted against the Bill's first reading[2] but their words perhaps indicate that Neil was a 'hedger' and Thomas a 'ditcher' from the start. Thomas took the principled stand that the existing Declaration could not be altered to soothe Catholic feelings while still ensuring the Protestant Succession and that the proposed reform was "stirring up religious strife the length and breadth of the land." Neil was far more measured, saying it would be a "pity" to remove "one of the safeguards" of the Protestant Succession.

In fact Neil's speech is more noteworthy for his ferocious attack on his fellow Liberal MP and devout Catholic, Hilaire Belloc on the ground of his anti-Semitism:

I have not been privileged to read his books, but I am told that, in one of them he has written in a style of some hostility against a race with which I am very proud to be connected. I should have hardly thought he was a man to lecture on religious toleration. I can only imagine, when my ancestors were compelled to follow the occupation of making bricks without straw, his ancestors were of those who imposed on them that uncongenial and laborious task.

Perhaps unwisely the Government, alarmed by the scale of opposition on first reading, now delayed the second reading until the final days of the session in order to rush it through before the Commons rose for the summer; so increasing Protestant paranoia.

During this parliamentary pause, Neil and Thomas agreed to address the Knox Club in Edinburgh as part of its public demonstration against the Bill.[3] In his speech Neil was careful to deny the charge of intolerance but Thomas arguably demonstrated his, and fuelled the sectarian atmosphere, with the rash words "I told my constituents at the last election the issue was between peers and people. Fool that I was, I forgot the Pope."[4]

When the Bill returned to the Commons, Thomas led the opposition and so followed the Prime Minister in the debate.[5] He advanced the extra-ordinary thesis that just as Charles II and his brother James II could not be trusted to make an honest declaration of faith, nor could monarchs 250 years later, and for that reason a specific repudiation continued to be required.

Once again, Neil was far more circumspect: "I have received letters from various people who are not my Constituents and who seem to be in a great state of agitation about the passing of this Bill." And that the Government's undue haste "will embitter feeling already bitter". On the following day, during the debate on the third reading, Neil clearly set out his political independence: "As a Liberal when the Leader of the Opposition happens to agree with the Government, I view the position with profound suspicion." The Bill easily survived its final vote in the Commons and five days later as the session ended received Royal Assent.[6]

Before Parliament rose for the summer Rosebery had left London for his usual summer spa visit, this year at Vichy, but on reaching Paris, Jimmy de Rothschild gave him a file of press cuttings on the matter. The result was the following headmasterly if benevolent letter to Neil, despatched from the Hotel Bristol on August 1st:

> Jimmy has lent me some speeches which I have read with the greatest interest. You have every reason to be pleased with the late episode. You have attached to your name a large and powerful following in the country which may be of the greatest use to you hereafter and you have become familiar to the House and to places like Manchester where otherwise you would not have been. And no one can be annoyed by the part you have taken up while a great many are delighted. I don't think you could stand in a better position. You have not attacked the Government but have shown that you can be independent on an occasion. And the country loves a little independence – it gets so little of it.[7]

In Neil's case Rosebery's conclusions were defensible, but the same cannot be said for Thomas, and surely the suspicion must be that where Thomas had led, Neil had innocently followed. Certainly Lord Birkenhead's 1922 memoir records that they were very much against mainstream opinion.[8]

Neil spent most of August in Deauville playing polo with his cousin Evelyn's Gunnersbury team[9] but in September he was rather more seriously engaged in accompanying his father to Vienna to make the formal announcement of King George's accession to the elderly Emperor Francis Joseph. The Special Mission stayed at the Hofburg as the Emperor's guests over three nights and, as well as a state dinner at Schönbrunn and a reciprocal dinner at the British Embassy, the visit also included meetings with the Austrian and Hungarian premiers. On conclusion of the visit *The Times* correspondent recorded that on all hands "the Rosebery Mission has been an unqualified success".[10] Rosebery's request to take Neil with him was perhaps an unusual one, but as in former years, Rosebery felt that the opportunity for his son to observe diplomacy at the very highest level was not one he should miss. On returning to London, father and son went north to Scotland but there they were divided as Rosebery was expected at Balmoral to report to the King on his diplomatic mission. Despite his royal surroundings, Rosebery was not happy with this separation as he told Neil in a letter edged in deep mourning black dated September 20th:

> It is very tantalising to be here, kind as are my hosts, while you are at Dalmeny but I shall get away on Saturday and then shall motor to join you at Dalmeny or Rosebery, let me know which.[11]

But just two days later, Rosebery's plans were upset by the King asking him to stay two more nights:

> I replied that I wanted to be with you as you were going off so soon, on which he replied that I was to ask you. It is extraordinarily kind but I must say I should secretly have preferred being alone with you at Dalmeny. Breaks are never warm at Balmoral; you had better come by the 10.53 from Edinburgh. I have my motor here and will send it to Ballater to meet you.

Rosebery then added a postscript "The King wants to speak to you about the Declaration! He has already mentioned it to me."[12]

If the King did discuss the matter with Neil, no record remains as to what was said (the King's diary merely notes Neil's arrival at the Castle[13]) but no doubt the King disclosed his own role in the genesis of the Accession Declaration Act, and his satisfaction that it was now in place in readiness for the next State Opening whenever it came.

16

A VERY FORMIDABLE OPPONENT

Rosebery had been so anxious to spend as much of September with Neil because on October 1st Neil was to leave England for a six-week tour of America. But unlike in 1905 this was not to be a solitary post-Oxford educational tour but a thoroughly decadent trip in the company of both Thomas and Jimmy. The trip started in New York and Neil would later reminisce about the voyage made "under such hilarious circumstances".[1] Of course the Commons was not expected to sit for many weeks and the trio of wealthy bachelors (aged respectively 27, 30 and 31) were spending their own money. On news reaching him by telegram that the trio had reached New Orleans, where they stayed at the Pickwick Club, Rosebery replied that it was "a glorious moment" and that even in his decrepitude, he almost envied them.[2] The trip did not entirely escape the notice of the press on both sides of the Atlantic and even *The Times*[3] recorded Neil and Thomas's return to Fishguard from New York on the Cunard steamer *Mauretania*. Perhaps fortuitously the pleasures of the trip stood Neil in good stead for the rigours of the weeks ahead, as three days after his return, Lord Crewe announced in the House of Lords that the Government was giving up on its attempt to reach agreement with the Unionists over the exercise of the Lords veto, and that Parliament was being dissolved.[4]

For Neil this second election of 1910 would be a far tougher and more bruising test than that undergone just ten months previously. This did not relate to some sudden shift in public opinion or grave error on Neil's part but was due to the unexpected fact that the Unionist candidate for Wisbech was another Prime Minister's son, Lord Robert Cecil. Even the firmly Liberal-leaning *Cambridge Independent Press*[5] called him "a very formidable opponent" notwithstanding his being "a Tory of the most reactionary type."

Cecil was a successful KC and Neil's senior by 19 years. He also had greater experience in the Commons having represented Marylebone East throughout the 1906 Parliament, although he had been out of the Commons since January 1910. One positive for Neil though was that Cecil was not personally known locally, and only arrived in the constituency three weeks before the poll. Even more significantly, Cecil's agent only arrived five days before that. Cecil himself openly acknowledged that the invitation to stand was belated, but his adoption on November 23rd undeniably enthused the local Unionists, as well as the local and national press.

In its November 25th edition the editor of the *Wisbech Standard* wrote of the rival candidates:

> The spectacle of these two sons fighting a battle in Cosmopolitan Fenland should provide an interesting picture and will doubtless be watched with more than ordinary interest by the rest of the country.

Seemingly the London press agreed and the town's hotels were filled with reporters. *The Times* sent a Special Correspondent to Wisbech and in his first column[6] he wrote:

> The fact that the rival candidates are the sons of former Prime Ministers lends a peculiar distinction to the election, and in this respect the contest is believed to be without parallel.

In assessing the likely outcome he said:

> Lord Robert's task is by no means an easy one. The seat has always been Liberal in Liberal years. Although Mr Primrose won the last election only by 200 votes, he has made himself a very popular member and his opponent may find a 3 week campaign in a wide-spreading constituency barely sufficient for his purpose. ... The chief Unionist stronghold is Wisbech town and among the farmers. Mr Primrose's strength is among the railwaymen of March and in the Nonconformist villages.

Both candidates were adopted on the same day in the town of March but thereafter they based themselves at rival hotels in Wisbech – Neil, as usual, at the White Hart and Lord Robert a short distance away at the Rose and Crown.

Unsurprisingly Neil's printed election address focussed exclusively on the House of Lords and the recent failure of the cross-party conference that had necessitated another election. However the document promised his supporters "reconstruction" of the House of Lords so that it would in future be "chosen without regard to hereditary privilege" which was far closer to his father's reform proposals than anything ever proposed by Asquith's Government. Therefore, fairly as things turned out, Lord Robert attacked those words on the ground that the Government's sole intention was to diminish the power of the Second Chamber so as to make it subservient to the Commons, without actually reforming its composition.

Not surprisingly Neil was sensitive to the small size of the majority he was defending. After the election in January he had heard rumours that the Unionist candidate had treated the electorate with free beer in several of Wisbech's many public houses. This time, if such bribery occurred, he wanted to gather the evidence to use in an election petition, in the event that he lost. As a result he secretly employed a London private detective agency to monitor the Wisbech pubs throughout the campaign.[7]

Cecil resisted using Lord Rosebery's attacks on the Government in the campaign, but nonetheless, as in January, Rosebery kept away. By December 1910 Neil had purchased his own motor car but as the following letter discloses, Rosebery could not resist making a contribution to the campaign:

I am sending a clock for your motor which may have to do for a New Year's present but it is useful at once. Asprey is to send instructions with it ... An occasional bulletin from the field of action will be very welcome but I know how busy you will be.[8]

Busy they certainly were, and *The Times* reported on November 28th that Cecil had already arranged to attend 31 village meetings. These meetings were lively affairs, as they were invariably attended by the rival candidates' supporters. Usually, but not always, the candidate's speech was listened to in respectful silence; but during the questions which followed the candidate might be tripped up. Given the number of journalists in attendance, rash remarks rapidly appeared in print.

This happened to Neil on December 2nd at Christchurch when asked if he was in favour of Home Rule. The word "Ireland" did not appear on Neil's Election Address and in answering the question "Are you in favour of Home Rule?" he was unwisely forthright, prompting headlines such as "Neil Primrose Against Home Rule". His exact words were quoted in the following day's *Yorkshire Post*[9]:

I am not a Home Ruler. I think it would be possible for them to manage a few more of their own affairs but I would never vote for anything which would give them full management of their affairs.

Home Rule was not exactly a burning issue in the Cambridgeshire Fens but later when the Home Rule controversy reached its Parliamentary apogee those words would come back to bite him.

At the other end of the country, when nominations closed in St Austell, Thomas found himself returned unopposed but any temptation to travel to the Fens to help Neil was resisted and he remained in Cornwall and spoke in support of other Cornish Liberal candidates who did face a vote.[10]

For Neil his last big speech of the campaign was made in the Public Hall in Wisbech. Despite extra stewards inside and numerous police outside there was some disorder and heckling but not so as to stop his speech. In it he re-iterated the charge that Cecil was against even the principle of old age pensions and that pensions were not safe if he was returned.

On polling day itself, which happened to be Neil's 28th birthday, the Unionists pulled out all of the stops and used over 100 motor cars in the constituency. The turnout was 10,285 (87.6%) and in consequence the declaration was not made until mid-morning of the following day. Neil had polled 5,401, the highest total for a candidate ever recorded in the seat's history[11], giving him a majority of 544.

Cecil was not the most gracious of losers and in his post-declaration speech made what *The Times*[12] termed a "vigorous protest" about the way his views on old age pensions had been misrepresented by Neil's campaign. Almost four decades later when Viscount Cecil of Chelwood wrote his memoirs[13] he was rather more generous to Neil:

There was also a charge that I was against Old Aged Pensions – inaccurate but understandable. My opponent – Neil Primrose – made the most of these arguments, and defeated me not unexpectedly.

Some days later Neil received his private detectives' report which exonerated Cecil of any illegal treating.[14] Elsewhere the report highlights how surreal the declaration of the result must have been for Neil, for while he was the victor, the partisan Wisbech crowd treated Cecil as if he were, and drew him round the Market Place in his carriage.

17

TORY MAGISTRATES

Nationally the second General Election changed almost nothing. Although fifty seats changed hands, the net totals hardly changed at all and the two main parties were left tied on 272 seats. However when the Labour and Irish Nationalist MPs were added to the Liberal total, Asquith's Government retained an enormous effective majority of 126 seats.[1]

On February 6th the new Parliament was opened by the King. He made the declaration that he was "a faithful Protestant" under the new Accession Declaration Act, before delivering the gracious speech. The main and almost only piece of proposed legislation that the King referred to was a re-introduced Parliament bill.

The previous month Neil had been troubled by his old foe (and fellow Liberal MP) Richard Winfrey[2], requesting a joint meeting in celebration of their respective re-elections to North Cambridgeshire and the neighbouring seat of South West Norfolk. The proposed celebration was to be held in the village of Upwell, then divided between the counties of Norfolk and Cambridgeshire, with half in each constituency. In the light of the wishes of the Upwell Liberals, Winfrey wrote: "I think … the time has arrived when I as the elder of the two ought to say that I am quite ready to meet at such a gathering and let bygones be bygones".[3] Neil promptly replied that while not bearing Winfrey malice, "I would prefer not to hold a joint meeting with you … we should each look after our own constituencies without mutual assistance and independently."

Winfrey though did not give up and now got his agent to reply and renew the request. This drew an even sharper put-down from Neil in which he reminded Winfrey's agent of "all the political injury he [Winfrey] has tried to do me in the past." Quite unknown to Neil, in January 1911 another letter

114

was being written that concerned him, by a fellow Liberal MP (and Home Secretary), Winston Churchill. This letter was sent to the Prime Minister and contained Churchill's detailed thoughts as to how the Government should now proceed and who should be honoured and rewarded. Inter alia, it contained the following suggestion: "if you could find a little place for Neil Primrose it would please Rosebery in spite of himself."[4]

Asquith did not follow Churchill's advice and find a role for Neil within the Government. In consequence he found himself soon burdened with a Liberal backbench problem. That problem was to be aggravated once again by Neil's public demonstration of his political independence.

The issue in question had been smouldering since the autumn of 1910 and concerned the appointment of magistrates to the Isle of Ely bench, and the perceived or even actual political bias in their selection which was resulting in a preponderance of Conservative-supporting JPs. Neil's grievance had previously been expressed by other Liberal MPs and in November 1909 a Royal Commission had been established to look into the matter. That Commission had recommended an Advisory Committee for each county to assist the Lord Lieutenant in selecting suitable men as magistrates and the Government adopted it. However in the Isle of Ely's case neither the Lord Lieutenant of the county (Cambridgeshire) nor the Advisory Committee had been involved. Nominations were being made directly to the Lord Chancellor by the principal Justice of the Peace, Lord de Ramsey[5], who was a most active Conservative.

While still recovering from his bruising election campaign, Neil's passions were stirred further by this letter from his agent, William House, on the subject dated 22 March 1911:

> I cannot understand how it is permitted for Lord de Ramsey as representative of the Crown in the Isle to hold the office of President of the Wisbech Division Conservative Association and [be] a regular attender at their meetings.[6]

On March 26th Neil wrote to the Lord Chancellor, Lord Loreburn, as follows:

> Six magistrates – all Conservatives – have been appointed in my constituency without the Advisory Committee having been consulted

… good men with even better claims could have been found among the Liberals in that district. It has caused great dissatisfaction there that the Party which raised your Lordship to the high position which you hold, should be treated with this studied neglect.

Loreburn did not appreciate at all the final part of Neil's letter and disdained to reply to it. Neil now raised the stakes considerably by sending a copy of the letter to *The Times* where it appeared on April 6th, along with Neil's covering note stating: "I feel that publicity should be given to this letter in justice to my constituents." Within days House was reporting from Wisbech that Neil's letter had delighted the local Liberals.

A few weeks later it became clear that the Government was itself happy to enter into a media campaign when Lord Loreburn consented to Lord de Ramsey's recent letter, and his reply, being released to the press.[7] In the correspondence both men admitted to avoiding the involvement of the local advisory committee on the grounds of de Ramsey's imminent departure for Egypt and the urgent need to appoint the additional six, due to a shortage of magistrates in the Isle. On Neil's charge that all six were known Conservatives, de Ramsey wrote "I cannot vouch for the truth of it but I can say they were the very best men that I could find for your approval."

In Wisbech Liberal circles, Lord de Ramsey's words were read with derision. Neil's agent William House reported to Neil that de Ramsey was a very regular attender at Wisbech Conservative Party meetings and that one of the six was a member of the Executive and "for his Lordship not to know his politics is a lie". A Wisbech constituent, Alfred Southwell, wrote in only mildly less stringent terms:

Lord de Ramsey's letter is as weak as dish water and he cannot hoodwink this constituency, for even fair minded Conservatives consider that he has gone too far.

In the Commons, on April 12[th,] Neil brought the matter to the Prime Minister's attention during the motion to adjourn for Easter but obtained no more than a promise to look into it. Asquith was pressed twice more in the Commons, first by Thomas and then by Cecil Beck[8], before on May 1st he made a statement on the matter. His statement consisted largely of the background to the institution of Advisory Committees before concluding that as some were still to be set up, it was premature to debate the matter.

This did not pacify Neil as the Isle of Ely Advisory Committee was in place and yet the system of appointments was still being abused. Seemingly, similar abuses were going on across the country and Neil received letters in support of his campaign for a full debate in Parliament from Shropshire, Nottingham, Southampton, Stoke-on-Trent and Warwickshire.[9] In the midst of all this furore, Neil and Thomas encountered Asquith socially and on a relatively intimate occasion – the christening of the infant son and heir of Lord and Lady Crewe at the Chapel Royal. The King attended and stood sponsor, alongside the child's only surviving grandparent Rosebery, and Neil was one of two ushers who conducted the small number of invited guests to their seats.[10]

Neil now tried to use the Chief Whip as his intermediary but that got him nowhere so Neil put down in the Commons notice-paper a 'Resolution on Justices of the Peace'.[11] Despite its neutral title it amounted to a politically explosive vote of censure on the Lord Chancellor. As Neil was reliant on the Government for debating time, there it remained undebated for almost five months. Eventually, but in a Whips' Office move designed to ensure its defeat, the debate was brought on, on the eve of the Christmas recess and in a fairly thinly attended House. But Neil was not to be discouraged and on 15 December he opened the debate and told the Commons that the Liberal Lord Chancellor was, in the case of the Isle of Ely, entirely failing to involve an Advisory Committee on the appointment of justices and simply accepting the recommendations of Lord de Ramsey. Neil added that de Ramsey was not only *Custos Rotulorum* of the Isle of Ely but also President of the Wisbech Conservative Association. The names he put forward were almost universally well-known Conservative supporters: in the latest instance, one was even a member of the Wisbech Conservative Association Executive Committee. For doing just as Lord de Ramsey asked, Neil charged Lord Loreburn with committing "a breach of faith" and suggested that his motivations may have been "social". This was explosive stuff to raise in the Commons against a Liberal Lord Chancellor and particularly so when the Prime Minister was himself there to answer for him. In responding the Prime Minister paid Neil a double-edged compliment that would have ended all hopes of advancement in the mind of a less illustrious young backbencher:

The Hon. Member (Mr. Primrose) made a lively and interesting speech. I regretted that it should be disfigured, as I think it was, by quite unnecessary personal imputations against the Lord Chancellor. The Lord Chancellor is a hard fighter in politics, and was for many years a much-respected Member of this House. It is sufficient to say there is no one who knows him, either as friend or opponent, who is not prepared to say, as I say, that there is no man in politics whose conduct is more scrupulously regulated by the highest considerations."

Later in the debate, Neil was congratulated by the Labour MP (and subsequent Party Leader) John Clynes[12] for bringing forward the resolution and for pursuing it from the beginning.

According to Lord Beaverbrook[13], Andrew Bonar Law, the Conservative leader of the opposition, was contacted by Lord Loreburn on the morning of the debate; knowing he was at risk, he asked for Conservative support to defeat Neil's motion. Bonar Law, while sympathetic to Neil's cause, did not (for reasons relating to Ireland) want to see Lord Loreburn resign and so voted with the Government against Neil's resolution. As a result the Government easily saw off the challenge by 121 votes to 39. Beaverbrook also discloses that while Lloyd George voted, as he had to, with the Government, he had covertly supported Neil's campaign.

Regardless of behind the scenes moves and the outcome, Neil could be pleased with his campaign, as it led to the far firmer establishment of the role of advisory committees in the process of selection and reduced the obvious cosiness of the old system. It had also raised further his national profile and in the Commons demonstrated his bravery and tenacity in pursuing a cause that the Prime Minister did not want aired. He had also demonstrated his independence from Rosebery who, as Lord Lieutenant of both Midlothian and Linlithgow, thought advisory committees an unwelcome innovation. Furthermore the cause was one of far greater substance than the King's Declaration of Faith in which Neil had followed Thomas's lead; a year later those roles had been reversed.

In April 1911, as the magistrates issue was raging, Neil was appointed to sit on a Home Office Commission on the constitution of the Isle of Man.[14] Neil was one of six members appointed by the Home Secretary, Winston Churchill, who had perhaps concluded that while the Prime Minister declined to give Neil a role in his government, he could at least give Neil this to do. The committee first met in London but in May 1911 held hearings in the island's capital Douglas. In November their report was issued and the main recommendations, limiting the Governor's term of office and making the island's legislative council and parliament more democratic, were implemented.

Churchill was also responsible for Neil being an original member of the cross-party Other Club, on its foundation by Churchill and F.E. Smith in the spring of 1911.[15] The object of the club was to dine, and membership was to be limited to fifty men, of whom no more than twenty-four were to be members of the House of Commons (twelve from each of the main political parties). Despite the club's cross-party nature it was not to be a political vacuum: by Rule 12 "Nothing in the rules or intercourse of the Club shall interfere with the rancour or asperity of party politics."

For Neil to be selected as one of just twelve Liberal MPs, including such stars as Lloyd George and Churchill himself, was some achievement after only eighteen months in the Commons and confirms Neil's early reputation as an ambitious Young Turk.[16] In fact Neil was the club's youngest Liberal member[17] and it has been said he was the "most promising of the youngsters".[18] Although Neil did not attend the inaugural dinner at the Savoy on May 18th, subsequent dinners would bring him more closely into the orbit of the Liberal Chief Whip and the Attorney General, Rufus Isaacs. Thomas was not an original member but in 1912 when he became established as a characterful rebel over Home Rule, he would join.[19]

On August 10th 1911 Rosebery voted in the key House of Lords division on the Parliament Bill with the Government (who won by seventeen votes) and the Bill received Royal Assent on August 18th. As he later explained to the King he only voted as he did "to protect the Crown from outrage and the Empire from the scandal" of a vast creation of new peers. Henceforth he would boycott the House of Lords for the rest of his life.[20] In consequence at the age of 64 his public life was now over and motivated by feelings of his own mortality Rosebery made his most generous gift to his younger son: the Postwick Estate in Norfolk. Postwick, located just five miles east of Norwich had come to the Primrose family in 1764 but after 150 years was considered remote and peripheral by Rosebery who hardly ever went there. With Neil now re-elected as MP for Wisbech, a tolerable distance away, Rosebery could both fulfil his wish to endow Neil with a country estate that was convenient to his constituency and end his own neglect of Postwick by giving it a resident landlord. The main residence of the estate was the Manor House overlooking the river Yare and hitherto used as a shooting lodge. With it came 2,000 acres - but as Rosebery's total land ownership at this time was around 35,000, the gift did not seriously diminish Lord Dalmeny's inheritance. Rosebery later explained the gift as enabling Neil "to lead the happiest of all lives – that of an English country gentleman". For Neil, Postwick would gradually and only briefly become a beloved rural retreat from London, where he could enjoy shooting and follow farming developments at the estate's Home Farm. After his death the *Eastern Daily Press*[21] would write "he went there essentially for a simple life in the country. He was seen by his tenantry when taking a quiet stroll or with a gun on the marshes."

Even when endowed with a country estate, Neil continued to spend weekends and holidays with his father. On Sunday April 2nd 1911, census night, Neil was recorded as being with Rosebery at The Durdans, in Epsom, along with his seven-year-old nephew Robin Grant, staying with his nurse, in addition to Rosebery's large retinue of resident servants.

Neil and Rosebery spent Christmas 1911 away from the rest of their family on retreat, in Oxford, where they stayed with the Dean of Christ Church. On Boxing Day, the *Daily Telegraph* reported them being present at the Christmas Day Boar's Head feast held at The Queen's College and them witnessing the magnificent procession of a 60lb boar's head, carried on a silver dish by the College Butler, to the sound of the choir singing the *Caput apri defero* carol. Far from feeling guilty about being away from his other children and his grandchildren, Rosebery confided to Herbert Fisher that he had much enjoyed Christmas in Oxford and having escaped "from the intolerable festival at home."[22]

18

A TRUER UNITY BETWEEN ENGLAND AND IRELAND

Early in 1912, Neil joined the National Insurance Committee under the chairmanship of the Liberal Chief Whip Alexander Murray, the Master of Elibank.[1] The Committee had the Party propaganda role of explaining and promoting the new scheme of National Insurance across the country. Funding for this came via the Liberal Party and Neil was given the role of Committee Treasurer. A succession of meetings and rallies were held and a vast number of leaflets printed to promote this controversial welfare provision. Contrary to some predictions the Unionist-dominated House of Lords did not reject this bill and the National Insurance Act came into force on July 15th 1912. Two days before it did *The Times*[2] sneered at the Liberal Committee's fruitless attempt to promote a national celebration of the Act, "Joy Day" as the paper termed it was "unlikely to be marked by uncontrolled rejoicing." Nonetheless and whatever its achievements, the Committee usefully brought Neil further into the Chief Whip's orbit and 'The Master' would successfully propose Neil for membership of the Reform Club in the spring of 1912.[3] Just a few months later Elibank unexpectedly resigned his post and seat and retired altogether from politics. When he did so Neil stated publicly that he regarded it as a calamity for the Party.[4] The resignation was also a personal setback for Neil in that Elibank was no longer in a position to propose that Neil should be given some junior role in Government. Also, and embarrassingly, the promotion of Percy Illingworth from within the Whips' Office to Chief Whip, led to false rumours in the newspapers that Neil would now be made a Junior Whip.[5]

Once the National Insurance Act was in operation the need for the Committee ended but its work was celebrated with a dinner at the National Liberal Club on January 17th 1913. The guest of honour was the Chancellor

David Lloyd George who celebrated his 50th birthday that day, and whose greatest achievement to date was the Act. In his rather fawning speech Neil claimed that:

> no man ever spent it [his birthday] under happier circumstances. He has been successful in his great work on the Bill and that was where he found his reward, as well as in every labourer's cottage ... and the gratitude of those benefitting by the Act to Mr Lloyd George would never die.[6]

The earlier passage of the 1911 Parliament Act opened the way for the enactment of Irish Home Rule and one of the bitterest ever parliamentary struggles, which would last right up to the opening of the First World War. The bland words of the 1912 King's Speech "a measure for the better Government of Ireland will be submitted to you"[7] hardly did justice to what was to follow. This was to be the third attempt at legislation to impose Home Rule on Ireland and it aroused feelings just as bitter as during Gladstone's two failed attempts. Unionists saw the 1912 Home Rule Bill as payment for the 'corrupt bargain' between the Liberals and Irish Nationalists, whereby they now received their reward of Home Rule, as payment for keeping the Liberal Government in power. However unless the Unionists could either secure a dissolution of parliament or amend the Bill during one of its required three passages through the Commons, it would inevitably become law under the Parliament Act during 1914.

In this constitutional maelstrom, Rosebery, even though now outside of Parliament, sought to steady the ship of state by being a bridge between the King and the new leader of the Opposition, Andrew Bonar Law, who became leader of the Conservative Party in November 1911. In consequence, Rosebery instructed Neil to ask Bonar Law to dine and meet the King for the first time at 38 Berkeley Square on April 1st 1912.[8]

The Home Rule Bill was first introduced just days later in April 1912 and Neil spoke in support of the measure during the second reading debate.[9] In so doing he acknowledged that he "had not always held these views". In summary he thought the Unionist fears were exaggerated, querying why, given their past successes, the "Men of Ulster" had "no faith in their political future" and stating that the measure would bring "a truer unity" between England and Ireland because it would put "2 heads under 1 hat."

Irish distractions in the summer of 1912 did not stop Neil from fully engaging with the flat racing season in both England and France. In late June Neil instructed James de Rothschild to back heavily two of Baron Edmond's fillies in the Grand Prix de Paris at Longchamp, using French francs that Neil kept for gambling in a Paris bank that he gave James access to.[10]

Later, when in committee, the Home Rule Bill was unexpectedly delayed by Thomas putting down an amendment to the Bill to exclude the four firmly Protestant counties of Antrim, Armagh, Down and Londonderry. This was a serious spoke in the Government's wheel and led to a three-day debate on the amendment, and once it became clear that Thomas would have Unionist support, the Irish Nationalist leadership were seriously discomfited.

In the vote, Thomas's amendment was defeated by 69 votes but Neil, rather than vote against his friend, absented himself from the division.[11] Thomas's amendment was not of course the end of the matter: in 1913 the Unionists put forward an amendment that all nine counties of Ulster be excluded.[12] Out of these beginnings would come the partition of the island of Ireland.

In January 1913 the Bill successfully completed its passage through the Commons but within nine days the Lords overwhelmingly rejected it by 326 to 69. In consequence, in order to bypass the Lords under the Parliament Act it had to be passed without amendment by the Commons in each of the next two Parliamentary sessions. As it did so Thomas consistently voted against it, while Neil consistently supported the Government. This difference between what the press had by now christened the "inseparables" and sometimes even the "inseparable twins" did not go unremarked; the following report in the *Warwick Advertiser*[13] captioned "Birds of a Feather" is not untypical:

It is impossible to catch a glimpse of Mr Primrose without seeing Mr Robartes close by. Being quite young men they both keep to the old fashioned custom of always wearing their hats on in the House. They are good speakers – clever rather than profound. Being such close friends it was a sad prospect to have to listen to each other preaching heresy. So on the night Mr Robartes rose to show the plight Ireland would be under Home Rule Mr Primrose went off and had a biscuit and on the succeeding night when Mr Primrose argued that Home

Rule would mean perpetual sunshine for Ireland Mr Robartes slipped off to have a cup of cocoa.

The newspapers were not alone in noticing these two prominent characters on the Liberal benches and, albeit posthumously, F.E. Smith wrote of them in similar terms:

The picture is vivid in the minds of those who met in the Parliament of 1910 of two young men upon the Liberal benches who differed in very evident fashion from most of those who sat upon those benches. They were more carefully dressed. They were always gay and often it seemed purposeless and even flippant.[14]

In July 1912 serious sectarian rioting broke out in Belfast. Not for the first or last time it occurred around the anniversary of the Battle of the Boyne. At the month's end and once order had been restored the disturbances were debated in the Commons.[15] Some Unionists saw these troubles as a useful peg to hang their opposition to Home Rule on. Among them was Lord Robert Cecil (who had re-entered the Commons as MP for Hitchin in a 1911 by-election) who used the debate to allege that Liberal candidates at the last General Election had deceived the electorate about Home Rule. This was not an uncommon Unionist charge – in fact the Unionist leadership, in pressing for a General Election on the issue, accepted that if the electorate sanctioned Home Rule they would concede it.

Cecil alleged that in his own case, in Wisbech, in December 1910, he had told his electors that curtailing the power of the House of Lords would inevitably lead to Home Rule, but that his opponent had said it would not. On this charge being made, Neil perhaps rashly responded. In doing so he did not deny being asked about Home Rule during the campaign and rather lamely conceded that his response had been: "I was in favour of some measure of self government for Ireland". Perhaps unsurprisingly Neil's words were met with "laughter" as Hansard records. Emboldened by this Commons reaction Lord Robert Cecil wrote to *The Times* and referred to newspaper reports of Neil's words spoken at Christchurch (already quoted). Two days later Neil's letter in reply was published.[16] In it he entirely avoided reference to his Christchurch speech and obfuscated by referring to other speeches he had made, where his words were rather less stark.

However Cecil's charge was not entirely unfounded and Neil was perhaps unwise to take up the bait and fuel the already overheated atmosphere.

Into this deeply polarised political situation entered what became known as the Marconi Scandal. Its background was the Imperial Conference of 1911 and its recommendation that a chain of wireless stations be set up across the empire. This led in March 1912 to the Government's acceptance of the tender of the Marconi Wireless Telegraph Company. Within a short time the Company's share price had risen more than tenfold in value and rumours abounded of ministerial insider dealing. The ministers alleged to be involved were Sir Rufus Isaacs, Attorney General (and brother of Marconi's managing director) and his friends — the Chancellor of the Exchequer, David Lloyd George, and the former government chief whip, the Master of Elibank. As a result in October 1912, a House of Commons select committee was appointed to investigate and report on the Marconi contract and Neil was appointed a member. It now seems extraordinary that this matter was the subject of a parliamentary rather than judicial inquiry as the Liberal members could hardly be expected to be dispassionate in judging a popular former chief whip and one of the most prominent members of the Government, David Lloyd George. Furthermore in Neil's case he was even further conflicted by Rufus Isaacs being tied by marriage to the Cohen family and so part of the financial network that was led by the Rothschilds.

Ominously for those involved, another member of the committee was Lord Robert Cecil and his exacting standards and severe judgment would lie behind the Government crisis that would follow publication of the committee's Report.

In December 1912, Neil celebrated his thirtieth birthday with an all male dinner at 38 Berkeley Square for those in his closest circle. He did so amid regular press comment that both he and Thomas were two of "the great partis of the day"[17] but however eligible a bachelor Neil was, those who sought him to marry their daughter remained disappointed.

19

MARCONI

In November 1913 the *Daily Sketch* gave a rare insight into Neil's life as a fashionable man in Mayfair:

> I saw him walking along Piccadilly ... and although deeply engrossed in conversation ... he stopped instinctively at Devonshire House to put a coin in the box of the blind beggar who sits there ... how many men richer than he pass a beggar in disdain.

Neil's social conscience for those far less fortunate than himself was also on display in Parliament when he introduced the Farm Servants' Holidays Bill[1] to give powers to local authorities to fix holidays for farm labourers. Although it was not to reach the statute book the proposed measure demonstrates that Neil could step outside the mindset of the wealthy landowning class and propose measures to help those smaller groups of disparate workers who were easy to overlook.

February 1913 saw Neil act as best man for Jimmy, when he married Dorothy Pinto at the Central Synagogue in Great Portland Street. The young bride was a fortnight short of her 18th birthday and Jimmy seventeen years her senior, but the marriage was to prove long and happy; Dollie, as she was known, was to be welcomed as an addition to their intimate group by both Neil and Thomas.

That spring Neil was appointed to the Government committee to consider the best means of celebrating the forthcoming centenary of peace with the United States. Among other things, the British Committee was to cross the Atlantic to confer with the corresponding American Committee at a conference in New York. This appointment may have come as something as a relief to Neil in that it enabled him to resign from the Marconi committee and so avoid judging the conduct of two Cabinet ministers with whom he was increasingly close. This was particularly so because in March 1913, Rufus Isaacs admitted that he, Lloyd George, and Elibank had dealt in the shares of the American Marconi Company and so the earlier rumours of dealing were not entirely untrue. However on the other side of the equation the American company had no interest, direct or indirect, in the profits of the English company and in fact the shares had fallen in value. Even so Isaacs's failure to mention his dealings in the House was an error of judgement that almost ended his political career.

Neil was plainly conscious of the trouble Rufus Isaacs was in and confided to Jimmy de Rothschild how "cut up" he seemed.[2] Notwithstanding Neil's pleasure to be removed from the Marconi affair he still had mixed feelings about the trip to the United States as he confessed to the newly-married Jimmy: "I feel greatly excited at visiting the great Republic of the West" but it was "to be a severe physical test. We spend the first 4 days in New York and then ... like a theatrical company on tour in a special train to Boston, Washington and Philadelphia ... then we are shut out at Atlantic City for one day's rest preparatory to going to Chicago."[3] In both this letter and the one that followed[4] Neil expressed disappointment that with its full itinerary of official banquets and receptions it would, regrettably, be no "repeat of 1910" when Jimmy and Thomas had last been there with him.

On arrival, Neil wrote to Jimmy from the Plaza Hotel to announce his great elation at being back and even went so far as to say if his circumstances were different he would like to live there:

> I do not know what the effect is which this place has on me but really I felt today that if I was engaged in a profession such as finance which is, so to speak, interchangeable between the two countries, I should like to settle here.[5]

Both the joint conference and resulting tour, during which they were received by President Woodrow Wilson, were judged a great success in strengthening Anglo-US ties; but the joint celebration of the signing of the Treaty of Ghent on December 24th 1814, was, owing to the outbreak of war in Europe, never to happen.

Neil was back in England for one of the annual fixtures in his diary – accompanying his father at the Epsom race meeting – and so he was present for that year's Derby. Rosebery recorded in his diary that it was "the most detestable day I ever spent on a racecourse. A woman ran into the King's horse, nearly killing herself and the jockey".[6] That woman was Emily Davison and she died from her injuries four days later, but this had no effect on Neil's opinions on female suffrage.

Neil was far from alone among Liberal MPs in opposing extending the franchise to women. Although he did not speak in the Parliamentary debates on the subject, he sat alongside Thomas on the platform of the Royal Albert Hall at the protest meeting in February 1912 organised by the National League for Opposing Women's Suffrage.[7] In June 1914 Neil was elected a vice-president of the Women's National Liberal Association and the normally supportive *Cambridge Independent Press*[8] noted "the announcement is particularly interesting in view of Mr Primrose's pronounced hostility to votes for women."

The Marconi Report was published on June 13th. In it the charge of corruption was unanimously dismissed but in a minority report written by Lord Robert Cecil the purchase of the American shares was condemned as "gravely improper" and the subsequent lack of candour that there had been dealings in those shares "failed to treat the House of Commons with the frankness and respect to which it was entitled."

On the back of this minority report and aided by the bitter party political polarisation that then prevailed, the Unionists attempted to embarrass the Government with a motion of censure and to end the career of David Lloyd George, one of its leading members. Both Lloyd George and Rufus Isaacs made personal statements of regret before withdrawing to await the House's verdict. This did not pacify the Unionists who were in full pursuit and determined to obtain their scalps. The debate ran into a second day of blisteringly heated argument. Neil intervened to ask the House to accept the ministers' acknowledgement of their mistake in buying the shares, and the expressions of regret at their lack of complete candour made at the opening of the debate, and not to unfairly hound them out of public life.[9]

The Government defeated the motion by 78 votes and so both ministers were left uncensured and undisturbed in office. However in the case of Rufus Isaacs, his ministerial career was short lived, as on the resignation of Lord Alverstone he was (to the Unionists' fury, but as precedent dictated) made Lord Chief Justice. Evidently Neil did not have any qualms about this as on a busy day in his constituency – "I have held 20 meetings and am still at it" – still found time to write to Lloyd George and propose a dinner for Rufus in celebration of his appointment.[10]

That summer on July 7th the Home Rule Bill completed its second journey through the Commons only to be rapidly crushed once more by the House of Lords. On August 15th the parliamentary session ended and the Commons did not sit again for six months.

Taking advantage of this long parliamentary break Neil and Thomas left Liverpool for New York on November 8th on the *Mauretania*.[11] This was to be their longest and most extensive visit and whatever disagreements they had had about Ulster plainly did not affect the fundamentals of their relationship. Rosebery, who was aware how long they would be away, left Glamis Castle, where he was staying with Lord and Lady Strathmore, to say goodbye to them in London.[12]

From New York they took a boat to Cuba and from Havana on November 22nd Neil sent Jimmy a postcard recording that "Thomas smoked 8 Corona cigars yesterday; he says carelessly 7 or 8."[13] The rest of their itinerary is not clear but it was late January when Neil was reported as coming back from New York to Plymouth.[14]

The new parliamentary session was opened by the King on February 10th and his speech unsurprisingly announced that the Government of Ireland Bill would be brought back before them. Later that day in the debate on the Address, Neil spoke about Ireland and paid a surprising public tribute to Thomas in "exhibiting a courage with which I do not agree, but which I must confess I admire, has voted consistently on every occasion against a measure of Home Rule for Ireland." He then proceeded to ridicule the opposition's charge of a lack of mandate for Home Rule before moving to his climax in attacking the hypocrisy of the Conservative Party's novel position that:

> a minority which is dissatisfied with an existing state of things is justified in resisting that state of things by force of arms. What will be their reply to any labour convulsion when the agitators of that convulsion feel that they are not only fighting for what they think right, but for the very necessities of their existence?[15]

The day following the speech Neil travelled to Wisbech, with Mrs Raymond Asquith, to attend a fundraising bazaar at the Corn Exchange. On arrival at Wisbech they were given luncheon by Lord Peckover at Bank House before Katharine Asquith cut the ribbon to open the bazaar. The event was to raise funds for the building of a Free Trade Hall in Wisbech. Owing to the outbreak of war and the subsequent decline in Liberal Party fortunes, the proposed hall would never be built.

Both Neil's vocal support for Home Rule, and his interaction with Asquith's daughter-in-law, in February 1914, while certainly not harming his ministerial prospects, were not enough to carry him over the line for promotion from the backbenches. On 16 February, Asquith had confided to Venetia Stanley[16] that he'd just appointed the "hardly known" Charles Roberts as Under-Secretary at the India Office, rather than "the other two possible outsiders – Dr Addison & Neil Primrose."

20

HAS THE IRISH GOVERNMENT SHOWN ANY SIGN OF EXISTENCE?

In March 1914 Neil was at Postwick where spring and the lambing season had arrived early as his letter to Dollie de Rothschild dated March 7th demonstrates:

> while walking through my demesne, my ears were assailed by a veritable babel of bleating and I came upon the sheep who seem to have multiplied exceedingly for there were masses of little lambs skipping about. Their guardian is justly proud of them but he declines to tell me how many there are till all are born: he thinks it unlucky.[1]

In early April Neil spoke again in the Commons following the Prime Minister's offer to the Unionists that each of the Ulster counties would, if they agreed following a simple majority vote, be permitted to contract out of Home Rule for six years. Carson rapidly threw the concession back in Asquith's face with the memorable words "sentence of death with a stay of execution for six years"[2] but this was still a significant moment as the Government had conceded the principle that Ulster could be treated differently.

Neil, in common with other backbench Liberal MPs thought the concession, even though rejected, was unnecessary and should not have been made:

> the Prime Minister was unduly generous when, at the head of a large majority, he came forward spontaneously and made his offer, the only condition that he asked being, not that constitutional resistance to the Bill should cease, but that rebellion and civil strife should cease.[3]

In fact not even acts of rebellion ceased – arms and ammunition were illegally landed at Larne by the Ulster Volunteer Force on April 24th as Asquith confirmed in the Commons three days later. Churchill told the Commons in a memorable phrase that this meant that although "the veto of the Lords is gone, there still remains the veto of force." But the Cabinet dithered and no prosecution was ever to be brought in respect of Larne, or the many other overt and illegal displays of Ulster defiance.

This failure to act stirred Neil into quite open attack on the Government and to ridicule some of its most senior members. At Prime Minister's questions on Monday June 15th, Neil asked Asquith why the Government could not enforce the law in Ireland as they had done in recent South Wales labour disputes. Asquith's icy reply was "I am afraid I do not quite understand the question". Just a few days later he told the Commons that Churchill's two-faced pronouncements on the Ulster Volunteer Force – condemnatory and then conciliatory - made him "the most perfect example of a human palimpsest extant".

The press loved these pieces of parliamentary theatre and Neil's words were widely reported but it also led to speculation as to what had led this young playboy to adopt such a weighty stance: the *Warwick Advertiser*[4] is not untypical in saying Neil was "much too young and much too good looking to be in such a moody state." Neil in taking the position he did was also putting himself in the unlikely company of the radical left of the Liberal party which given his parentage seemed incongruous; but perhaps he was finally breaking away from his father's influence. In January 1914 Rosebery underwent an operation on his prostate[5], followed by five months of recuperation.[6] The fact that his son's radicalism reached its zenith as he did so may not be a coincidence.

If Neil is to be accused of opportunistically joining a radical bandwagon he had at least tried at first to get the issue resolved quietly and in private by leading a deputation of Liberal backbenchers to see the Prime Minister in his Commons room on May 14th.[7] But the Prime Minister, never adept at disarming his opponents, only made things worse by brushing their views aside. Perhaps for Neil, having endured similar rebuffs and feeling long overlooked, this was a turning point in his relations with Asquith. Like the Ulster Unionists he would now exhibit his own open defiance. Within a fortnight Neil was addressing a public meeting in Tunstall, Staffordshire[8] and saying that "a principle of great magnitude" was involved "that of even-handed administration of the law". Neil held a similar meeting in Merthyr Tydfil and a very rowdy one in Glasgow[9] at which he said amid much heckling from Ulster sympathisers: "without even-handed administration of the law no property was secure and liberty itself could not survive". Of course his sentiments were sound but he did not specify how, regardless of whether prosecutions were made, Ulster was to be successfully coerced into accepting Home Rule while avoiding a civil war.

In the midst of this speaking tour Neil spent a happy interlude at the annual Yeomanry exercises, this year held on Salisbury Plain. *The Times*[10] reported that the 2nd South Midland Mounted Brigade "forms an imposing encampment at Hamilton Camp"[11] and that one of its component regiments the Royal Bucks "has 20 officers, 428 other ranks and 406 horses – a noticeable feature of this regiment is that 70 - 80% of its horses are privately owned ... Second Lt. Neil Primrose is among the officers present."

In June, the *Suffragette* (no admirer of Neil) reported his letter to the *Daily Mail* condemning the Government's policy of coercing militant women while permitting law breaking on the part of militant men.[12] For all of the speeches and newsprint, the Government remained entirely unmoved and the Chief Secretary for Ireland[13] told the Commons on July 2nd "In the present state of the controversy, I do not think any action on the part of the Government would be wise" and that prosecution must always be a matter of discretion even where breaches of the law were admitted. At this, Neil rose to ask the Chief Secretary (amid opposition cheers) "Has the Irish Government shown any sign of existence at all?" to which Hansard records "no answer was given."

In late July, the febrile political atmosphere was interrupted by the King trying to find a consensual way forward at the Buckingham Palace Conference. This unexpected move, made as the parliamentary session was drawing to a close, led to fears on the backbenches of a Government sell-out to the Unionists under royal pressure, which might in turn lead to a sudden dissolution of Parliament before the Parliament Act had been used to enact both Home Rule and Welsh Church Disestablishment.

Neil fully shared these fears and the existential threat the situation posed for Liberalism. The past three years had seen the passage of little progressive legislation and had largely been spent treading water to satisfy the three-fold passage under the Parliament Act. If even these two measures, fought so hard over, were to be abandoned how were Liberal candidates to defend their Government's record?

Such grave concerns and the pressing need to stiffen the Government's resolve led to a hastily organised but crowded meeting on July 29th at the London Opera House in Kingsway under the chairmanship of Sir Henry Dalziel. Those attending largely represented the radical left of the party and were surprising soul mates for Neil. However he did not stay in the shadows but proposed the meeting's motion, urging the Government to complete its legislative programme and so demonstrate that the Parliament Act was a living force.[14] Following Neil in the list of speakers was Arthur Sherwell[15] the radical Liberal MP who told the cheering assembly that they would never assent to a dissolution until their programme was carried. If the Government yielded to Tory pressure they "would do their best to overthrow you as a Government and to re-establish Liberalism ... on a sound democratic basis." After such firebrand speeches the motion passed unanimously.

On the very day of the London Opera House meeting the Prime Minister first spoke publicly of the extremely grave international situation. Patriotic unity would now end the long period of great cross-party partisanship and bind together the fractious Liberal Party.

21

MOBILISED

The outbreak of war just a few days later would soon repair Neil's broken relations with the Liberal leadership, although Neil's relations with Asquith were destined never to be close. However many Liberal MPs, including some in the Cabinet, needed to be convinced that Britain should enter the fray and not stick to the tried and tested policy of staying aloof from continental disputes that did not threaten its vital interests. As Lord Birkenhead wrote in 1922, Neil was not then an established believer in the German menace, and it was only the German ultimatum to (and then following its rejection, invasion of) Belgium, that convinced him otherwise.[1]

Neil's hesitation over the international situation in early August is reflected in Jimmy's letter to Neil of August 4th: "When last I saw you, you were hesitating as to whether you should oppose in the House any Government proposal embodying the principle of war."[2] But as Jimmy had anticipated, Sir Edward Grey's statement to the House of August 3rd, which first publicly alluded to the German ultimatum to Belgium to allow free passage of its troops through it en route to France, and Belgium's refusal of it, changed everything – "Thank Heaven Grey's statement was so splendid … Germany looks to have begun her war under rather worse conditions than could have been expected."

In fact Jimmy was so delighted with Grey's words and anxious to communicate the fact to Neil that on the same day as his letter he sent Neil a telegram from Paris saying "overjoyed at yesterday's statement. Edmond[3] and I send all love. Jimmy".[4]

However, events in London were moving so fast that as the telegram was sent 2nd Lt. Neil Primrose received mobilisation orders to join his regiment in Buckinghamshire and so the telegram was actually delivered to Neil "c/o

Bucks Yeomanry, Aylesbury" later that day and just hours before the 11pm deadline that the Government had imposed upon Germany to respect Belgium's neutrality. As a result of his mobilisation Neil was not in the Commons on August 5th to hear the Prime Minister announce "since 11 o'clock last night a state of war has existed between Germany and ourselves."

On the following day many newspapers printed a list of 72 MPs subject to mobilisation for being either in the regular or territorial forces. The *Wisbech Standard* informed its readers that "The North Cambs Member [has been] called to service".[5] Neil was one of fourteen Liberals but they were massively outnumbered by the Unionist list of 58. Thomas's name was not listed: he had formerly been a Lieutenant in the Royal 1st Devon Imperial Yeomanry[6] but had resigned his commission in January of the previous year[7] and was now caught out without a commission. For one so chivalrous and honourable this was plainly seen by him as an immediate problem, both in terms of his reputation and of separation from Neil. But the problem was rapidly solved by his accompanying Neil to Aylesbury on August 4th where he volunteered and was promptly accepted as a subaltern in the Royal Bucks Hussars (RBH). Obviously Neil and his Rothschild cousins were deeply enmeshed in Buckinghamshire society and its county regiment; that would undoubtedly have helped in obtaining Thomas's commission in a regiment with which he had no other connection. But the matter was almost certainly clinched by the regiment's commanding officer, Colonel Cecil Grenfell[8], who had briefly been the Liberal MP for Bodmin during the first parliament of 1910 and would have known Thomas personally. Certainly his joining the RBH was rapid; although the London Gazette took weeks to list all of the appointments made at the war's start, when Thomas's commission made it in, it dated from August 5th 1914.[9] In 1957 when Colonel Cripps, a subsequent commanding officer of the regiment, published his memoir, he made no bones about Thomas joining "our regiment on mobilization because of his great friendship with Neil".[10]

At the point of mobilisation the RBH had four squadrons A-D based respectively at Buckingham, Aylesbury, High Wycombe and Chesham. The officers of B squadron were almost exclusively drawn from the House of Rothschild – the three brothers Lionel, Evelyn and Anthony and their cousin Neil all being officers of the same squadron. Lionel a Major (and Conservative MP for Aylesbury) was the squadron commander; and his two brothers Evelyn and Anthony each held the rank of Lieutenant under him. Neil as 2nd Lieutenant was the junior squadron officer. This close knit family aspect was not missed by the local press and the *Bucks Herald* reported on August 15th that Miss Alice de Rothschild[11] had come to Aylesbury from Waddesdon several times during the preceding week to visit her relatives in the local RBH squadron. In the same report it was noted that the RBH were the first regiment of the Brigade[12] to report mobilisation complete. The local squadron remained at Aylesbury for the remainder of August, parading and training, but its main utility in those first weeks was as an advertisement for local army recruitment.

As the month came to an end the regiment's squadrons rendezvoused at Reading Market Place before moving on to Churn Camp on the Berkshire Downs, five miles south of Didcot. At Churn the entire mounted Brigade assembled before going under canvas and undertaking field work, firing practice, and munitions instruction. Coinciding with the move to Churn was Neil's promotion to full Lieutenant and his cousin Evelyn to Captain.[13] This promotion gave Neil a higher rank than his Sandhurst-trained brother, who had remained on the General Reserve of officers since 1906, and who was gazetted 2nd Lieutenant in the Foot Guards on August 25th 1914 when he embarked for France.[14] Dalmeny's initial role in France was to act as a GHQ messenger and driver, alongside the Duke of Westminster.[15]

Via Didcot, Churn was not particularly remote from London by rail and both Neil and Thomas were noted[16] as being back in the Commons and dressed in khaki on September 15th. Because of the pressures that the newly declared war was expected to bring, the Government and Opposition made a conspicuous effort to complete contentious legislation then in progress. As a result, the Home Rule and Welsh Church Bills were passed on this day[17] (but with their operation suspended for the war's duration). The Unionists remained unhappy that the Bills were to be enacted (even if on a deferred basis), and Bonar Law made a bitter speech in protest. To quote his biographer Robert Blake: "At the end of his speech he announced that the Unionists would walk out of the House and take no further part in the debate."

Rosebery had been in Scotland when war was declared, as due to his operation he had taken his annual cure in May (some months earlier than his usual custom) when he had travelled to Vichy.[18] His travelling abroad was now ended and on August 12th he gloomily reported to his sister that "this terrible thunderburst of war has changed the whole aspect of everything".[19] In the following month Rosebery was fretting that Neil's support for the conflict "might bring him into uneasy relations with Lloyd George".[20] But Rosebery need not have bothered as days later, at the Queen's Hall, in London, on September 19th Lloyd George delivered his first great patriotic speech of the war which was the foundation stone of his later reputation as a great war-time leader. Naturally given his Boer War record he was conscious of the need to prove his sincerity and so started as follows:

There is no man in this room who has always regarded the prospect of engaging in a great war with greater reluctance and with greater repugnance than I have done throughout the whole of my political life. (Hear, hear.) There is no man either inside or outside of this room more convinced that we could not have avoided it without national dishonour.

He moved on to his most memorable phrase 'the road hog of Europe' crushing those in its path:

Small nationalities in his way are hurled to the roadside, bleeding and broken. Women and children are crushed under the wheels of his cruel car, and Britain is ordered out of his road. All I can say is this: if the old British spirit is alive in British hearts, that bully will be torn from his seat.

The speech had a profound national impact and was widely applauded by those of all parties and indeed none. Neil, out of things and kicking his spurs at Churn, was doubtless anxious not to be forgotten and so sent the Chancellor alongside his congratulations a box of his favourite mild cigars.[21]

At this time he wrote to an un-named friend – who passed his words to the newspapers – "we are daily expecting command to start for the front".[22] But that command to the RBH was not to come. Their hopes were raised when the Oxfordshire Yeomanry (The Queen's Own Oxfordshire Hussars) of the same brigade did receive orders to leave Churn for embarkation to France on September 19th. But Oxfordshire was to be a special case, probably on account of the regiment's link to Winston Churchill, and the remainder of the Brigade, for all of their eagerness to go, resentfully remained at Churn.[23]

However Neil was also to be treated as an individual special case when he received orders to leave his regiment and embark for France on September 25th. He was to join the Staff of the Indian Army Corps and in consequence was immediately promoted Staff Captain.[24] This appointment was both extraordinary and in military terms indefensible. Apart from a negligible few weeks spent over the previous five and a half years at Yeomanry camps and exercises, Neil had no military experience whatsoever. He also had no readily-apparent connection with India and for all of his extensive foreign travel had never even been there. Neil's only relevant connection with the sub-continent was that his brother-in-law Lord Crewe was Secretary of State for India[25] and it was that family relationship that lay behind his appointment.

22

INDIAN TROOPS

On the war's outbreak Indian Expeditionary Force A was shipped from India to France and Lord Crewe later told the House of Lords that from the outset it was considered by his Department that "some special steps should be taken for the purpose of supplying authentic information in India itself."[1] This was not only to aid morale and recruitment but also to scotch false rumours and prevent opposition to the war in India. The result was, as Crewe retrospectively told the Lords in November, that: "three officers have been deputed to serve with the staff of the Indian Expeditionary Force. Their sole duty is to supply accounts of the doings of the Indian troops. These accounts as they are received at somewhat uncertain intervals, are telegraphed to the Viceroy for him to disseminate in India".

Although not named by Lord Crewe, Neil was the second of the three officers. The first was Major F.E. Smith MP and the third Major Steel who was a regular Indian cavalry officer and former military attaché at Teheran and so, as Crewe later admitted in the House of Lords, was in a position to "supply technical knowledge with which those other two gentlemen [F.E. and Neil] were not so fully acquainted."[2] Crewe's suggestion in the Lords that the appointment of the Indian Press Officers to look after the despatch of news to India had an orderly planned gestation is not supported by his correspondence with Lord Kitchener.[3] Only on September 20th did Crewe write and thank Kitchener for agreeing to the plan, and in a further letter from the India Office next day Major Steel is first mentioned and Crewe presses Kitchener to "give instructions for this to be put in train, so that both may be put under General Willcocks's orders?"[4] Fortunately this was rapidly done as the Indian troops were due to arrive in Marseilles harbour within a week. In neither letter is Neil's name mentioned and his appointment seems to have been an after-thought agreed upon orally by the two ministers; the exact reasons for it remain unclear. It may be that Kitchener and Crewe thought that F.E. with his maverick and unpredictable personality required monitoring. A further reason may have been that having a Liberal MP officer (and it had to be an army officer as Kitchener resolutely refused to have civilians in France) at his side avoided any Liberal Party criticism of the Conservative F.E.'s appointment.

It can be taken as read that Crewe knew from Neil's sister Peggy that Neil was frustrated and restless at Churn Camp; and Kitchener knew of Neil via Rosebery, and rather more recently through their common Other Club membership. Such jobbery and favouritism were not at all untypical in the early months of the War but in Neil's defence there is no evidence that he set out to use his connections to jockey for this position. In fact there was no time for him to do so between Crewe's letters to Kitchener and his embarkation as a Staff Captain just four days later.

Neil and F.E. crossed the Channel together and then rushed to Marseilles so as to meet General Willcocks on arrival. Major Steel who arrived in France with the Indian troops met them both there on September 29th.

For Neil this unexpected appointment had the attraction of getting him to the front and giving him a job to do but on the negative side it separated him from his regiment and his fellow officers. To ease his conscience about this Neil extracted a promise from Kitchener and Crewe that "whenever his regiment was ordered on active service, he should be given immediate leave to rejoin it."[5]

Of course prime among his fellow RBH officers was Thomas, who had only joined the regiment six weeks earlier to be with Neil, and this appointment plainly rather left him in the lurch. What his feelings were about Neil's departure are not recorded but Rosebery's posthumous tribute states that Thomas never resented Neil's successes. Also Neil seems to have retained the belief, albeit erroneous, that the RBH would be coming out to France soon and so their separation would be brief. On November 6th Neil wrote telling his sister Peggy that he had sufficient warm clothing and there was no need to send more "as I intend to join the Bucks Yeomanry when they come out and my amount of luggage will be limited."[6]

Neil was in Marseilles to witness the extraordinary spectacle of 24,000 Indian troops disembarking. The quays and wharves were choked with cheering crowds and as the transports passed other ships their decks were crowded with passengers and crew waving hats and handkerchiefs in welcome. At the quayside Neil and F.E. met General Willcocks and followed him with the rest of his Staff through the streets to Parc Boreli and the race-course where they were to camp. As they passed bars and cafes, the customers stood on their chairs and shouted "Vive l'Angleterre! Vivent les Hindous! Vivent les Alliés!"[7]

Although General Willcocks and his Staff proceeded north first, the full transfer of Indian troops by rail from Marseilles to Flanders, via Orleans, took several weeks. As a result it was October 23rd before the Indian troops joined the British Expeditionary Force. They were immediately deployed and throughout the First Battle of Ypres they held approximately twelve miles of the British line.

F.E. Smith in a letter to his wife did not hide the horrors of their initial baptism of fire:

> Poor wretches, they were marched straight from motor omnibuses into a style of warfare of which they knew nothing, and many of them shoved into trenches too deep for them, so that they could not even fire from them, and so handicapped, they were exposed to the hideous concentration of shell fire.[8]

It has been said, not unfairly, that Neil and F.E. had been given "a ringside seat" from which to experience "the personal suffering of the forces at first hand from a personal position of some comfort."[9] They were certainly given privileged access to General Headquarters and were free to roam about with both army transport and drivers supplied. Neil also had taken out several of his favourite hunters, so he could get on horseback beyond the useable road network. This mobility certainly helped him to assess the situation and by early November, Neil was reporting to Lord Crewe "as an unofficial source" that the bravery of the Indian Army during First Ypres had been both mixed and very costly of lives:

> It has already suffered heavy losses, but the Sikh regiments behaved very gallantly. I am afraid that it not so with one of the Ghurkha regiments. It is true that they had to undergo a terrific shell fire for many hours, but they left their trenches and most of their British officers were killed or wounded ... the rate of mortality has been so

heavy among them [British officers] that some of the Indian troops here cannot for the moment be employed.

Turning to his personal situation, Neil reported: "Everyone has been charming to us and we have had many opportunities of hearing about how things are going on. There is only one refrain; we must have more soldiers."[10]

In the same letter he made it clear just how awful things were for those in the trenches, whether in the Indian or British army:

There are regiments who have been 10 days or more in the trenches because there is none to relieve them. They come out, if they can be relieved, having acquitted themselves like heroes but dead beat and sometimes hardly knowing what they are saying or doing after no sleep and awful shell fire.

These conditions on the ground he found a world away from the accounts appearing in the British press which remained available to him at headquarters: "It makes me angry to read the English newspapers that are so full of sanguine swagger." This most candid letter, if written by an ordinary infantry officer, would have brought considerable trouble from the military censor; but as a Member of Parliament writing to a Cabinet Minister, Neil's letters were completely untouchable. Neil did at least use his privileged position to communicate practical matters to Crewe such as the need for more warm clothing from the Indian Soldiers' Fund (a charity based in London and established in October 1914) to the Indian Army advance depot rail-head. Neil also suggested food supplies that would be acceptable to the Indian troops:

1 cwt tins of mutton have been promised and it is most desirable that they should be sent out at once ... some generous private donor has given some Horlicks malted milk to the troops. The General [Willcocks] is practically certain the Indian troops will eat it or drink it – I am not sure which you do.

For Neil, while he was in Flanders, was certainly not on a diet of Horlicks – in February 1915, F.E. wrote to tell his wife that Jimmy de Rothschild had sent six dozen oysters, a hare and two bottles of 1811 brandy.[11] In October soon after they arrived in Flanders, Neil himself wrote to F.E.'s wife describing their life at war:

> I am irresistibly tempted to write you a line to describe the appalling hardships which your husband undergoes ... tonight ... I was sitting in his bedroom after dinner ... F.E. lying in an enormous bed ... after an excellent dinner well tempered with burgundy, with an enormous cigar in his mouth and a glass of rum and hot water by his bedside. I feel you must give him an appalling time at home if he is not to be considered as living a most luxurious life.[12]

In another letter to Crewe[13], Neil sought to excuse F.E. for the absence of any articles on account of the large number of injuries to the troops' left hands – out of 1,848 wounded, 1,049 had hand wounds. It is unclear exactly how many of these hand wounds were self-inflicted[14] although a great many were considered to be so and two soldiers were court martialled and executed for deliberately wounding themselves. In these circumstances, Neil reported to Crewe:

> a very large percentage of the wounded had received injuries in the left hand undoubtedly inflicted by themselves. This has of course been kept very secret and was due most probably to agitators and also possibly with a view to a pension. Strong measures have been taken and it is believed it has been stopped but no doubt you will agree it is not an auspicious moment to write their successes. A further reason against having sent any lately is ... a certain jealousy at headquarters at the idea of the Indian troops being mentioned preferentially to those of the British troops. However F.E. is writing an article tomorrow and thenceforth will continue to send them regularly.

Evidently Neil did not see it as his role to produce articles, although perhaps he assembled the material or devilled for F.E. by writing first drafts. From his letters Neil seems to have seen his role as being Crewe's eyes and ears in France. But the relationship was not entirely one-sided and Neil quite obviously attempted to use Crewe as an intermediary to Lord Kitchener by including sentences such as "I am sure a word from you at the War Office would do such a lot" and "I do hope you will urge re-inforcements on Lord K."

Neil also favoured his brother-in-law by giving him that autumn's partridge shooting at Postwick: "I am delighted that you had such a pleasant shoot at Postwick and I wish I could have been there to entertain you in person. As you may have found, Waters [Neil's gamekeeper] is a little old-fashioned in his ideas of driving partridges."

In early December and with the Ypres sector still raging, Neil, who was almost in a parallel universe, obtained a fortnight's home leave from General Willcocks. Even in war-time the newspapers continued to report his movements, including his leaving London for Scotland to see his father on December 8th.[15] By this stage of the war, the railways were considerably disrupted by troop movements and the journey entailed an untimetabled night in a railway carriage on each leg of the journey. Neil found his father in considerably reduced circumstances, living between his eponymous shooting lodge near Gorebridge, and an Edinburgh town house at 5 Randolph Crescent. This change in circumstances had come about because the Army Council had requisitioned Hound Point (a headland on the Firth of Forth) for a defensive artillery battery, and rather than share his estate with the army, Rosebery preferred to vacate Dalmeny House[16] and to let it be used as a military hospital.[17]

The other person Neil spent part of his leave with, in London, was Thomas who managed to obtain a few days leave from a sympathetic commanding officer. Since November 17th the Bucks Hussars had been in Norfolk, in the tiny village of Great Ryburgh, two miles outside Fakenham. They were there to defend the Norfolk coast following that autumn's German invasion scare. For Thomas this move was no improvement on Churn Camp as it put off indefinitely the possibility of joining the BEF on the western front. Also Ryburgh was a rural backwater even more remote from London, further from his beloved Cornwall and not even easily accessible from Wimpole. At Ryburgh the men were billeted with the villagers and the officers a short distance away and in considerable comfort at Sennowe Park. The Edwardian splendour of Sennowe did not entirely compensate for the monotonous routine of riding out to the coast north of Fakenham to observe the grey, cold and empty North Sea. Excitements for the regiment were few – their first Zeppelin sighting in January 1915 and then the King, while on a visit to Sandringham, coming over to inspect them.

Thomas, like Neil, having taken leave before Christmas, spent Christmas away from his family in Norfolk[18] and on Boxing Day wrote to inform them he had applied for transfer to the Brigade of Guards, to ensure getting to France. It seems Thomas's decision to seek a commission in a Guards regiment was not unconnected to his having seen Neil earlier that month; for just as Neil has arranged his commission in the RBH, now Neil's military connections would extricate him from the Yeomanry and get him into the Guards, and so to France.

Neil was back in Flanders early in the week leading up to Christmas and so witnessed the last British attack in the Ypres sector before Christmas Day. In a subsequent letter to Crewe he did not hide the fact that nothing permanent was achieved "except that a good many men were lost. I believe that many corps lost about 1,000 men with no result, except that they took a trench, which subsequently had to be abandoned. I understand that much the same occurred on our [Indian] lines".[19]

On Sunday December 18th the Germans made a counter-attack and as Neil told Crewe this "met with a large measure of success. No doubt we shall hear the Indian army criticised for this result, but I think this is unjust" and Neil proceeded to list their lack of reserves, inferior munitions, fatigue and poor weather, in justification of the situation. In fact that part of the line held by the Indian Army had buckled so badly that on December 21st General Haig was sent by the Commander in Chief to the Indian Corps headquarters at Hinges Chateau[20] to assess the situation. On entering the Chateau, Haig witnessed a scene beyond parody: "a big salon where tea was still going on. It was now past 5pm".[21] In this surreal atmosphere Willcocks gave Haig his stark and panicky view that "the Indians were done: they would not fight any more and they simply ran away. And he begged me to relieve his Corps at once."

This Haig did on the following day and he also took over Hinges Chateau as his own HQ. This eviction much upset F.E. (and by implication Neil) who wrote to his wife on December 29th and described, without a blush, the inconvenience caused:

We got beautiful rooms here (I a large bed with electric light on each side to read) and that damned fellow Haig the General came and turned us out. Then on a wet morning we searched everywhere in vain for billets and at last found a picturesque old chateau with a moat round it ... We have got the sole possession of it. We have enormous fires everywhere, including our bedrooms, and on the whole are very comfortable. It is huge and we are waited on by Ward and the two chauffeurs – quite amazing.[22]

The comforts enjoyed by these two highly privileged and under-employed Staff Officers in the opening months of the war could not have contrasted more with the privations of the men in the trenches, of all ranks, just a few miles away.

However, if Neil was troubled by this contrast he certainly did not communicate it to Crewe. On December 28th, once newly ensconced in their latest comfortable chateau, Neil wrote "the weather has been awful. Rain practically every day and I believe in some trenches, the men were up to their knees in water." In the same letter he gave news of the latest heavy Indian casualties – 3,000 killed or wounded in just three days of fighting from the German counter-attack, to when they were relieved.

As his nephew William Wyndham, an officer in the Life Guards, had been killed at Ypres in November 1914, Rosebery was perhaps understandably relieved that both of his sons were serving in Staff roles, and so in relative safety and comfort. He told Herbert Fisher on New Year's Day 1915: "The boys are well, moving chiefly in Chariots like the ancients i.e. motor cars."[23]

Neil's conscience may have been eased by the alternative to the Indian Staff being one of dull drudgery in an obscure part of north Norfolk. However the same could not be said of F.E. who did convey his unease to his wife: "The Oxfordshire Yeomanry are actually in the trenches ... I feel rather a cad when I think of my comparative comfort and safety".[24] The other issue of conscience was whether they were actually producing articles for India that were of any value. That issue was later directly addressed by Crewe in the House of Lords when in answer to Lord Curzon's question he said:

From Mr. F. E. Smith and his colleagues, between October 14 and February 9, seventeen communications have been received. They have all been either sent by telegraph or by mail to the Viceroy for translation and dissemination in India. Only four of them have appeared in the Press in this country, and they were published as

147

containing matter which would be regarded as of general interest in this country and which was not supplied through the ordinary means of information or through the Despatches of the Field-Marshal Commanding-in-Chief.[25]

Seventeen articles over a period of almost four months does not seem very much. However this lack of productivity scarcely mattered because as General Willcocks was later to admit, even of this output, hardly any of it got through censorship and so what did appear in print in India was only "in the baldest form."[26] This meagre output and lack of achievement did not stop both Neil and F.E.'s names being mentioned in the Commander in Chief's despatch from France dated January 14th 1915[27] – although whether they had really done anything to justify the despatch description of "gallant and distinguished service in the field" must be in doubt; many far braver men were omitted.

One undoubted achievement of Neil's months in Flanders was that it turned what had been a mercurial cross-party amity with F.E. into one of close and intimate friendship. Given they were together constantly over almost four months this is scarcely surprising and once Neil left the Indian Army Staff he wrote to F.E. that their deepened and strengthened friendship "has become a great thing in my life. Time can never congeal it".[28]

Ironically the one press release that did appear in print with Neil's name on it concerned the centenary of the Treaty of Ghent and saluted "our American cousins with greetings of goodwill" while apologising that our "defence of the faith of treaties and the rights of smaller and weaker nationalities" had compelled the postponement of celebrations of Anglo-US friendship. It also rather milked the opportunity for propaganda, by reminding its American readers that Ghent, where the treaty was signed, was now under hostile occupation.[29]

23

UNDER-SECRETARY TO THE FOREIGN OFFICE

In mid-January 1915 Neil received an unexpected and unexplained order from the War Office to return to London. Although Neil did not know it, the reasons behind his recall were political and not military and arose from the sudden and unexpected death of the Chief Whip, Percy Illingworth, on January 3rd.

Within days this led to newspaper speculation that Neil would be appointed in his place. If he knew about this it seems unlikely that he took it seriously and even on reaching London, Neil was left in limbo by the War Office, who merely told him to await further orders. The reason for this was that Asquith was hesitant about filling the unexpected vacancy and saw deficiencies in all of the possible candidates. Lloyd George was unquestionably in favour of Neil's appointment and he might well have sparked the newspaper rumours. Asquith, perhaps unsurprisingly given their troubled history, was far from persuaded but did at least ask his intimate confidante and possible mistress, Venetia Stanley, what she thought. Evidently she gave Neil the thumbs down as Asquith, writing to her on January 16th, made clear: "Your veto on Neil for Chief Whip is heartily endorsed by both Violet [Asquith] and Bongie [Maurice Bonham Carter]. I wonder why Ll.G. is so enamoured of the idea? I am beginning to think that faute de mieux, it will be the line of least resistance to promote Gulland".[1] In his next letter, Asquith almost gleefully recorded "Neil's stock is quite at a discount."[2]

John Gulland was promoted from the number two position and as *The Times* noted on announcing his appointment "if seniority within the Whips' Office is any test, Mr Gulland had a very strong claim".[3]

Of course, if that was the test, Neil with no Whips' Office experience was entirely unqualified but perhaps it was typically complacent of Asquith not to realise why Lloyd George still wanted him as Chief Whip. Neil was certainly in contact with Lloyd George in the days leading up to Gulland's promotion. Margot Asquith's diary entry of January 23rd records Lloyd George telling her at dinner that he had dined with Neil and Churchill at the Café Royal the previous evening and that following a political argument Churchill had sulkily complained about Neil to Lloyd George: "Didn't you hear the young ____ say to me "I don't agree with you". Margot records Lloyd George's response as being "I roared with laughter, it's so childishly absurd."[4]

Notwithstanding this dinner with two prominent Cabinet members, it seems Neil was still largely in the dark about these Downing Street machinations and so was still expecting to be ordered back to France and his role on the Indian Army Staff. Certainly this is reflected in Rosebery's letter to Neil of January 23rd:

I am delighted to hear you are in our island once more … you must not think of travelling down here with two nights in the train again. Of course it would be a delight if you came but I know how short your time must be and I would rather think of you being happy with friends of your own age, than toiling down here [Rosebery was at his eponymous shooting lodge in Midlothian]. I shall not be in London until next week when you I fear will be gone.[5]

Although unspecified by Rosebery, one of Neil's "friends of your own age" was undoubtedly Thomas who had managed to extricate himself from Norfolk by obtaining a transfer to the Coldstream Guards and was then in London pending embarkation. The fact that Thomas's commission was to that particular Guards regiment is almost certainly explicable by Neil's intervention: his brother-in-law Major Charles Grant[6] had been an officer of the regiment since 1897, but more significantly, he was then commanding a company of the Coldstream Guards, in Flanders, that had just suffered heavy losses during the First Battle of Ypres, and which Thomas was now to join.

Thomas's transfer took effect on January 5th and was not ignored by the press who gleefully reported that "the Beau Brummell of the Commons" was made a Lieutenant "in the Coldstreams". Some newspapers even reminisced about him and Neil being the smartest and best-dressed pair in the Commons.[7] According to his fellow officer in the Bucks Yeomanry, Fred Cripps, Thomas could no longer stand being stuck in England[8], while the *Eton Chronicle* records his determination "at all costs to get to the Front."[9] Doubtless he was understandably and genuinely bored by Norfolk and anxious to see and engage the face of the enemy. But surely another motivation was to get him to Flanders so as to be closer to Neil.

Once Gulland was appointed Chief Whip, any chance Neil had of this position was stilled but that was not the end of the prolonged period of reshuffle. Asquith had another Cabinet vacancy, that of Chancellor of the Duchy of Lancaster. The vacancy arose from Charles Masterman's inability to get re-elected to the Commons, as the law then required, following his appointment. Prior to the outbreak of war he had stood and lost in his old seat of Bethnal Green and again in Ipswich, with the embarrassing result that he had been a Cabinet minister for almost 12 months without a seat in Parliament. The final straw for Masterman came in January 1915 when he had failed to be selected as Liberal candidate in two bye-elections. With Parliament set to resume in February the situation could not continue and Asquith accepted his resignation. That one cabinet resignation led to three consequent promotions and meant that Neil's wait for office was over. He was at the age of 32 in Government as the new Under-Secretary at the Foreign Office. Although his appointment explained why the War Office had kept him in limbo, it was still unexpected as he confided to Jimmy: "when I came over [from France] I had no idea of this. I did not know till I arrived in London that Masterman was going to resign and this re-shuffling depended on that".[10]

Edwin Montagu took Masterman's place in the Cabinet and Francis Acland left the Foreign Office to succeed Montagu as Financial Secretary to the Treasury. Neil's appointment to succeed Acland completed the re-shuffle on February 4th. By happy coincidence Rosebery returned to London from Scotland on the day of Neil's appointment and was the first person Neil informed on arrival at 38 Berkeley Square. As the following letter from Neil to Sir Edward Grey written later that day demonstrates, Rosebery evidently took charge of the situation:

Mr Asquith has offered me the Under Secretaryship to the Foreign Office and as he must have consulted you, I write to thank you for what you have done for me. My father who has just arrived from Scotland was the first person to whom I told the news and he was delighted that I should be serving under you. He told me that I should await your instructions as to when I should come and see you, which accordingly I shall do.[11]

Neil and his father were correct in their assumption that while the appointment had Asquith's sanction, the initiative behind it was Grey's.[12] It also transpires from Asquith's letter to Venetia Stanley of January 25th that Lord Crewe had lobbied the Prime Minister to give Neil a role:

I had a letter from Crewe this morning: he is very anxious that something shd. be done for Neil who needs to be 'steadied by responsibility': an Under Secretaryship for instance.[13]

Other letters from Asquith to Venetia indicate that Lloyd George had continued to press him about "bringing in Neil" in another capacity, after Gulland's appointment, but perhaps more crucially, they indicate that Neil went to the Foreign Office with Venetia Stanley's blessing.[14] That her support may have been decisive, is perhaps indicated by Asquith reflecting that Neil was "devilish lucky to find himself" a Foreign Office minister.

The Times of February 5th characterised the appointment as "most interesting" and pointed out that Grey had himself been Lord Rosebery's Under-Secretary during his last term as Foreign Secretary from 1892-1894. Other papers pointed out that the Foreign Office Under-Secretaryship was a well established route to higher preferment; Lord Curzon who had served in the role under Lord Salisbury being a further example. The *Daily Telegraph* suggested that the appointment of Neil had cross-party support; this idea is supported by the following letter Neil wrote to the Conservative leader on his first day at the Foreign Office:

Dear Mr Bonar Law,
I was most pleased by your kind letter of congratulation and I thank you for it very much. It is a very pleasant moment for me to make acquaintance with official life as the political truce helps a debutante.
Yours sincerely, Neil Primrose[15]

A century ago the Foreign Office had only two Government Ministers and so in the absence of the Foreign Secretary the Under-Secretary would answer for him in the Commons. Neil's debut at the despatch box came at the beginning of the following week, when it was reported that he was "loudly cheered by all parties" on first rising to speak.[16] The *Scotsman*[17] praised his performance as demonstrating "the ready self-possession which his previous record had led the House to expect." Later that day Neil wrote to Jimmy in France and confided that he had got the "plum job" in the re-shuffle. He also described the events of his first day in post:

> I started on my duties at the Foreign Office last Friday in a charming sitting room of mine own in that august office and was given the Cabinet keys for the despatch boxes, because I see all the telegrams, also a key for the door into the F.O. from the Park and selected my secretary who is a charming fellow there called Locock[18] about my age, when all this happened my feelings were indescribable.

His day did not end there though, and henceforth his evenings and weekends would be interrupted by a relentless succession of red boxes:

> After dinner at Berkeley Square a messenger arrived with a red box containing the latest telegrams; it felt good. I am babbling like a child but as this is only for your eyes it does not matter.[19]

24

NEIL IS SHAPING EXCELLENTLY

Although there is some record of Neil engaging in 'pure' diplomacy in his first weeks – courting the Bulgarian minister in London to join the allied side[1] – much of Neil's initial work at the Foreign Office concerned the welfare of British civilians who had had the misfortune to find themselves in Germany when war was unexpectedly declared. Although women, children and men beyond the age for military service had gradually been permitted to leave, in February 1915 over 5,000 male British subjects of military age were being held at Ruhleben internment camp, at Spandau, Berlin. Their conditions (described as "revolting") were frequently raised in the Commons at Foreign Office questions. There was, in the circumstances, nothing the British Government could do other than request that the United States Ambassador raise the issue on its behalf with Germany. However as Neil kept telling the Commons, Germany remained unresponsive and after six months was yet to supply a list of those interned.[2] Added heat was given to the issue by the presence, among those interned, of wealthy civilians and retired military officers who had been receiving medical treatment at the fashionable clinic at Nauheim in August 1914. Many of these gentlemen had influential friends in the Commons who persistently raised their poor conditions at Ruhleben.

On a more positive note as February progressed Neil was able to report on the successful exchange of injured prisoners of war and of captured non-combatant army medics, via neutral Holland.[3] Holland itself had interned British soldiers and sailors who had managed to reach its neutral territory from Belgium and Foreign Office moves to improve their conditions with the Dutch government also formed part of Neil's workload.

At Commons questions Neil also had to answer for the Government in respect of unexpected events that in peacetime would have been nothing to do with the Foreign Office. An example of this occurred within days of his appointment when the German steamer SS *Wilhelmina* bound for Germany sought refuge in Falmouth harbour after being battered by an Atlantic storm. On docking its crew were arrested and the cargo of food impounded.[4] But what was to be done with the cargo? This was ordinarily a matter for the Prize Court but in the press there were calls for it to be donated to relieve Belgian refugees.[5]

On February 22nd Asquith records in his daily letter to Venetia Stanley: "Grey is very pleased (by the way) with Neil, who he says is shaping excellently."[6]

Neil's joining the Government led to a thaw in relations between Rosebery and the Prime Minister and in consequence Asquith attended what he termed a "men's dinner at Rosebery's" in Berkeley Square on March 22nd. It is unclear whether Neil was present but Asquith did not appreciate the absence of female company as he later confided to Venetia Stanley:

Not at all interesting – except for the wonderful pictures and portraits wh. R has on his walls. On the whole my experience of men's dinners without women is a minus mark. Certainly to-night when there was a really good cohort of intelligent & rather distinguished men, points that way. It was simply a competition in the telling of old chestnut stories.[7]

Exactly one month after Neil joined the Foreign Office his surprise engagement to Lady Victoria Stanley was announced by the Press Association. Almost ten years his junior, Lady Victoria was the only daughter of the 17th Earl of Derby, a leading Conservative peer. As such the match united two rival political families. The then Tory-leaning *Observer* commented: "the engagement might almost have been made in heaven". The *Sketch* rather less respectfully called it "An Engagement in the Earldoms." The usually anti-Tory *Cambridge Independent Press*[8] judged the match "appropriate ... at a time when ordinary controversies are silenced by the common danger from without."

The acceptance of his marriage proposal certainly united his constituents on either side of party divide. The engagement was also popular across the

Commons and, on his first appearance at the despatch box following the announcement, Neil "was greeted with a cheer that emanated from all parts of the House."[9]

However at the very top of the Liberal Party, Neil's cross-party engagement was not so widely welcomed and the Prime Minister characterised it as "Neil's adventure".[10] The married Clementine Churchill, who was probably not the only Liberal lady to have developed a platonic crush on Neil, also felt ambivalent about the match.

Lady Victoria was young and pretty and in social terms her hand was something of a coup for the younger son of a far less ancient (and Scottish) Earldom - although of course Neil was not a typical aristocratic younger son, thanks to Great Aunt Lucy's bequest and Rosebery's gift of Postwick. Neil was also blessed with good looks belying his 32 years and by common consensus he had a promising political career to look forward to. In terms of mutual interests they both shared a love of hunting and racing. Some newspapers stated that her face was almost as well known in the paddocks of leading race courses as his. Via their mutual interest in racing, fuelled by each of their fathers being leading owners, the couple had known each other for quite some time. In fact a year earlier in March 1914 Neil was a guest at Lord Derby's Knowsley House party that always surrounded the Grand National meeting at Aintree.[11] But evidently nothing then came of the highly eligible pair being under the same roof for several nights. Doubtless in the intervening year Lord Derby considered that Neil's value as a suitor in the marriage market had risen on account of both the political truce and his joining the Government. However there is no evidence that Neil was rebuffed in 1914 – and plainly given that they had invited him, the Derbys did not then consider him a radical pariah.

Obviously something had changed over the intervening year to prompt Neil towards marriage to Lady Victoria and perhaps the War and its consequences had matured him. However there remain several odd features of the match and the speed with which it was concluded. First and foremost among them must be that Neil had demonstrated almost no interest in the opposite sex since adulthood. His almost constant companions hitherto had been his father, Thomas and Jimmy and it may be significant that none of them was with him in London when the proposal was made. There is also no hint whatsoever of a budding relationship in his surviving correspondence and the press who followed his every move had not even hinted at it in advance of the engagement. Also given the chronology of Neil's life during 1914-15, there was scarcely any opportunity for romance or for deeper feelings to develop between him and Victoria before the engagement took place. In fact the engagement seems to have been made almost on impulse and the suspicion must be following the urging of a more senior political mentor such as Lloyd George. However the indications are that Lloyd George had emphatically not urged Neil to marry Victoria Stanley and on first hearing the news from Churchill mixed her up with the far more acceptable Liberal stalwart, Venetia Stanley.[12] When Churchill explained his mistake, Lloyd George apparently exclaimed "Good God – poor Neil – I am so sorry."

Neil had sent first news of the engagement to Jimmy and Dollie in Paris by telegram but in his next letter the engagement is only obliquely referred to in his close - "love from us both to you both."[13] Thomas had been in the trenches with the Coldstream Guards since mid-February and it is unclear exactly how or when Neil informed him. The Cornish newspapers were quickly writing of the engagement of Thomas's 'conspicuous' friend and the *Cornwall Advertiser* wrote later in March "the matrons of Mayfair are wondering how long before the member for St Austell follows his example."

It appears that Rosebery received the news in Scotland with both surprise and alarm - that he was losing his closest companion to matrimony. It is also apparent that he barely knew Lady Victoria: his son-in-law Major Grant wrote in an effort to pacify him over the engagement on March 7th: "Sybil and I know Victoria very well and she is a dear little thing. I am afraid, however, that you will miss Neil very much; he has been the most dutiful of sons."[14] A day later Rosebery received a letter of congratulation from Herbert Fisher on Neil's engagement, which he acknowledged on March 10th from Berkeley Square, rather curtly, with the line "Many thanks. Neil's marriage seems all that is happy and auspicious," before changing the subject to the news that Fisher had just been appointed a trustee of the British Museum.[15]

Another odd feature was that the period of their engagement was markedly brief. Admittedly it was war-time; so reducing the length of engagements for those in uniform, but Neil was now in the Foreign Office and at no risk of being ordered abroad. Nonetheless, *The Times* announced on March 13th that the wedding would take place in London on April 7th – during the parliamentary recess and on the Wednesday following Easter (as they could not be married in the Church of England during Lent). Again this must surely allow for the suspicion that an impulsive engagement was now to be solemnized before minds could be changed and promises withdrawn.

Amid all the fuss that the engagement provoked, Neil calmly continued his Foreign Office duties without distraction. On March 10th he was able to announce in the Commons that following the intervention of the Pope, Germany had agreed that all invalid civilians would be released and exchanged via Holland. Later that day during a debate on the treatment of British prisoners of war in Germany, Neil strongly rejected the idea that German prisoners here should be similarly mis-treated in revenge for the mis-treatment by Germany: "I think it would be a most deplorable policy to follow to try and pay back on those who are in our hands now any ill-treatment which British prisoners are receiving."[16]

On the same day he attended the inaugural meeting of the Russia Society, formed to foster 'good feeling and a better understanding between the peoples' of Britain and Russia. At the event Neil made a speech on behalf of the Government and (with the Russian Ambassador at his side) defended Russian territorial aspirations in the Baltic.[17] The speech caused some difficulty in Scandinavia and Neil was compelled to give an interview with a Stockholm newspaper, in which he said Sweden had no need to fear Russia's westward expansion.[18]

In mid-March Parliament rose for the Easter recess, so lightening Neil's duties and enabling him to spend two nights with Lady Victoria and the Derbys at Knowsley. However the indications are that the visit was far from relaxed or informal; on the first night Neil had to help entertain Lord Kitchener who was staying in advance of watching 12,000 newly recruited local soldiers march past him at St. George's Hall in Liverpool. The newspapers reported that next day Lord Derby, with Neil and Lady Victoria, were among the group standing by Lord Kitchener as he did so over several hours.[19]

As well as visiting his future parents-in-law, Neil also needed to introduce Victoria to his political circle, many of which did not know her. Among those who had never met her were Lord Reading, the former Rufus Isaacs, but fitting this in, amid the frantic dressmakers, was evidently a struggle: "I will telephone to you one morning and bring Victoria round to see you about 6. She is very much occupied with trying things on, so I cannot tell you for the moment which day it will be."[20]

As the wedding day plans were made there was evidently sensitivity about the ceremony and celebration appearing overly lavish and expensive in time of war. Even *The Times* was enlisted on April 2nd to lower expectations with the announcement that: "the event will be very quiet owing to the war". However this was not the only problem the couple faced in the weeks leading up to the wedding. Neil's house in Great Stanhope Street, which had been profitably let for many years, was perhaps understandably not quite as Lady Victoria wanted it and the necessary improvement and decorative works could not be completed in the short time available before the wedding. In consequence Jimmy and Dollie de Rothschild offered to lend their house in Park Street, Mayfair. Neil, seeing no reason not to start their married life where he had always lived, in his father's house in Berkeley Square, politely rebuffed the offer in a letter from the Foreign Office written on Easter Saturday:

> Very many thanks for your kind offer of your house. We are however going to stay at Berkeley Square till 5 Great Stanhope Street is ready.[21]

The letter continues in almost mournful tone:

> I shall be married in the absence of all of my intimate friends as I do not think Thomas or Harry will get leave, Jimmy is enchained at Paris and the Rothschilden will probably depart with the Bucks Yeomanry about that date, I expect, for Egypt.

In fact Neil's pessimism was partly misplaced: both Thomas and Harry did obtain leave and made it back to London to perform their respective duties as best man and usher. The others were not so lucky: Evelyn and Anthony de Rothschild, with the rest of the South Midland Mounted Brigade[22], left Fakenham by train for Avonmouth shortly before the wedding, and Jimmy, as Neil predicted, was unable to leave Paris to attend.

Rosebery came down from Scotland following the Easter weekend. The wedding ceremony did not begin until 2.30pm and in the morning Neil and his father took a walk in Hyde Park and were much photographed doing so. This interest accurately predicted what was follow, as for all the families intentions to keep it "quiet"; the London populace, feeling both deprived of society weddings and depressed by events, were not going to overlook a now rare bit of pre-war glamour and spectacle. The following day's *Times* recorded that the crowd started to assemble hours before and by 2pm there were thousands lining the approaches to St Margaret's. The *Tatler* later estimated the crowd at 5,000 - 6,000 and after the ceremony the police apparently struggled to control them.

Despite Neil's great enthusiasm for motor cars, Thomas and he arrived at the church in a horse-drawn coach. The crowd was not disappointed and the congregation was described in print as 'brilliant'. It included four royal ladies – Queen Alexandra, Princess Victoria, the Princess Royal and her daughter Princess Maud of Fife. The French ambassador arrived to loud cheers; and both main political parties were well represented. Asquith did not attend but his wife did. Bonar Law was also absent but the previous Conservative leader Arthur Balfour was there. Mr and Mrs David Lloyd George and Mr and Mrs Winston Churchill were also, unsurprisingly, there, but as well as the great and the good, a large number of Rosebery and Derby estate workers and servants attended.

Neil and Thomas's buttonholes were bunched wild primroses brought up from Mentmore. Queen Alexandra also displayed her partiality for the bridegroom's family with primroses pinned to her ermine stole. As the next day's *Times* recorded, as the royal party arrived

a little incident occurred which greatly interested the spectators. A number of poor children, some of them shoeless had got onto the pavement outside the awning, and as Queen Alexandra approached they pushed their heads under the canvas to get a better view. Her Majesty was much amused and stooping down patted some of their heads.

The bride arrived by carriage and was attended by seven bridesmaids; she was met at the church door by the Bishop of Liverpool who officiated. After the ceremony the national anthem was sung and Queen Alexandra followed the newly married couple into the vestry and signed her name as a witness besides theirs. The one major concession to the war was the absence of a reception for all of the guests. Instead there was a family luncheon at Derby House[23], that Queen Alexandra also attended.

Rosebery, never one to deprive his younger son of an extravagant gift, gave the couple a Sunbeam 12/16hp motor car, with a then list price of £535, and a top speed of 50mph.[24] Neil's constituents gave an inscribed silver tray as a wedding present and an album containing the several hundred names of those who had subscribed. As the *Wisbech Standard* later remarked the names were drawn almost equally from supporters of the two political parties.

The honeymoon was spent at Cowarth Park, near Sunningdale, Derby's Berkshire seat, but their stay there was a brief one of only five nights. Parliament returned from its Easter break on April 14th and there was no break at all for Neil from Foreign Office telegrams and the other contents of his red boxes that awaited him on the couple's return to Berkeley Square.

On first rising to speak in the Commons, Neil was accorded "a general cheer of congratulation on his recent marriage"[25] but within his first week of married life, he was back to answering questions on greater post-war autonomy for Turkish Armenians, whether raw cotton should be made a contraband item, and the treatment of British prisoners of war in Germany.

The vexed issue of British prisoners of war continued to dominate Neil's workload throughout April and May. The newspapers were full of allegations of mistreatment and their anxious relatives applied pressure on MPs for a Government response. However there was little the Government could do, other than ask, via the American embassy, for American diplomats in Germany to seek information and inspect the camp's conditions. At the end of April the Commons held a debate on prisoners and emotional accounts were given of British officers being spat upon, deprived of warm clothing and denied Red Cross food. Neil spoke for the Government and attempted to deflect the accusation of Government inactivity by roundly denouncing what he referred to as "the Prussian spirit of brutality", while at the same time holding out against the demand that the British treat their German prisoners in like fashion.[26]

The situation was made more complex by the British treatment of captured submarine crews responsible for sinking merchant ships and fishing boats, often without warning. Such conduct was outside the normal rules of war and although not internationally defined as such the British Government effectively considered the submarine crews to be war criminals. By the end of April Britain was holding 39 submariners that it considered to be within this category; and although it denied treating them inhumanely, it was confirmed by Churchill in the Commons[27] that they were being held separately from all other German prisoners. In response Germany took reprisals against a similar number of British Army officers who were now transferred into solitary confinement. Rather more rationally the German Foreign Ministry asked the American Embassy in Berlin to arrange for American diplomats in London to visit the submariners to ascertain their conditions. This visit was eventually agreed to by the Foreign Office but not before the objection of the Admiralty had been over-ruled by the Prime Minister.[28] Seemingly the initial decision to treat German submariners as a different category of prisoner had been Churchill's; the policy was rapidly dropped by his successor, who informed the Commons[29] on June 9th that their treatment was from now on to be "absolutely identical".

A month after his return to the trenches, Thomas was wounded, and although not severe, it was bad enough to justify a period of recuperative home leave.[30] Once recovered and on his last day in London he lunched with Neil and Rosebery at 38 Berkeley Square. Lady Victoria was not present at what was to be Neil and Thomas's last meeting. Rosebery included the following account of it in his posthumous memoir of Thomas:

The last time that I saw Thomas was when he lunched with Neil & me and Sybil (who loved him too) in the parlour in Berkeley Square. We were a gay party, we provided him with champagne & then he left to go to the station & then to the front. Neil went with him to Victoria, I would not.[31]

25

THE PRIME MINISTER'S DIFFICULT TASK

During the Commons' final sitting before the Whitsun recess, Asquith told a stunned House that the Government was to be reconstructed on a "broader political basis".[1] Which meant replacing an exclusively Liberal Government with a cross-party coalition. Following the unexpected announcement came the difficult task of allocating Government offices between the parties and the inevitable sacrifice of some Liberal Ministers to make way for Conservative replacements.

The new Coalition Cabinet was announced on May 25th and Sir Edward Grey remained in post as Foreign Secretary. But what was to be the fate of his Under-Secretary? The highly supportive *Cambridge Independent Press*[2] predicted that Neil's "excellent work" in the Department would be safe if, as was suggested, Under-Secretaries were of the same political complexion as the Heads of Department. However Asquith and Bonar Law applied no such universal rule for junior ministers and some departments had two ministers from the same party while others did not.

That Neil's job was in jeopardy was first reported in the *Daily Chronicle* on May 27th but it was another four days before it was officially confirmed when his long time adversary, Lord Robert Cecil, was announced by Downing Street as his successor. Seemingly even Sir Edward Grey was not consulted - according to Margot Asquith's diary:

At the Wharf Sunday 30th May Henry got a very hard letter from Grey insisting on keeping Neil Primrose. H. 'So like Grey! He never thinks of anyone but himself in all of this. I've made every personal sacrifice for the whole; he thinks himself an injured man if he has to make one.' He tore up a dry little letter which he read to me and threw it in the waste paper basket.[3]

For all of Asquith's self-pitying, his prime motivation in forming a coalition was to save his own career and that of those closest to him. That Neil did not fall within this category is scarcely surprising, but Asquith's cold ruthlessness is particularly shocking given the explanation about the Under-Secretaryship that Lord Robert Cecil gives in his 1949 memoir:

I received a message offering me to be Under-Secretary at the War Office or the Foreign Office ... I was very glad to accept and chose the War Office ... it then appeared that Jack Tennant – Asquith's brother-in-law was not ready to leave the War Office, where he was Under-Secretary, for the Foreign Office, I therefore went to the latter.[4]

As this account demonstrates, Asquith's partiality for his wife's family that gave rise to the jokey adage '*Asquith looks after his Tennants*' was not to be compromised by the sudden formation of an unexpected coalition.

The newspapers, unaware of Asquith's nepotistic preservation of his brother-in-law's job, still commented freely on the harshness of the abrupt termination of Neil's role "through no fault of his own"[5] and exacerbated by the choice of his bitterest rival as his successor. Interestingly, the Conservative leader, who would have been aware of the Jack Tennant aspect, was unimpressed by the Prime Minister's move and wrote Neil a letter sympathising (and possibly disowning responsibility) over Neil's sacking. Neil's gracious (and charitable to Asquith) reply, written from the Foreign Office on his final day in post[6], is preserved in Bonar Law's papers:

My dear Mr Bonar Law,
I am very grateful for your kind letter which coming at this moment in my life has left a deep impression on me. The Prime Minister must have had a very difficult task and I have no doubt that he had good reason for the course he took. I am not much of a letter writer, so I will only reiterate my thanks to you and I can assure you they are very real.
Yours sincerely,
Neil Primrose[7]

Neil's calm and dispassionate words almost certainly belie his real feelings. After only three months he had been deprived of the job he loved. Also on a personal level his sacking could not have come at a worse time. On May 17th he'd written to Dollie de Rothschild looking forward to commencing his occupation of Great Stanhope Street[8]; although rather less to "the disagreeable task of payment" for the works. In the event more than a year would pass before Victoria and he lived for any time together in the house.

Certainly the Parliamentary reporters suggested that Neil was forlorn and a little lost in the days following his sacking: "Neil Primrose ... looked in at the House of Commons for a little while this afternoon. He loitered about the front bench of the opposition side but was not present when his successor Lord Robert Cecil made his debut."[9] Thomas expressed his anger about Neil's treatment in a letter from the trenches in June: "I am so awfully sorry about Neil – it maddens me that the old Jesuit Cecil should displace him." In London Lord Reading wrote privately to Lloyd George and asked him to "think of Neil if you find an opportunity."[10] This appeal was followed by a piece in the *Daily Sketch*[11] "Mr Gossip" column that Neil was set to receive an important appointment in the near future, but it was not to be.

Without a Government job to do, honour dictated that he rejoin his regiment. However doing so was not so straightforward as the RBH had been in Egypt since April 23rd and Neil, after nine months without cavalry experience, was in no condition to immediately rejoin them. However the RBH's Reserve had remained in Buckingham, training new recruits, and it was there that the War Office now sent him. In order to circumvent any accusation of shirking his duty, the Cambridgeshire press regularly updated his constituents about his whereabouts during the summer of 1915.[12] However his training regime was not unrelenting and he was spotted at the July Meeting at Newmarket on July 13th.[13] With August and the war's first anniversary, Neil was daily expecting orders to embark for Egypt.

On August 9th the RBH and the rest of the 2nd South Midland Mounted Brigade in Egypt received orders to proceed to active service as infantry on the Gallipoli peninsula. Neil was well informed of these developments via his Rothschild cousins, but Rosebery on learning that Neil was destined for Gallipoli was horrified. In a candid letter to Herbert Fisher he frankly confessed that he was in a state of turmoil following Neil's departure:

my mind has been occupied by one fact – that Neil has gone to the Dardanelles, to that slaughter house. Of course he was right to go – but the pity of it. He is not the least military, and has brains, and was at the beginning of a happy married life and seemed to have a future – if that be worth having.[14]

Thomas, now promoted to Captain Agar-Robartes, had a rather different perspective from Rosebery's and his regret expressed to Dollie de Rothschild was that Neil's departure would prevent their meeting on his next leave: "I am so sorry to hear that there is a chance of Neil going off to Egypt soon as I expect to be in London about September 23rd".[15] In fact Thomas got leave slightly earlier than he expected, in order to be back in place for the battle of Loos which commenced on September 25th and during which he was to be mortally wounded.

He wrote what was to be a final letter[16] from Wimpole Hall, where he had been shooting partridges, on September 18th bemoaning the absence of all of his "intimates." On Thomas's final day of leave in London, he visited in hospital Major Fred Cripps whom he knew from RBH days and who had been wounded a month earlier at Gallipoli. Cripps was about to undergo an operation on his wounded knee and Thomas secretly brought him a bottle of Martini cocktail, mixed at the bar of the Carlton Hotel, and disguised as soda water.[17]

Neil sailed from Folkestone on a ship bound for Alexandria on August 22nd. He took with him his polo ponies and what had become his beloved white greyhound Falcon[18] (a wedding gift from Lord Winterton[19]). He also had a quantity of luggage unthinkable for any cavalry officer on the western front.

26

GALLIPOLI

Although he did not know it, just as Neil was making final preparations for his departure to Egypt, the RBH, without any prior combat experience, was being shipped across the Mediterranean, to go into battle dismounted, something that they were completely untrained for and which was to prove a most expensive failure.[1]

At 4.00am on August 18th the Bucks Hussars as part of the 2nd South Midland Mounted Brigade disembarked at Suvla Bay, Gallipoli. The British Army had first landed there twelve days before in an attempt to relieve the pressure on Anzac Cove to the south. However problems with the landing meant that the planned rapid advance onto the hills above never occurred. Any element of surprise was lost; and the Turkish enemy significantly reinforced its defences in the area.

Within 48 hours their Brigade was on the move, marching eight miles by night across the sandy bay before assembling in relative safety behind the hill of Lala Baba. At 3.00pm on August 21st the attack on the enemy, who were by now strongly entrenched on the hills above, commenced. Initially the yeomanry were kept in reserve but with the fighting underway and without any cover they marched out from Lala Baba in open formation and crossed the dried up salt lake in full view of the Turkish artillery. As a result, even at this preliminary stage, their slaughter commenced, as General Sir Ian Hamilton did not bother to conceal in his subsequent despatch:

During this march they came under remarkably steady and accurate artillery fire. The advance of these English Yeomen was a sight calculated to send a thrill of pride through anyone with a drop of English blood ... Ordinarily it should always be possible to bring up reserves under some sort of cover from shrapnel fire. Here, for a mile and a half, there was nothing to conceal a mouse, much less some of the most stalwart soldiers England has ever sent from her shores.

Once those who had survived the march reached the cover provided by Chocolate Hill they were thrown into the battle in a futile attempt to save the day. As the Brigade War Diary frankly records, they were attacking an invisible enemy – "owing to the skilful way in which the enemy's trenches had been sited it was impossible to see them." A further problem, as if one were needed, was that the ground over which they were advancing was ablaze or as the War Diary records "a large amount of scrub which had been burnt made the advance difficult."

Notwithstanding these seemingly insurmountable difficulties the Brigade did make progress and started to ascend towards Scimitar Hill. After nightfall they even reached some of the Turkish trenches and took significant parts of Scimitar or Hill 70 as it was also called, but prior to daybreak all of these gains were given up as the exhausted yeomen were forced to retire. The Brigade Commander, the Earl of Longford, was killed during the attack along with twenty other officers. That day's total allied losses were 5,300 killed, wounded or missing. The 2nd Mounted Brigade, along with the other units involved that day, had been sacrificed for nothing. Subsequently *The Times* reported:

It was the Second Brigade under the Earl of Longford consisting of the Bucks, Berks and Dorsets, which made the final glorious charge, in conjunction with the 87th Brigade, and obtained temporary possession of Hill 70, which had to be subsequently abandoned in the night. The losses of this brigade were very heavy, the Bucks regiment losing almost all of their officers and men.

Lord Longford, whose body was never found, was shot at close range while calling his men on and carrying nothing more than a map and walking stick.[2] Among the wounded officers was Neil's cousin Tony who had been shot in the arm[3] - such a wound was considered fortunate as many of the immobilised wounded were burnt alive in the burning scrub. Tony's brother Evelyn had had the good fortune to be unwell and so had been held back at the British forward base at Mudros. Following the attack, he landed at Suvla on August 23rd and two days later wrote to his mother with news that Tony was injured but not seriously and had been evacuated on a hospital ship:

I will tell you as much as I have been able to gather always keeping within the censor ... They had to advance in the afternoon across a mile and a half of open country under very heavy shrapnel and rifle fire and moved as steadily as if on parade. They reformed under a hill and at dark moved on to attack. Our brigade went right on through our first line trenches and got into the Turkish trenches on the next hill but there was nobody on the flanks and the position was enfiladed and untenable and they eventually had to retire ... Longford led the brigade in attack in the gallant way we expected and it is very sad that he was killed. It was a very high trial to come straight into an action like that but I think from all accounts the regiment were splendid and the men fought magnificently. I always felt the Buckinghamshire farmers would do well and they have certainly done so and I only wish I had been with them. It is very sad coming back and finding all the gaps and our casualties are terrible ... five out of eight of our officers hit, seventy-two men wounded and fifty-four killed or missing.[4]

After this legacy of the battle, no further open attack was undertaken and the survivors dug in for trench warfare beneath the Turkish positions. As well as being shot at, the yeomanry units had to endure the terrible heat, flies and widespread disease. The Brigade War Diary gives a candid account of these conditions in the entry for September 30th:

During the last 4 weeks of trench life sickness has been on the increase. Chiefly dysenteric diarrhoea amounting in some cases to true dysentery. Also owing to constant digging even while in reserve, septic sores are very common and the vitality of the men is very low.

27

HE HAS LEFT AN EXAMPLE I SHALL TRY TO LIVE UP TO

Just as the war in Gallipoli descended into deadlock, thousands of miles away in Flanders the British Army was attempting to break out at Loos. The battle commenced at zero hour (6.30am) on September 25th but success, along with the chlorine gas that was first used there, was patchy. On the morning of the second day Captain Thomas Agar-Robartes commanding 2nd Company, 1st Bn. Coldstream Guards was in a forward trench at Chalk Pit Wood, north-east of Loos. At 6.00am two of Thomas's company sergeants Hopkins and Printer went out into no man's land in front of Bois Hugo to bring in a wounded man. The whole area was easily observable by enemy machine gunners and while bringing the man in, Sergeant Hopkins was shot but Printer carried on and dragged the wounded man into their trench. Now Thomas and Printer left the trench again to retrieve Hopkins and while carrying him and under heavy machine gun fire, Thomas was himself severely wounded.[1] In fact he was hit twice – first by a bullet in his groin and then by another that passed right through his right lung before exiting through his back.[2] Amazingly he survived both being retrieved himself and then being stretchered back to the 18th Casualty Clearing Station. The hole in his lung was later described as being as big as a hen's egg.

Given the extent of his lung injury and resulting blood loss, Thomas's wounds were considered hopeless and the Army Doctors decided it would be pointless to evacuate him further back from the Casualty Clearing Station. As a result he lay there for four days quietly weakening until his death on September 30th.

Two days before he died and while he was tenaciously clinging to life, the Coldstream Guards recommended him for receipt of the Victoria Cross on account of his conspicuous gallantry in rescuing Sergeant Hopkins while under machine gun fire. However, much to his family's distress the VC was not awarded after his death; in fact was withheld on the questionable ground that by acting as he did he was in breach of the Commander in Chief's orders to do all in his power to prevent unwounded soldiers risking their lives in the rescue of the wounded.[3] Evidently in the parallel universe at GHQ it was considered reasonable for men in the trenches to sit tight and watch men of their own company die slow and agonising deaths in no man's land and within clear sight of their own trench.

By way of small consolation to Thomas's family, his bravery was posthumously mentioned in despatches[4] and they received many letters from Thomas's brother officers who testified to his remarkable bravery that was exhibited throughout his time in Flanders. Sergeant Hopkins survived the war and subsequently sent a letter of thanks to Viscount Clifden.[5]

The awful pall of Thomas's death reached Rosebery on October 2nd when Lady Clifden came round from Great Stanhope Street to 38 Berkeley Square to inform him in person. After she left, Rosebery immediately put his highly emotional feelings in writing:

I have just received, from his mother, the news of his death.

I loved him as a son ... He was bright & full of fun, reckless, dissipated, extravagant ... Neil loved him especially, they were twins in parliament. He ... rejoiced in Neil's successes, in his accession to office with a generous joy, devoid of the least jealousy ... Poor Neil, he will hear the news at Alexandria alone.

If God had spared him ... he would have returned a new man, weaned from the follies of youth ... But it was not to be ... He has taken this noble fellow from an adoring family and adoring friends, and all that remains are their sore hearts and their tears.

The note of his character was chivalry, the rarest of qualities in these days. Gay, loyal, chivalrous, that was the lad, for he was always young.[6]

Rosebery was not alone in fearing Neil's reaction; Jimmy de Rothschild went so far as to express the fear to his wife that Neil might suffer a breakdown – "It will be very hard for Neil to hear about it so far away. I long he can pull through [from this]."[7]

Two days later Neil received the news by telegram in Alexandria and a day later he wrote confidentially to Jimmy (from the Club Mohamed Aly) for comfort in his overwhelming sorrow:

He has left an example which I shall try to live up to. He was always very affectionate and the war brought this more to the surface. Every letter I had from him was full of affection. In the awful searchings of that which intrude on one in such a crisis I wonder whether I was as unselfish to him as he was to me and I am afraid that I was not ... If we survive this war ... I hope you will find me a more chastened character. Do write me full details. Perhaps you could find the doctor or nurse who looked after him and ask them whether he was unconscious all the time and whether he said anything. I hope you will locate his grave: perhaps we could jointly buy the ground where it is: very few can realise what he was to his friends.[8]

It is hard to interpret what Neil describes as his own selfishness as applying to anything other than his marriage and his acceptance of the role on the Indian Army Staff that had first separated them and that had caused Neil to pull strings so as to get him transferred to the Coldstream Guards. As to Neil feeling chastened, F.E. Smith later wrote: "The death of Robartes and the glory of his unquenchable courage was always in Neil's thoughts. He was it seemed to many of us never quite the same after his friend's death."[9]

Before Jimmy received Neil's letter, he had already anticipated what was required, and along with Thomas's brother Gerald[10] visited the Casualty Clearing Station where Thomas had died on October 5th:

I went today on this melancholy expedition ... Thomas poor boy, seems to have been the Dame as ever and laughed an hour or so before he died and insisted on shaving himself and saying half seriously that he knew so well that cleanliness was next to Godliness ... the end came very quickly I daresay after the exertion of shaving.
We saw his grave[11] and think it will be well looked after.[12]

Thomas was the fourth MP to be killed in the war and quite naturally his death was widely reported; and his relationship with 'his most intimate friend' Neil Primrose was not overlooked in the coverage. Even *The Times* of October 4th reported that "Mr Agar-Robartes and Neil Primrose were inseparable companions". Some newspapers went further and compared the two to Damon and Pythias[13], a comparison with strong homoerotic overtones, albeit safely couched in ancient Greek myth. Rosebery's own close relationship with Thomas was also not overlooked. The *Daily Record*[14] reported: "he was almost like another son to Lord Rosebery and by none will his untimely death be more deplored." That this assessment was correct is confirmed by Rosebery's letter to his sister of October 6th: "Yes I loved Thomas Robartes as a son … Horrors rain thick upon us all and we must always be prepared for the worst."[15]

In preparation for Thomas's memorial service that was to take place at St. Margaret's, Westminster on October 13th, Rosebery prepared and had typed a three-page address two days before.[16] It is far less personal than his original grief-stricken reflection and makes no mention of Neil, but deserves quotation:

> Few who approached him escaped his charm, for he had exquisite tact, ready humour and unbounded sympathy. Wherever he went he brought sunshine and joy. But above all each felt he was in the presence of a loyal soul. Thus no man excited more unbounded devotion.

Rosebery's tribute was never delivered and in fact Rosebery left London for Scotland ahead of the service. Why remains a mystery – perhaps Rosebery was put off by Thomas's family who feared further press scrutiny (they certainly had reason to – Thomas's brother Gerald, a diplomat in the Foreign Office since 1906, was homosexual and subsequently lived with Lord Berners[17], and his youngest brother Alex was to commit suicide in 1930, apparently on account of his sexuality[18]), or perhaps Rosebery himself realised that his words might cause an unwelcome sensation. In Rosebery's absence a rather less flowery tribute was made by the fellow Cornishman (and Thomas's then Liberal Association Chairman) Arthur Quiller-Couch.[19] Many if not most of those attending St. Margaret's had to grapple with the memory of their last seeing him in that very church, six months earlier, at Neil's wedding and by his side. The list of those who did attend is an odd one, almost all of the truly significant being absent – Neil, Rosebery, Harry (Dalmeny) and Jimmy (de Rothschild). The next day's *Times*[20] listed Lady

Victoria and her father Lord Derby as being present (presumably representing Neil), alongside Mrs James de Rothschild (representing Jimmy). Crewe was the most senior member of the Government to attend but Lady Peggy and her sister Lady Sybil were other notable absentees.

Whatever the true reason for Rosebery's absence, he and Neil certainly did not forget Thomas, and in November Rosebery asked his sister Constance to suggest "a man who makes artistic mural tablets, as I am anxious to erect one to dear Thomas Robartes".[21] By July 1916 the tablet, made of Derbyshire alabaster was finished and ready for erection in Cornwall. The design was Rosebery's and the placing on the north wall in Lanhydrock Church, behind the family pew, indicates Lord Clifden's blessing. The Times[22] reported it as "as a tribute of Lord Rosebery and his immediate friends to one whose intimate friendship they so highly cherished."

The quite severe neo-classical design reflects Rosebery's conservatism, and expensive taste; the inscribed tablet is bordered by fluted Corinthian columns and the gap in the broken pediment is filled with Thomas's arms and crest. At the foot is the crest of the Coldstream Guards. The wording is derived from Rosebery's private tribute – "The many who loved him as the Soul of chivalry, honour and friendship have erected this tablet in the church of the house which he cherished."

28

MUDROS

When Neil first heard of Thomas's death in Egypt he was already aware that the War Office's appetite for further disastrous slaughter on the Gallipoli peninsula was ended. Much of the initial blame was directed at General Sir Ian Hamilton who was relieved of his command by the Dardanelles Committee of the Cabinet on October 14th.

His successor General Sir Charles Monro was given the task of assessing the military situation on Gallipoli and of advising on the alternative options of evacuation or a fresh offensive.[1] In consequence the landing of fresh troops on the peninsula was suspended.

These decisions rapidly impacted on the Yeomanry units in Egypt that Neil had joined in September as he reported to Jimmy:

The draft I was going with to Gallipoli is off. Most of our Regiment here is under orders to go to Greece and I shall probably go there or to Gallipoli.[2]

Perhaps Neil's desire to see for himself the situation on the peninsula was natural; but in his desire for privileged access to observe the situation at Suvla Bay, there perhaps remains a hint of his former role as a privileged Staff Officer in Flanders. However there was no comparable safe and comfortable space to that enjoyed by the Staff in France and Neil was to be denied setting foot on this bit of Ottoman soil. Even if there had been, it seems certain that the War Office would never have wanted Neil, an influential Member of Parliament who was free to write letters without censorship, to witness the awful situation there.

By Greece, Neil meant Mudros, a port on the Greek island of Lemnos, in the north-east Aegean and the island closest to Gallipoli (the Straits were thirty-one miles away). Lemnos, which had only been part of neutral Greece since 1912, was first occupied unopposed by the Royal Marines, and then used as a forward base by the Allies throughout 1915. Neil arrived on Lemnos during the final week of October and remained there, and largely idle, for a month. He later wryly commented of his prolonged stay – "I was sent off with a draft to Gallipoli but got no further than Mudros ... verily a military life is taking me into strange places."

While perhaps appropriate for Neil to joke that Mudros would never have been a port of call, in happier times, while sailing with Thomas on the *RYS Zaida*, he was mightily lucky not to be at Suvla Bay and enduring the dreadful conditions then prevalent there. Aside from persistent shelling, a combination of heat, flies and insanitary conditions was causing a developing medical emergency during those still scorchingly hot autumn months. Diarrhoea, dysentery, jaundice and paratyphoid were becoming common and the RBH officers were suffering just as much as the men. Neil's cousin Evelyn became increasingly unwell with jaundice and abdominal pains during October and his fellow officer Major Fred Lawson[3] wrote from Suvla to his great-uncle Lord Burnham[4] on October 15th, mentioning his condition: "Evelyn, I am sure will not be with us long, but he is sticking it extraordinarily well, but looks very ill. I am moderate with this infernal diarrhoea".[5]

This prediction was quite accurate and on October 24th Evelyn left Suvla by hospital ship.[6] Initially he was taken to Malta and hospitalised. In mid-November he was brought back to England where he was granted a further six weeks of medical board leave. He would not rejoin the regiment until April 1916.

Even for those in the regiment who remained well, conditions were very hard and Fred Lawson told his wife that he had overheard one of his troopers say that while he had enlisted to fight on a horse, he was now 60% navvy and 40% pack mule. There was also growing anger with the politician most closely associated with the disaster – Winston Churchill. Fred Lawson in another letter confessed "I should very much like to have Winston tied to the end of the pier here every morning at 9 when the shelling commences with regularity and watch him from the seclusion of my dugout."[7]

Evacuation finally came on the last day of October. What was left of the regiment marched to Lala Baba and under cover of darkness embarked. At the end of a disastrous campaign, even the embarkation was not problem free; according to the War Diary[8] the night was "very dark and stormy, causing difficulty embarking from lighters to ships." At 7.00am the ship carrying them sailed out of Suvla Bay and docked at Mudros harbour three hours later. Their ordeal was over; but of the original 260 officers and men of the RBH who had disembarked in August, just 60 were judged fit for service following their arrival at Mudros. They all would have been emaciated, sallow skinned and grey with fatigue and for Neil, fit, healthy and entirely unscarred by the war, this sight was surely one which haunted him. It helps explain his subsequent costly determination to be with them whenever they saw active service again. Some of his troopers would have been known to him since his youth at Mentmore and have attended the Countess of Rosebery's School, and now those fine specimens of farming stock were reduced to this and dressed in filthy ragged uniforms. They remained on Mudros recuperating under canvas for just over three weeks and their number was gradually supplemented by those rejoining like Neil.

In November 1915 Kitchener left London for the Dardanelles to inspect the situation himself. The Royal Navy cruiser *Dartmouth* brought him from Marseilles to Mudros[9] and after visiting the peninsula he wrote his final report to the Cabinet at Mudros on November 21st. As Neil later confided to Jimmy, while at Mudros, Kitchener sent for him and they spent half an hour talking alone together.[10] This demonstrates that just as Neil was never an ordinary backbench MP, he was also never an ordinary junior yeomanry officer. What Neil told Kitchener is not disclosed but hopefully he used his highly privileged access to recount what he'd been told by his fellow RBH officers who had seen action. Neil was also sent for and interviewed by General Sir Charles Monro – possibly at Kitchener's prompting. Kitchener had given Monro command of the Eastern Expeditionary Force and the delicate task of closing down the Gallipoli front.

Soon after these VIP interviews, Neil's regiment left Mudros harbour in *HMS Hannibal* and, after three days of successfully avoiding German submarines, docked at Alexandria on November 29th. From there they went by train to Cairo and their former base at Mena Camp where they were re-united with their horses. Neil's polo ponies had been taken there when he had left for Mudros and put under the care of the Regiment's Veterinary

Officer. As Neil later confided to Jimmy he had entered one of them in that November's Cairo race meeting and it had won. Within days of their arrival at Mena the process of re-organising the RBH and the rest of the Yeomanry Brigade back into a mounted cavalry began.

News of Neil's safe return to Egypt rapidly reached Lady Victoria at Knowsley from where she wrote in the following gushing terms to Dollie de Rothschild on December 5th:

Isn't it splendid Neil has gone to Egypt and there I hope he will remain for some time. It is perfectly maddening that I am not allowed to go out there to join him; a winter in Egypt would be perfectly delicious though I should hate the journey out there with lots of German submarines in the Mediterranean.

Perhaps Lady Victoria's longing to swap winter in Lancashire for Cairo and its uninterrupted social scene was understandable but her optimism that Neil was quite safe there was to be rapidly displaced: on the very next day the RBH B and C squadrons received orders to proceed to join A squadron which was already on active service with the Western Frontier Force and to engage a new enemy.

On Boxing Day 1915, replying to Herbert Fisher's Christmas greetings, Rosebery did not hide both his relief over Neil and his fury over the senseless Gallipoli slaughter: "Neil is in Egypt having been detained at Mudros and never having got to the Dardanelles … I am glad he has been preserved from our Walcheren expedition[11], the most ghastly enterprise of modern times."[12]

15. Declaration of Neil's election to Parliament, January 1910

16. Neil with his sister Peggy, Lady Crewe in March, Cambridgeshire, 1912

17. Neil with Mrs Raymond Asquith and the Peckovers, 1914

18. Lady Victoria Stanley, 1915

19. 5 Stanhope Gate, London

20. Evelyn de Rothschild in Royal Bucks Hussars full-dress uniform

21. *Officers of the Royal Bucks Hussars, Churn Camp, September 1914. Neil seated middle row far right; Thomas at his feet*

22. *Neil and his greyhound Falcon in the Egyptian desert, 1915*

23. Neil home on leave, 1916

24. Neil before his final departure for Palestine, 1917

TO THE BELOVED MEMORY OF
CAPTAIN THE RIGHT HON.
NEIL JAMES
ARCHIBALD PRIMROSE
M.P. FOR WISBECH AND M.C.
BORN AT DALMENY DEC.14 1882
AND KILLED NOV.15 1917
WHILE LEADING A CHARGE
OF THE ROYAL BUCKS HUSSARS
AT THE HILL OF GEZER
NEAR WHICH AT RAMLEH
HE LIES BURIED
THIS TABLET IS ERECTED BY HIS
PROUD AND SORROWFUL FATHER

NOW HE IS DEAD
FAR HENCE HE LIES
IN THE LORN SYRIAN TOWN
AND ON HIS GRAVE
WITH SHINING EYES
THE SYRIAN STARS LOOK DOWN

25. Memorial, St Mary's, Mentmore

29

THE SENUSSI

That new enemy against which Neil was first to see action was a force drawn from the Sufi Senussi clan that emanated from the Libyan interior of the province of Cyrenaica. During the Italo-Turkish war of 1911-12, Ottoman officers had played on the Senussi's devout Islamic sentiments to mobilize them in opposition to the Italian coastal invasion. The result was that even after Italy and Turkey signed a peace treaty in October 1912 the Italian army did not succeed in pacifying this part of Libya. As a result when the Ottoman Empire allied itself with the Central Powers and entered the war on their side, the German-Ottoman allies now saw an opportunity to exploit the situation in eastern Libya so as to bother the British in Egypt.

By 1914 the Senussi regular force the Muhafizia numbered several thousand and were a disciplined uniformed body supplemented by nomadic Bedouin tribal irregulars.[1] They received arms, money and ammunition from Germany and were led by the Ottoman General Ja'far Pasha al-Askari. The Senussi were never in a position to actually conquer Egypt but the British feared even limited success might provoke a jihadi uprising in the populated Nile delta and lead to serious disorder.

The Senussi first struck against the border town of Sollum in November 1915; soon after, 134 Egyptian coastguards deserted to the Senussi[2] and disorder broke out in Alexandria, 280 miles away – suggesting that British fears of a general jihad might be realised. Sollum was far too isolated, given the paucity of water resources, to be counter-attacked and so the British pulled back to Matruh, 120 miles closer to Alexandria and the best place to make a base for Western Frontier Force operations. The first engagement, in which RBH A squadron took part, took place at Wadi Shaifa west of Matruh on December 11th and over the following two days. The attack was not decisive and demonstrated that the Senussi force's strength lay in its mobility; further re-inforcements were going to be required to eradicate it. On the following day, December 14th, Neil and the other RBH squadrons arrived at Mutrah.[3] This re-united all units of the RBH but they had to wait until Christmas Day before a second thrust was made. Alongside Neil was his cousin Tony de Rothschild who had returned to service following his injury at Gallipoli. They had ridden in a yeomanry column from Alexandria with heads shaven to impede the nuisance of the desert sand. On Christmas Eve, Neil reported this to Jimmy by letter:

Sollum is in the hands of the Senussi and we are camped at Mutrah about 160 miles west of Alexandria on the coast. I understand they have machine guns and show an unwarranted disregard of death. Of course the Germans have many fingers in this pie. We are to make an advance soon but today, at any rate, we shall probably remain stationary as there is a sandstorm. Tony and I have cropped our hair which gives the sand smaller opportunities for asylum.[4]

The following day, Christmas Day, was one of clear still weather and before dawn the Western Frontier Force moved out of the safety of Mutrah to attack. The main Senussi force of about 5,000 had been identified by aerial reconnaissance near Gebel Medwa, a hill eight miles south-west of Mutrah.[5] A few days after the attack Tony de Rothschild sent his father a detailed description of the day's events:

I will now attempt to give you some kind of account of how we spent Christmas Day. We paraded at 4.30am and moved off in the dark leaving a few sick and transport to shift camp inside the inner perimeter. It was quite a formidable column, of which we found ourselves to be part, perhaps the most noticeable part being an Indian Regiment which has already done right well in France[6] ... The majority of the cavalry was out on the flank to do a turning movement, we were with the infantry, as advance guard ... or anything that was needed. The country is bare and stony, broken with steep dongas and nullahs, capable of hiding any number of men and quite impossible for horses to cross at any pace, or even in many cases at all. We marched out some 8 miles, a long serpent winding along the dusty track: it was quite cold and it seemed a long time waiting for the sun to rise. We then saw the alarm beacons of the enemy burning, and afterwards our advanced points were fired on.

He then describes the attack and alludes to his cousin Neil's part in it:

We were busy on the flank most of the day trying to dislodge an unknown number of men from a large donga: they fired on one of our patrols, and then Neil led his squadron up in a dismounted attack, this with a troop on their flank made the Senussi 'quit' and the nullah was empty when we got there.

Later in the day as the enemy became surrounded on three sides they retreated en masse, as Tony describes:

in a moment, to our astonishment, from where we thought there were only 12 or so, we saw about 300 streaming away in odd groups with about 70 camels, etc: 2 of our squadrons galloped up to within about 500 yds., but did not dare go up closer because of our own guns, and from there did some execution with rifle fire. It was really a most remarkable sight, rather like bolting rats from a hole ... It was too late, however, and there was no means of communication between the different units of our force, so it was impossible to round them all up as we were afraid of being left out there in that difficult country in the dark, so we came home, leaving a great deal of loot uncollected.

Among this 'loot' was a quantity of carpets:

I feel I might have secured a far better bargain at a cheaper rate in carpets than I shall ever get in Bond Street and it would have been delightfully 'chic' to stand in front of the fireplace with one's legs on a carpet secured in this fashion.

As it was later reported that General al-Askari's flight from the Christmas Day battle had been so rapid that his office and personal effects had been left behind[7], it seems likely that the carpets were his and thus highly collectable as battle trophies.

We marched back to camp ... got in at 8 o'clock and gave the horses their first drink of the day. As bad luck would have it, it came on pouring with rain and we were drenched.

The day was on the whole a great success but might have been much greater, and, personally, I see no end to these operations, as the enemy disperse as soon as any force is sent against them. Many interesting papers were found with German proclamations, etc.

That was our merry Xmas, I hope yours was equally successful.[8]

After the return to Mutrah on Christmas night Samuel Lawrence, a trooper in B Squadron, prepared the officers' dinner – roast turkey from tins – but they declined to eat it and told him to give it to the men.[9] The problem was not lack of appetite but that they had their own rather more appetising food that had been sent out from England by Harrods and Fortnums and which continued to reach them, even at Mutrah. This is reflected in Tony de Rothschild's letter to his father dated December 30th:

on my return to camp today I found a most magnificent array of parcels spread out in my tent, and I thoroughly enjoyed myself unpacking them, and I hope to carry the process of enjoyment one stage further during the next few days and eat a large quantity of the many acceptable things which they contained.

British Christmas Day battle casualties were light – fourteen killed and 50 wounded as against 370 Senussi dead and 82 wounded prisoners.[10] As it had been not possible to collect and bury the dead the previous day, on Boxing Day the RBH squadrons returned to the scene of the battle to retrieve their dead. Many of the British corpses had been mutilated and they actually caught a group of Arab women still engaged in violating bodies. The troopers were ready to shoot the women but Trooper Adams recalled in 1985[11] that Neil drew his revolver and threatened to shoot the first man who did so. As a result they just drove the women back before collecting the bodies for burial.

From Boxing Day onwards the weather remained unusually wet. This meant that when the next attack on the Senussi took place on January 23rd the ground was so waterlogged that the fast movement of mounted troops was not possible and so the RBH played no significant part in the attack.

However, just as Tony de Rothschild had predicted, this clash did not decisively defeat the highly mobile Senussi force.

With February the weather improved and the sand dried enabling the RBH some recreation in hunting foxes houndless, using their drawn swords for the kill.[12] Doubtless this was a great boon for Neil's greyhound Falcon who accompanied Neil throughout the Senussi campaign – a photograph of him in the desert was subsequently included in the *Times History of the War*.[13]

The big logistical problem that the yeomanry faced in the desert was, of course, the lack of water for both troops and horses and this was why, even as the Senussi were driven further away westwards, their base camp remained at Mutrah and there each night, following operations, they returned. Gradually though the availability of drinking water improved by the use of steam pumps to draw water from the historic wells that existed to the west of Matruh. The Camel Corps were also used to bring up water to forward operations: each camel could carry up to 40 gallons.[14]

By February 20th both security and water provision had improved sufficiently for the base camp to be shifted further along the coast to the port of Barrini; fourteen miles south-east of there at Agagia, on February 26th, the decisive clash came. The battle plan was somewhat different from that adopted on Christmas Day – the infantry were to attack in isolation and break the Senussi's resistance; as soon as they showed signs of giving way and fleeing the yeomanry and armoured cars were to rush up and complete the rout.[15]

The infantry went in at 11.00am while the bulk of the yeomanry and two armoured cars remained assembled behind on the infantry's right, and Neil's squadron of RBH and two cars on the left. After two hours of contact the Senussi started to buckle. Their camel force and baggage, escorted by irregulars, left the battle first and were pursued at speed by Neil's squadron and the two cars.[16]

The main fighting force of Muhafizia and their maxim guns formed the rear and flank of the Senussi as they pulled back and at 3.00pm they were charged by the main force of yeomanry, and the armoured cars. Neil was perhaps fortunate to miss this cavalry charge as the Senussi's maxim guns caused significant casualties. The charge, while lauded at the time, has since been described as reckless.[17] Nonetheless the battle's object was achieved: the Senussi force was put to flight and the Ottoman General al-Askari was captured. Their force now dispersed and while skirmishes followed it never re-assembled for battle. While Neil's squadron of RBH's attack on the retreating camels did not represent the *coup de grâce* on the Senussi it was important enough to be recognised in the distribution of battle honours and both Neil and his fellow officer John Crocker Bulteel[18] were awarded the Military Cross for leading their squadron in pursuit of and for capturing the Senussi's camel baggage train.

Following the battle of Agagia the British forward base remained at Barrini but Sollum remained to be captured. Once re-supplied by sea, the mounted yeomanry force under General Peyton advanced along the coastal road towards Sollum. At 9.00am on March 14th the air scouts reported that the enemy was breaking up its camp at Sollum and retreating into Libya. As a result, Sollum was occupied later that day without resistance.[19] Following the retreating Senussi into Cyrenaica in Libya was not practicable and the Senussi campaign ended with the raising of the British flag over the fort at Sollum.

30

LEAVE

Just a week after Sollum was re-taken, the RBH received orders to return to Alexandria – a 320-mile journey that took several weeks to undertake. Neil arrived back in Alexandria in mid-April, in time to celebrate Passover with Tony and Evelyn who had just returned from England after months of sick leave following Gallipoli. On the following day Neil wrote to Jimmy to inform him that he was safely returned from the Senussi campaign:

We are now in Alexandria and we rode back the whole way from Sollum – some 320 miles. I have applied for leave and if I get it shall be in England by the second week of May.
Last night I was the only Christian at a Jewish Passover dinner.[1]

On the very day Neil wrote, April 18th 1916, although he did not yet know it, his daughter Ruth was born at his house in Great Stanhope Street. Her birth was reported in the newspapers within a few days under the heading 'Lord Derby's Grandchild'[2] – her birth made Derby a grandfather for the first time whereas she was Rosebery's sixth grandchild.

Almost certainly on account of her birth, his leave request was quickly granted. Lady Victoria, eagerly anticipating his return after over eight months absent, wrote Dollie de Rothschild a postcard from 5 Great Stanhope Street saying "isn't it glorious that Neil has got leave."[3] Rosebery was equally delighted by Neil's leave. On April 29th he proudly told Herbert Fisher "he is very happy with his daughter and has really distinguished himself in action."[4]

Within a few days of this, Neil was home; arriving to their mutual delight on his father's 69th birthday.[5] Next day he was seen in the Commons chamber where his appearance did not go unreported:

judging from his appearance his experience at the front has agreed with him entirely. He is bronzed and looking very fit and was in the most cheerful spirits. Mr Primrose was home in time to spend Sunday, Lord Rosebery's birthday with his father.[6]

On the same day Winston Churchill also returned to the Commons from Flanders where he had been in the trenches trying to remove the stain of Gallipoli by commanding the 6th Battalion of Royal Scots Fusiliers. As former ministers both Neil and Churchill were entitled to sit on the opposition front bench and so, unsurprisingly their being there together was noted in the press gallery:

Mr Winston Churchill clad in mufti took his place on the Front Opposition Bench next to Sir Edward Carson and was joined by Neil Primrose who remained for some time in animated conversation with him. Mr Neil Primrose like Mr Churchill was in civilian dress.[7]

This report demonstrates the complete transformation that the war had brought to the Opposition Front Bench; anyone who had predicted this scene of Carson, Churchill and Neil sitting there, happily side by side, during the 1912-14 Home Rule debates would have been considered mad.

Neil remained the prominent flâneur in Parliament, notwithstanding the war or the loss of Thomas. During the following week the *Daily Mirror*[8] reported that he was one of the first MPs to don a summer morning coat – "summer grey, with a scarlet flower in his button hole". On May 15th Neil unsuccessfully challenged the Chancellor of the Exchequer, Reginald McKenna[9], about making Australian silver coinage legal tender in Great Britain, in order to simplify life for the great number of Australian troops here.[10]

It would be misleading to suggest though that Neil's leave in London, which was extended by a further month from May 19th,[11] was entirely dominated by Commons attendance. He attended Windsor Races[12] on Friday May 12th and on Tuesday May 23rd his infant daughter was baptised at

Westminster by the Speaker's chaplain, in the Chapel of St. Mary Undercroft.[13] She was given four names – Ruth Alice Hannah Mary, Alice and Hannah in honour of her maternal and paternal grandmothers.

On the day of Ruth Primrose's christening, Colonel Churchill (as Hansard now referred to him) made a searing attack on the War Office's use of military personnel. He followed this up on May 31st with an attack on the failure to utilise the manpower of the Empire to strengthen the country's fighting strength. Rather more ominously for Asquith's government the Liberal MP Sir Ivor Herbert followed Churchill in the debate and moved a resolution to reduce Lord Kitchener's salary by £100. Although the amount was a token, this was the traditional means for the Commons to show its lack of confidence in a minister. Neil's old radical friend Sir Henry Dalziel joined the onslaught on Kitchener towards the debate's end and wrung from Kitchener's hapless Under-Secretary, Jack Tennant, the concession he had come prepared with, that Kitchener would himself meet with MPs and address their points and questions. After this announcement Sir Ivor withdrew his motion, and next day, the last before the Whitsun recess, the House was informed that Lord Kitchener would meet MPs the following day in Committee Room 14 at 11.30am.

Neil, as ever the press's darling, was widely reported as an early arrival at the subsequently packed Committee Room.[14] The proceedings were private and no minutes were taken but Neil subsequently told Fred Cripps that Kitchener had addressed them like "a schoolmaster addressing schoolboys" and no MP was brave enough to interrupt him.[15] Kitchener's departure from the political scene was though otherwise achieved; three days later, he was drowned when *HMS Hampshire* struck a mine off Orkney.

Neil's Military Cross was announced in the King's Birthday Honours of Saturday June 3rd; just four days later he went to Buckingham Palace and was invested with it by the King.[16] But both the Palace and Downing Street were reeling from the double blows of Kitchener's death and the inconclusive great naval battle at Jutland. That night after dinner at 10 Downing Street, Lord Reading let slip to Margot Asquith that Lloyd George wanted to succeed Kitchener at the War Office.[17]

While avoiding making the difficult decision of who should replace Kitchener, Asquith himself temporarily took charge of the War Office. However a month after Kitchener's death it was announced that Lloyd George would be his replacement. How much Neil knew of these manoeuvres during his final weeks of leave is unknown but given his closeness to both Lloyd George and Lord Reading, it seems highly likely he did know. Lloyd George may even have held out to him the possibility of his own return to the government. However with his leave already extended once and in the absence of any announcement from Downing Street he had no option but to return to Egypt and await developments there.

31

MUNITIONS

Neil's extended leave expired on June 20th and so he only learned after disembarking at Alexandria that Lloyd George was now in charge at the War Office; furthermore, Neil's father-in-law Lord Derby had joined him there as Under-Secretary on July 7th. Within a week of these appointments (and Edwin Montagu replacing Lloyd George at Munitions) rumours that Neil would go to Munitions as a Parliamentary Secretary were printed in both the *Pall Mall Gazette*[1] and the *Daily Mirror*[2]. The vacancy at the Munitions Ministry was, they said, set to occur in the event of Colonel Arthur Lee[3] MP accompanying Lloyd George from Munitions to the War Office.

These newspaper rumours were to prove entirely accurate but there was quite a considerable delay before Neil's appointment was confirmed; exactly why is now obscure. It seems likely that the problem lay with the limited number of permitted ministerial salaries. As a result even the wizard Lloyd George could not just create a second Under-Secretaryship at the War Office when there had only ever been one. The issue was eventually solved by Lee agreeing to go to the War Office on an unpaid basis and with the creative job title of 'Personal Military Secretary to the Secretary of State for War'. Not until Lee's appointment on this basis was confirmed by the *London Gazette* on August 12th, did a vacancy at Munitions exist, which Neil could be asked to occupy. There was then a further delay while Frederick Kellaway MP was instead considered for the post[4] and only on August 24th did Neil receive the command to return to London.[5]

Before he was recalled he was promoted to Captain on July 19th. This promotion followed his second mention in despatches for his service against the Senussi.[6]

It seems doubtful that Neil was given anything useful to do in Cairo during July and August 1916. The months that followed the defeat of the Senussi were not productive ones for the Egyptian Expeditionary Force. Officers were left alone to lead a sybaritic existence and wealthy ones, such as Neil and Evelyn, abandoned the officers' mess for the luxuries of Shepheards Hotel and the Mohammed Aly Club. When interviewed in the 1980s one elderly veteran of the regiment, Trooper Samuel Lawrence[7], recalled that while acting as Evelyn de Rothschild's army batman, he had also been put up at Shepheards, so as to be on hand when needed by Evelyn.

As well as achieving nothing of military use, Neil's pointless journey to and from Alexandria in the summer of 1916 exposed him to the considerable threat posed by German submarines to British shipping in the eastern Mediterranean. One victim during August 1916 was Rosebery's yacht *Zaida* on which Neil had spent many happy hours with both his father and Thomas in pre-war days. Handed to the Admiralty in 1915 she had been converted by the Royal Navy into to HM Armed Yacht *Zaida* with a crew of six officers and 30 men. She was on detached service in the Gulf of Alexandretta[8] engaged in destroying Turkish petrol stores when she was hit and sunk on August 17th. Most of her crew were captured but three officers and ten ratings were lost with her.[9]

Neil left his greyhound Falcon in Egypt under the care of his fellow officer Fred Cripps to whom the dog became most attached. In Cripps' 1957 memoir[10] he recounts how Falcon would manage to come and seek him out at the Mohammed Aly Club in Cairo and even took a train to do so. Falcon's end would come during the Palestinian campaign, in 1917, as a result of a misadventure while chasing a quail.

Neil was back in London and in post at 6 Whitehall Gardens, where the Ministry of Munitions was based, by the second week of September. The huge and growing Ministry was now in its second year of existence and was responsible for the complete supervision of both private and state armaments factories. The degree of state control over these enormous factories came to be known as 'War Socialism'.

At the time Neil joined the Ministry, a significant problem was the pressing need to release male workers for the army. This was to be done by reducing the number of skilled male workers and replacing them with unskilled women. The process was referred to at the time as 'combing out' but, as the engineering workers who were going to be sent off to fight were highly unionised, there were increasingly frequent disputes and threatened strikes for the Ministry to resolve. Neil was perhaps an unlikely conciliator of industrial disputes but that was the role he was assigned[11] on appointment by Edwin Montagu and the First Parliamentary Secretary, Dr Christopher Addison[12].

Neil would in time confess that he loved receiving munition worker delegations, as they gave him an insight into the life of industrial workers that he had never previously had. However Neil was not always adept at managing his time and on one occasion Addison had to rescue him from a much over-run meeting with a deputation of women workers from Barrow-in-Furness.[13]

Neil's interaction with women workers, while at Munitions, is interesting in the context of his previous opposition to any form of female suffrage. The issue had not disappeared, even in Neil's largely rural constituency; that December the campaigning suffrage journal *Common Cause*[14] reported a meeting of the March Women's Suffrage Society passing a resolution to their MP, to help include them on the electoral register.

Neil's new ministerial workload was worlds away from his former Foreign Office role but the newspapers remained just as adoring as they had been eighteen months earlier. The London correspondent of the *Hull Daily Mail* wrote on September 30th:

> Everyone is glad to hear that a new sphere of usefulness has been found for Mr Neil Primrose. He is such an able speaker that the fear is that he will rather cast his new chief Mr Montagu into the shade when he rises to speak from the Treasury Bench.

Certainly Neil's abilities as a word-smith were in evidence when he wrapped up a long debate[15] on a motion critical of the unregulated activities of the Central Control Board in restricting the sale of alcohol to munition workers in the Carlisle and Gretna areas. Neil masterfully demonstrated that the ends justified the means, however unacceptable in peacetime, and that those affected, far from Westminster, were not unhappy:

> I do not think I am giving away any great secret if I refer to the gigantic factory at Gretna. A year ago Gretna was a rural district connected in our minds principally with romance. Another page has

been written in its history which is perhaps as romantic as any that has been written before. Within ten months, owing to the labours of several thousand workmen, a great factory has sprung into being, which is already contributing its quota to the munitions of war.

Since I have come back to England I have been dealing largely with the labour side of the Ministry of Munitions. I have seen a great many of the trade union representatives, not only in this country but in Scotland, and I can assure the House that from not one single trade union representative have I heard any complaint made against the Liquor Control Board.

The concentration of munitions factories in and around Carlisle gave rise to complaints from other large employers that the Ministry was so dominant an employer that it was distorting the labour market and causing housing shortages. Neil, increasingly seen as an able and tactful conciliator, was given the delicate job of addressing and listening to these concerns at a conference in the city.[16] Back in the Commons, Neil was frequently given the job of answering questions in the House that related to munitions. In answer to one concerning the dilution of male workers at the Woolwich Arsenal, Neil disclosed that in August 1914 just 125 women were employed there whereas by November 1916 the female workforce at Woolwich had reached 18,000.[17] Later that month Neil was challenged in the House as to why the Munitions Department was still using accountants who were of military age. Neil explained that as the work was highly specialised it could only be entrusted to members of one of the recognised institutes of accountants and there were not enough unfit or ineligible members. He also added that the department's total expenditure, that was required to be audited, was greater than the entire Government's had been before August 1914.[18]

Although Neil was the third and most junior minister within the department, the war had, by now, so transformed the Whitehall machine that he had some access to the very pinnacle of Government, the War Committee, which had to a degree displaced the Cabinet. Although Neil was never to be a member of the War Committee, when items on the agenda concerned munition labour questions he was invited to attend and speak. In this way he was able to observe and assess both Asquith's chairmanship[19] and Lloyd George's contributions as Secretary of State for War.[20]

Of course Neil was not an impartial judge and there is ample evidence that his close and sociable relationship with Lloyd George continued throughout Neil's time at Munitions.[21]

During these busy autumn months of 1916 Neil had no time to visit his constituency but the ever-supportive *Cambridge Independent Press* reminded its readers of his talents and potential on October 6th:

> Undoubtedly one of the most brilliant men of the day … He is considered to be a coming front rank man and was certainly born under a lucky star. He is good looking, clever and pushful … Mr Neil Primrose is sometimes talked of as a future Prime Minister which is not at all unlikely as he has got the pertinacity and ability to carry him anywhere.

In October 1916 a serious 'unofficial' strike broke out among the engineers employed on the Clyde ship-building yards and added to his burdens. Strikes during the war had been made illegal and the Clyde shipbuilders wanted it broken up by force and even suggested using soldiers of the 'Dockers Battalion' who had been recruited from the same shipyards. Resolving this explosive situation brought Neil into the orbit of the Labour Party Leader, Arthur Henderson, who was then acting as the Government's labour adviser and effectively fixer of industrial disputes.[22]

Neil and Henderson subsequently met with the Clyde employers and a delegation of workers in Neil's room in Whitehall Gardens and got the dispute peacefully resolved.[23] This settlement was then followed up by a morale-boosting conference of the Federation of Engineering and Shipbuilding Trades at Westminster Central Hall, that both Neil and Arthur Henderson addressed.[24]

Neil spoke in the Commons[25] on behalf of the Munitions Ministry on December 4th and shortly afterwards Asquith made a brief statement on the pending reconstruction of the government.[26] This was to be his last address to the House as Prime Minister.

32

REGIME CHANGE

The complex sequence of events that led to Asquith resigning as Prime Minister on December 5th 1916 are, a century on, still a matter of vigorous and even heated debate. Here is not the place to engage in the controversy. From Lord Beaverbrook's account[1] we learn that Neil was present, albeit in the shadows, over the key weekend of December 2nd-3rd. Beaverbrook records seeing Neil at Sir Henry Dalziel's house in London on the Saturday. This was the day before Dalziel's *Reynolds's Newspaper* carried the sensational and inspired leak that:

> Mr Lloyd George has arrived at the definite conclusion that the methods of dilatoriness, indecision and delay which characterise the action of the present War Council are such, in his opinion, as to endanger the prospects of winning the war.

Whether Dalziel was actually briefed by Lloyd George, or by Neil as his agent, or simply put the article together himself from bits of information he had accumulated, may never now be known.

In any event while the *Reynolds's* piece cause quite a tremor on the Sunday morning, it was quickly trumped by *The Times*'s earthquake of Monday. *The Times* was apparently given its information by Sir Edward Carson[2] (although he can only have got it from Lloyd George himself or one of his authorised friends). It not only published details of the plan to reconstruct the government but also strongly attacked Asquith.

Later that day Asquith (without Lloyd George) met with his other Liberal Cabinet colleagues; excepting Montagu, they were universally supportive, while indicating that accepting Lloyd George's proposal to reform the War

Council was a step too far. This meeting probably led Asquith to withdraw his offer of accommodation with Lloyd George, and next day Lloyd George resigned from the Government. On the Monday night, December 4th, Beaverbrook saw Neil again:

> I had a talk with Neil Primrose, who did not conceal his certainty that the Prime Minister would offer no terms now, but would resign, and thus follow the Conservative plan for getting rid of Lloyd George and coming back without him.[3]

Had Asquith managed to pull this manoeuvre off it would have left Neil dangling in the wrong camp but it would have also been very damaging for his father-in-law, as Lord Derby had now become publicly associated with Lloyd George. Perhaps fearful of this outcome Derby made a final appeal to Asquith to make peace with Lloyd George (as the car waited outside to drive him to the Palace to resign). Asquith though declined to discuss the matter, and although he did not know it, by proceeding to gamble on the inability of his opponents to form a government, sealed his own fate.

When Christopher Addison later wrote[4] about the final days of Asquith's premiership he was careful to deny any intrigue and scheming, although he freely admits that within an hour of Asquith's resignation he was summoned to the War Office by Lloyd George and thereafter continually assisted with the formation of a new government. The exact degree of Neil's involvement with Lloyd George in the days that followed Asquith's resignation is far from clear but what about his participation in scheming and intrigue in advance of it? There are a few snippets – for instance it may be significant that as soon as things had settled down in Downing Street and he had recovered from an inconvenient cold, Lloyd George wrote in a letter dated December 22nd:

> I did not get my lunch until 2.20 having asked Dalziel & Neil Primrose to lunch ... Clearing things up. Parliament up. General feeling we have started well.[5]

Another is Margot Asquith's record of a conversation with Jimmy de Rothschild when at Walmer Castle on Sunday December 3rd, in which he indiscreetly pointed out the benefits of a Lloyd George premiership; Margot suspected Neil to be his informant.[6]

Neil certainly owed Asquith no loyalty after his 1915 removal from the Foreign Office, which just added to a series of snubs that he received from Asquith in the years before it. Conversely Lloyd George had been a consistent friend and it was he who had rehabilitated Neil by bringing him into his Munitions fiefdom. While there Neil had gained first-hand experience of the War Council structure and Asquith's faltering chairmanship of it.

At 7.30pm on December 7th the King appointed Lloyd George Prime Minister and later noted in his diary "he will have a strong Government". The crisis was over and Lloyd George could form his own coalition government; but the issue of how much support it would have within the Liberal Parliamentary Party remained open. Even before Lloyd George kissed hands Christopher Addison was busy canvassing the back benches. He concluded that if Lloyd George managed to form a government he would have the support of 126 Liberal MPs. Given this canvassing work it is scarcely surprising that Addison was the new Prime Minister's first choice for Liberal Chief Whip; however he declined the role and instead was rewarded with promotion to Minister of Munitions.[7]

Addison's declining the role of Chief Whip for Munitions raises the interesting but hypothetical question of whether in place of Addison, Neil might have been promoted to run Munitions, or whether Montagu might have been kept on there.[8] Regardless, it was not to be and instead Addison was given the job of persuading an equally reluctant Neil to be the new Liberal Chief Whip.

On December 12th Neil received the following letter from 10 Downing Street:

My dear Neil,

I am very anxious that you should, at least for a short time till things settle down take the Chief Whip-ship. I know you prefer the Labour job, which I talked to you about, but I am asking this as a real favour to myself at the present juncture. I promise you that it will only be temporary if you prefer work of another kind.

Do say yes, and take it in hand at once.

Ever sincerely, David Lloyd George[9]

196

This letter, which was delivered by hand to Neil in his ministerial room at Munitions, is interesting because it discloses that Neil and Lloyd George had earlier met face to face and discussed Neil's future role. The cryptic reference to "the Labour job" refers to the new Ministry of Labour that was created by merging the Labour Sections of Munitions with those of the Board of Trade. As Neil had experience (although only of three months) in running this part of Munitions, it was perhaps natural, if in normal times a little bold, to seek to head the new ministry. Unfortunately though as the price for obtaining Parliamentary Labour Party support for his government Lloyd George gave the post to the Labour MP John Hodge[10]. Hodge was without prior government experience; Arthur Henderson, the Labour Party leader who had helped Neil resolve the Clyde shipbuilding dispute that autumn, was perhaps a more natural choice. However Henderson was given a far bigger prize for pledging Labour Party support – a seat on the new five-member War Cabinet.

Neil had first been identified as Chief Whip material by Lloyd George in January 1915 but had instead gone to the Foreign Office. Whether Addison knew that fact is unclear but now he evidently shared the Prime Minister's view that Neil was suitable for the job. Although without prior Whips' Office experience, Addison had noted two relevant qualities in his diary entry of November 16th – Neil's "fine temper" and "that he does not worry over things too much".[11] Neil also had the strong advantage of being able to reach right across the Liberal Party to both its Whig and Radical wings.

Of this though Neil was far from persuaded as he evidently confided to Addison who that day wrote in his diary "much as he dislikes it (Chief Whip) we shall have to force it on him." The forcing was necessary because Neil had already replied to Lloyd George's letter in decidedly negative terms:

My dear Lloyd George,
  I am deeply touched by the kindness of your letter. I need hardly say that I have always been proud of the friendship which will I trust always exist between us. My feelings against taking the position of Chief Liberal Whip are insuperable. I have neither experience nor inclination for the office, which is one which has no attraction for me.

Neil then adopted Addison's tactic of proposing another MP for the role – William Pringle: perhaps a perceptive choice of Neil's as he was to become one of Lloyd George's most vocal critics.[12] Neil continued:

If there is no vacant place for him, I shall be quite happy that he shall have mine and by doing this you may be making a friend of him while I shall be ready and happy to give you any support from outside which is in my power.[13]

Lloyd George was not to be tempted by this suggestion and Dr Addison continued to apply thumb-screws to Neil throughout the next day. That evening, as Addison recorded in his diary, Neil buckled, but his agreement was limited to just three months and Addison wrote "I am sure he will escape for active service at the first opportunity".[14] In a handwritten letter he confirmed his acceptance to the Prime Minister:

In view of the urgency of your request and the extreme kindness which you have shown me I will fill the position of Chief Liberal Whip to the best of my ability on the understanding that you will relieve me of that office if I ask you to do so after a few months.[15]

As well as making his acceptance the subject of this time limit, Neil also made clear that while doing the job he must have:

access to yourself personally when I think it necessary and also that I shall have your entire confidence.

Lloyd George, who was then suffering from a severe cold and so doubly desperate to complete the formation of his government, gladly accepted all of Neil's conditions and the following day was Neil's first in Downing Street. Neil was soon advising the still unwell Lloyd George, by letter, that to put Under-Secretaries of the same party colour as the presiding Ministers of the new departments of Labour, Pensions and Shipping would arouse "great hostility in the Commons and the Press ... Hope you are better".[16] That evening as Lord Stamfordham recorded[17], Neil went to the Palace and "brought the list of Household and further minor appointments in the Government" for the King's approval. Neil's old friend Cecil Beck MP remained Vice Chamberlain of the Household as he had been under Asquith, thus ensuring that he had a reliably friendly face at his side in the Whips' Office.

33

LIBERAL CHIEF WHIP

In purely Liberal Party terms the formation of the Lloyd George coalition was a revolutionary moment. No Liberal member of the previous Cabinet, excepting Lloyd George himself, remained in government. Lord Grey (as he now was) and Neil's brother-in-law Lord Crewe went with Asquith and did not return; and the same was true of McKenna the former Chancellor of the Exchequer and Home Secretary Herbert Samuel. The fact that Montagu would probably have accepted office from Lloyd George, so long as it was not a demotion from his previous role at Munitions, was not then widely known. Winston Churchill would also have accepted office at the outset of Lloyd George's premiership, but he was unacceptable to the Conservatives and had to wait until July 1917 before doing so.

In these circumstances the new government was Liberal light and Lloyd George needing ballast despatched his new Secretary of State for War, Lord Derby, to ask Rosebery to add weight and lustre by becoming Lord Privy Seal. As Rosebery had not set foot in the House of Lords since 1911 he considered it "a preposterous mission" on that and other grounds, but he confined himself to giving Derby the excuse of decrepitude.[1] Alas what Neil made of this extraordinary meeting between his father and father-in-law is not recorded. The Earl of Crawford and Balcarres was given the post. More welcome to Neil, if unexpected, was his former New College tutor, Herbert Fisher, joining the government as President of the Board of Education.[2] Neil, while still at the Ministry of Munitions, wrote a congratulatory letter that did not mask his surprise: "I have always looked back with the greatest pleasure to our former association and I never dreamt it would be renewed in this way, which makes the realisation all the more delightful."[3]

On the Conservative side, Neil doubtless especially welcomed Derby's promotion to lead the War Office. Balfour at the Foreign Office in place of Grey was also not too hard to swallow. Far less palatable to Neil would have been Lord Robert Cecil, who not only remained as Foreign Office Under-Secretary but was now given the additional role of Minister of Blockade. Amusingly, Lloyd George's secretary (and more importantly mistress) Frances Stevenson shared Neil's dislike of Lord Robert and wrote in her diary for December 7th: "We do not want Bob Cecil in the government at all. He is spiteful and malicious & will do D [Lloyd George] no good."[4]

Doubtless Lloyd George had also not forgotten either Marconi, or their severe spat over the disendowment of the Church in Wales, but current political reality, and patriotism, called for personal feelings to be set aside.

Setting aside personal feelings was and remains easier for those closest to Downing Street but the repercussions of Lloyd George's ascent rapidly rippled out, causing disquiet among the Liberal rank and file across the country. In these circumstances Neil could not ignore his constituents' own concerns about why he had accepted office, and these he addressed in a letter he sent, for onward circulation[5], to his Association President[6]:

12 Downing Street
December 15th

Dear Sir William,

I am writing to you as I find it impossible at present for me to go down to Wisbech and I think my position should be made known to my constituents.

At the request of the Prime Minister I have temporarily assumed the position of Liberal Chief Whip as I consider it the duty of all to try and help the Government at this time in whatever way they may be called upon to do so.

I most sincerely regret that Mr Asquith has at present no share in the government of the country. There is no one who knows him who does not feel affection and admiration for him and all members of our party owe him a debt of gratitude for his services to the Empire and to Liberalism. Party politics are not to be thought of but as I am writing to a constituent, I feel it is not out of place to state that I, and I believe I can speak for all of those Liberals who are members of the new Coalition Government, have in no way receded from our former political principles. We are still Liberals serving under a Liberal Prime Minister.

Yours sincerely,

Neil Primrose

On December 19th Lloyd George made his first big speech in the Commons. It lasted 2 hours and the following day's *Daily Telegraph* wished that "our men on the sea and at the front could have heard the more moving parts of it ... that they might feel and know ... that hesitation, indecision and over-caution are at end." Three days later on December 22nd the Commons rose for the Christmas recess but Neil remained at work at 12 Downing Street until the evening of Christmas Eve. One of his tasks was to tell the Prime Minister that the new Liberal MP for Derby, elected unopposed, had just telegraphed to promise his support for the new government "in achieving victorious consummation of aims for which war was entered upon."[7] Neil added his comment "this is quite satisfactory. Best wishes of the season to you."

Given this schedule, Neil unsurprisingly spent Christmas 1916 (his daughter's first) in London and entertained Lloyd George to dinner at Great Stanhope Street on Boxing Day. The Prime Minister had just returned to London after spending Christmas with his mistress at his house at Walton Heath in Surrey.[8] How much of this Neil knew is unclear but it seems unlikely, given the presence of Lady Victoria and their servants, that Miss Stevenson also dined at 5 Great Stanhope Street.

Two days after entertaining the Prime Minister, Neil left London for the first time in over a month, in order to see in the New Year at Postwick. There the Primrose family were joined by Jimmy and Dollie de Rothschild. After all the stresses that month had brought him, it and the old year, was to end with a relaxed gathering, that Neil said gave him "the most inexpressible pleasure."[9]

34

I MUST REJOIN MY REGIMENT

At the beginning of 1917, Neil was still trying to sort out the messy legacy of the Liberal Party split of one month before. Curious as it may seem now the old Liberal Party central organisation, the Liberal Central Association with its office in Abingdon Street, remained loyal to Asquith and under the control of his former Chief Whip, John Gulland. Although Lloyd George was unable to take control of it, he was also not happy to let the matter rest, and instructed Neil to establish a new rival Liberal organisation that was loyal to his leadership. Such a move, while understandable, was likely to entrench the schism, as was pointed out by the political correspondent of the *Manchester Guardian*.[1] Neil though had no option but to obey; offices were taken at 49 Parliament Street and a secretariat employed.

On February 2nd Neil accompanied the Prime Minister and Mrs Lloyd George on his first visit to Wales since gaining the premiership.[2] They travelled from Euston to Bangor on a special train with a large press contingent in attendance. The visit was largely a publicity exercise to promote the new Prime Minister against the backdrop of his remote constituency, and that was why Neil and no other member of the government accompanied him. On arrival at Bangor they continued by car via Snowdonia to Criccieth.[3] Every detail of the journey was widely reported, even down to the detail that the Prime Minister sat in the open front of the car alongside the driver, while Neil and Mrs Lloyd George sat covered behind as the Prime Minister pointed out and gestured towards the stunning scenery.[4] It was also pointed out by the press that the Prime Minister also chatted freely with the driver at his side – while not stated expressly, the point that this was in great contrast to Asquith's haughty grandeur was surely obvious. At Criccieth, Neil stayed in the Lloyd

Georges' house and late that afternoon the Prime Minister saw his ailing uncle, Richard Lloyd for what was to be the final time. According to Frances Stevenson, this part of the visit was why she remained in London – Lloyd George being convinced that Uncle Richard would immediately see through the fiction that she was merely his secretary.[5]

On the Saturday evening Lloyd George made his big speech of the visit at the Pavilion in Caernarvon. He did so before an audience of 5,000 and beneath a banner proclaiming "Britons Today Honour the Great Man of Wales". The final part of his long and rousing speech he repeated in Welsh and then 'Land of My Fathers' was sung.[6] Neil had the difficult job of delivering a brief follow up, in which he said how pleased he was to be present on such a historic occasion. He then added a bit of partisanship to the Prime Minister's apolitical patriotism, by saying that he had seen it said that "Liberals serving in the present Government had changed their principles, but, I will only say, the measures the new Government have taken, are measures to win the war."

On the Sunday morning, Neil and the Lloyd Georges attended what was termed by the press as 'an English service for soldiers' at the Welsh Baptist Chapel in Caernarvon.[7] Church was followed by another car journey across the mountains, this time to Colwyn Bay where Neil and the Prime Minister lunched with F.E. and Lady Smith, who were staying there, before returning to London by the afternoon train.[8]

As soon as they were back from Wales, Parliament reconvened and the King opened the new session on February 7th. This meant that the ousted Asquithians now faced Lloyd George across the despatch box. There were also grumblings about the Parliament Street office being a breach of the political truce, and that the Prime Minister was not present for the debate that followed the ceremonial.[9] Spats in the Chamber such as these mainly fell to Bonar Law to deal with, in his capacity as Leader of the House, and in all but name Deputy Prime Minister. Relations between Neil and Bonar Law in the main remained close, but in March an unexpected issue blew up that put them under severe strain.

Within the Coalition, Austen Chamberlain, a Conservative, was Secretary of State for India. He now proposed that raw cotton imported from India be subject to tariffs. (The underlying idea was to free up shipping capacity by promoting cotton-processing in India.) This hit a raw nerve with Liberal MPs as it was a fundamental tenet of Liberalism to promote Free Trade and resist tariffs where possible. For a few days the issue threatened to re-unite the divided Liberal Party - but not in the way the Prime Minister wanted. Lloyd George's War Cabinet had backed the move and the Prime Minister had no real option but to support his Secretary of State,[10] but Neil was enraged and there were rumours of Liberal government resignations as the Commons vote approached. As Bonar Law was both Chancellor and a War Cabinet member, many saw him as responsible for not foreseeing an issue that imperilled the Government. As the following letter marked 'Private' that Neil wrote on March 11th demonstrates, things in Downing Street were at boiling point:

My dear Bonar,
Please forgive me for the violence of my language the other night. All that I can plead in extenuation of my behaviour is that my feelings are very deeply roused by this question but that is no excuse for rudeness least of all to one who has always been a friend to me.
Yours most sincerely,
Neil Primrose[11]

In the midst of the storm over the Indian cotton duties, Cynthia Asquith records Neil (without Lady Victoria) being present at a decidedly louche evening of supper and poker at Edwin and Venetia Montagu's house in Queen Anne's Gate. The relevant part of her diary entry reads:

After eleven I went across to Venetia's house having been bidden for poker. Found Neil Primrose and Scatters Wilson awaiting their host and hostess who had been dining with Winston. Mary and Goonie came with the Montagus, and Diana, Patrick, Duff, Osbert Sitwell, Phyllis Boyd, Frances Horner, Mrs Arkwright and Lord Stanley trickled in. We sat down to an oyster, baby potato, and champagne orgy... After a long, quite amusing supper, Osbert, Diana, Phyllis, Lord Stanley and I settled down to poker. The others all played bridge. Alas, we played till 3.30 – arrant folly which was all the more appreciated by me because I lost my five pounds.[12]

Notwithstanding Neil's bout of hedonism, the Government carried the Commons vote on the increase. However the episode caused many

205

unwelcome newspaper inches and even the leaking of Neil's whip to his supporters:

> Your attendance on Wednesday next, March 14, is most URGENTLY AND SPECIALLY requested to support the Government in a vital decision on the Indian Cotton duties.
> Neil Primrose[13]

Whipping on unpalatable protectionist tariffs was not the only headache Neil had. In late February he had to mediate a row between Derby and Lloyd George over the names submitted for membership of the Army Canteen Committee.[14] This row also had historic Liberal v Tory fault lines: Derby's nominees were objected to as being closely connected to the liquor trade, while Derby was refusing "anyone connected with the Temperance Association".

Throughout all of these troubles, Neil was being continually bombarded with requests for political honours; even requests for Irish honours initiated by the Lord Lieutenant, Lord Wimborne, landed on his desk.[15] This aspect of his job, the Prime Minister's patronage secretary, he always found highly distasteful.[16]

In late March 1917, Neil received news from his regiment in Egypt that the long-planned advance into Palestine, that he had always planned to join, was now imminent. At the end of 1916 Ottoman forces had withdrawn from the Sinai peninsula, to a defensive line between Gaza and Beersheba and the British mounted a full-scale assault on Gaza over 26-27 March. News of this encounter from his Rothschild cousins soon reached Neil in London. The attack, which became known as the First Battle of Gaza, had not been a success and as there could be no advance on Jerusalem (the Palestine campaign's prize) while the Turks still held Gaza, it was obvious that further attacks were required. This news when coupled with the imminent Parliamentary Easter recess on April 5th caused Neil to waste no time before writing to the Prime Minister to tell him that he must now exercise the option of returning to his regiment that he had always reserved:

12 Downing Street
2nd April 1917

My dear Lloyd George
As you were not alone I did not broach the subject to you this afternoon and therefore I write to tell you that I feel I must rejoin my regiment. I need not tell you what a pleasure it has been to me to work under you not only because of my affection for you but because I really believe you to be a great War Prime Minister.

I had however always resolved to rejoin if my regiment went on active service and in the last two days I have had letters from friends there which show that they are progressing slowly towards Jerusalem. The Government is now quite rightly calling up everyone and if I continued in civilian life here I could never reconcile it with what I believe to be the course I should follow.

I think you will sympathise with me or I know if you were my age you would never hesitate. I have spoken to Derby about it and he is naturally sorry but he feels that I am doing the right thing. The W.O. have not yet heard what the casualties are out there and he says if my regiment has had none I might not be able to go for the moment but I think it would be very unwise for me to take on a position in your secretariat which I might have to leave at any moment or this would give rise to other interpretations.

I think I may count on your approval and sympathy as will my wife who while she is naturally sorry says she would never try and persuade me to follow a course which might hereafter cause me remorse.[17]

Neil's reference to the Prime Minister's secretariat refers to the new body, known as the Garden Suburb, that Lloyd George had set up to improve contact between Downing Street and the various departments. It was located in temporary offices in the 10 Downing Street garden and that was how it acquired its unofficial title.[18] In February 1917, on the secretariat's foundation, there had been rumours (that were swiftly denied) that Neil was to leave his post as Chief Whip to head it.[19] Plainly Lloyd George kept this place in mind in order to answer Neil's dissatisfaction with the Chief Whipship and now Neil, knowing how hard the Prime Minister's will was to thwart, wanted to kill off any proposal that he abandon his regiment, remain in London and merely move within Downing Street.

35

TRAFFIC IN TITLES

On April 1st the United States had declared war on Germany and naturally the Prime Minister was much pre-occupied with that, when he first saw Neil's letter. Rather than respond himself when time became available, he used Lord Reading as his intermediary to press Neil to reconsider.

That year's Easter weekend fell over April 7th/8th and Neil spent it in Bournemouth from where he answered Rufus on Easter Sunday. In his reply[1] he remained resolute, although he admitted that writing to Lloyd George had been "a great wrench" but that "personal disappointments must go by the board" regardless of whether they were his own or the Prime Minister's, as the only thing that counted was the great work of winning the war. Neil knew that this resolution would be unwelcome but this time he was determined to resist pressure by keeping his head down and slacking "away from Town a little longer."

As the Prime Minister was away from London twice in April[2], first of all visiting the Grand Fleet at Scapa Flow, and then in France and Italy at inter-government conferences, Neil did not in fact see him until his return to Downing Street on Saturday April 21st. That afternoon, according to press reports, Neil and Lloyd George left Downing Street together in Neil's car for Surrey.[3] The press suggested that they were to spend the weekend together but this was not in fact so. Lloyd George's house at Walton Heath was only a short drive from The Durdans, Neil's destination, and Neil was simply giving him a lift. As Frances Stevenson was with them in the car[4] it seems certain that Neil must have known the real basis of their relationship. From what soon followed, it is clear that Lloyd George now accepted the hard reality of Neil's resignation; but before he would release him Neil had not only to recruit his successor, and fill the vacancy in the Garden Suburb; but also to conduct one final bit of highly secret work as Liberal Chief Whip.

Neil's secret mission involved the American Ambassador and concerned obtaining a settlement of the Irish Home Rule question that had been shelved on the war's outbreak. What Lloyd George wanted was to trigger an intervention by the American President suggesting an Ulster compromise agreement in aid of the war effort. This it was hoped would work on the most intransigent Unionist in the government – Sir Edward Carson. However a second Liberal Party advantage that it was hoped would be obtained, if this worked, would be to detach the votes of the Irish Nationalist MPs from their continuing alliance with the rump of Asquithian Liberals in the Commons.

Plainly this scheme, which if revealed would upset both the Conservatives and those Liberals who wanted to conciliate and not aggravate their former Liberal colleagues, had to be kept secret and entirely away from the War Cabinet.[5] Neil knew and was trusted by the United States Ambassador, Walter Page, who agreed to forward messages from the Prime Minister to the President that Neil was to secretly supply. Neil and Page had had many prior dealings, in particular during Neil's time as a Foreign Office minister, over the treatment of prisoners of war. Prior to that Neil and Page had first got to know one another during the initiative to celebrate the 'Centenary of Peace' and, during the delegation's visit to Washington, Neil had of course met President Wilson. When that visit was added to his numerous and well publicised private visits to the United States, Neil's name was well known in the White House of 1917.

Neil acted as agreed and passed on the message but on being chased up by Lloyd George, Neil wrote the following rather delphic note to the Prime Minister from the Whips' Office on April 25th:

Mr Page's private secretary tells me that the cable, of which you spoke, went to the President 4 or 5 days ago and that you may be certain that the President has followed the advice in it.[6]

This initiative eventually led, shortly after Neil had left the Whips' Office, to Lloyd George's offer of an Irish Convention in Dublin. This was accepted by both Nationalists and Unionists, who met at the Convention in July.

Although the Convention's final report was overtaken by events in April 1918, it had at least neutralised the Irish issue for almost a year of the war.

Neil's other task to be accomplished before he was to be allowed to leave Downing Street was to recruit his successor. Lloyd George had decided that his first choice of successor was Cecil Harmsworth[7], the rather less well-known younger brother of the newspaper Lords, Northcliffe and Rothermere.

On April 26th Neil met Cecil Harmsworth in Pall Mall and told him that he was the PM's choice to follow him as Liberal Chief Whip. Cecil recorded in his diary "I indicate my dislike for this office but promise to let him know."[8] Cecil's particular dislike was the patronage element and the role of conferring "honours and titles" as he told the Prime Minister, over lunch, alongside Neil, at No. 10 on May 1st – "we are a party of 3 in a snug little panelled room." He later records in his diary:

> afterwards in Neil's room in the House of Commons we argue the subject of the traffic in titles … I plead that I could never share in that work. … Neil doesn't like the business himself and confesses … it is one of the reasons of his giving up the Chief Whip's office and joining his regiment in Palestine.

On the following day:

> Neil Primrose telephones to say PM like to see me at 3 just before War Cabinet and am to be offered a place in his secretariat.[9]

Cecil accepted the Prime Minister's offer and took on liaison with the Labour Department that had previously been offered to Neil as an alternative to being Chief Whip.[10]

The Prime Minister's second choice for Chief Whip was Frederick Guest[11] and his appointment was now rapidly arranged. *The Times* of May 3rd recorded both appointments, as well as Neil's resignation. A whole month after his hard-written resignation letter, Neil was finally free of Downing Street.

36

A PRIVY COUNCILLOR

While Neil had been detained in Downing Street, the Second Battle of Gaza had taken place over April 17th-20th, but the attack on the city was no more successful than the First Battle in March.[1] This time though the RBH suffered heavier casualties and Fred Cripps records in his memoir that his squadron suffered 30.[2]

Probably because of his despair at the continuing lack of breakthrough on the Western Front, Lloyd George was taking a close interest in the Palestinian operation and after this second setback determined on the recall of General Murray[3] from Palestine, and was considering the great Boer general, Jan Smuts, in his place. The Egyptian command was then considered by the War Cabinet and Smuts was offered the role on May 1st; but after a month of consideration, Smuts declined. Lloyd George now turned to seek a General who could conveniently be removed from the Western Front. On June 13th the problem was finally solved when General Allenby was appointed to replace Murray and told by the War Cabinet to report on the feasibility of defeating the Turkish forces in Palestine.[4]

Obviously these War Cabinet moves were highly secret but as Allenby's ADC was Harry Dalmeny[5], it seems quite safe to assume that Neil knew quite a lot more than the average officer in Egypt. Allenby proceeded to Egypt and took over command of the Egyptian Expeditionary Force in early July but until he had assessed the situation in Palestine himself, and advised London what further was required, all fresh offensive operations at Gaza, and Neil's participation in them, were suspended.

Irrespective of how much Neil knew, so far as the press and public were concerned his departure to rejoin his regiment was imminent. On May 10th following the Commons sitting in secret to discuss the war without reporters, there was a farewell dinner for Neil held in one of the House of Commons dining rooms. The *Pall Mall Gazette*[6] noted that it was "well attended by representatives of all of the different parties". A week later a government dinner was held for Neil hosted by Sir Alfred Mond[7] MP at his house in Lowndes Square. The Prime Minister and nineteen Liberal members of the government attended.[8]

Neil was also able to spend more time with his family in the weeks following his resignation. Rosebery had decidedly mixed feelings about Neil's resignation: for while on the one hand he welcomed his son's removal from Lloyd George's close orbit, it also returned him to active service, with the attendant risk of death and injury. Rosebery's long memory meant he could not forgive Lloyd George for old offences; and in his eyes those were compounded by the Prime Minister's innovation of abolishing full Cabinet government. In these circumstances, Rosebery had found his son's service as his Chief Whip quite indigestible. Tellingly in January 1917 Rosebery had written to Herbert Fisher to say that his appointment to Lloyd George's government "is the one that I most welcomed for public and private reasons."[9]

Rosebery who had turned 70 on May 7th was ever more conscious of his mortality and, as he viewed it, his increasing ill health. His mood was not lightened by the death of Leopold de Rothschild on May 29th at the age of 71. Rosebery and Neil attended his funeral together at the Jewish Cemetery in Willesden. As they stood by Leopold's grave, just a short distance away was the grave of Hannah Rosebery, their wife and mother, lost to them almost 27 years earlier. The mourners were led by Leopold's eldest son Lionel and his youngest Tony, home on leave[10], but Evelyn was absent, still on duty with the RBH to the south of Gaza.

A few days later the King's birthday honours announced that Neil was made a Privy Councillor. This was his reward for his service as Chief Whip but also surely anticipated his bright political future. Not long before this, Rosebery had privately recorded his disapproval of the Prime Minister's policies[11] but he delighted in Neil's youthful promotion and shared his feelings with Herbert Fisher: "It must make even you a little older to see Neil a Privy Councillor! Me it makes a centenarian, for I was admitted 36 years ago. I only hope the honour will not excite jealousies."[12]

Notwithstanding what he viewed as his great age, Rosebery could not resist a rare attendance at the meeting of the Privy Council at Buckingham

Palace on June 13th in order to see Neil sworn in. In fact, as the King's diary entry discloses the meeting was something of a family affair in that Lord Derby acted as Lord President: "At 12.0 I held a Council at which Eddy Derby acted as President & several were sworn in amongst them being Neil Primrose"[13]

The following day's *Daily Record* speculated whether it was unique for a father and son to be privy councillors simultaneously – in fact it was not, as Joseph and Austen Chamberlain had achieved the same feat in 1902. The same newspaper also pointed out a more obviously unique feature of the meeting – that it took place during an air raid and to the accompaniment of booming anti-aircraft guns. This daylight air raid on London involved 20 Gotha bombers and led to 162 civilian deaths and 432 civilian injured; and it would prove to be the worst air raid on Britain of the war.

On the very day he joined the Privy Council, Neil received orders from the War Office to proceed to Aldershot and to join the 3rd Reserve regiment of cavalry there. That after ten months out of uniform he required further fitness and other training is hardly surprising, but the Aldershot regime was not too demanding, and he was reported in the Commons dressed in uniform on June 21st. He remained the darling of the parliamentary correspondents and it was reported, "he looks very well in his captain's uniform and seemed in the best of spirits."[14]

At the month's end, again in uniform, he travelled to Glasgow with other MPs of Scottish birth, in a special train, to witness Lloyd George receive the Freedom of the City and to hear him make another of his great morale-boosting speeches.[15] On July 4th Neil was in the Commons chamber in uniform, when he attended[16] to vote, in the free vote, on introducing proportional representation under the Representation of the People Bill. Neil voted in favour along with a significant, but defeated, minority of others.[17]

On the third anniversary of the war Lloyd George made another great set-piece speech and Neil watched him from the platform of the Queen's Hall in Langham Place. As he did so he was just days away from receiving his much delayed embarkation orders for Egypt. This coincided with the War Cabinet's instruction to General Allenby to strike the Turks as hard as possible during the coming autumn.[18] The Prime Minister separately advised Allenby that the capture of Jerusalem was to be the nation's 1917 Christmas present.[19]

In his final days before shipping out to Egypt, Neil visited his father at The Durdans. Ever the pessimistic fatalist, Rosebery assumed, rightly as it transpired, that this would be their last meeting.[20] As Neil drove away past the ornamental eighteenth century front gates[21], it is said that a tearful Rosebery locked them and vowed never to use them again until Neil returned. Save for the purposes of conservation in 2013, they have apparently remained locked ever since.[22]

Neil's orders were to embark at Folkestone on August 17th but in the days leading up to then, the *Daily Mail* printed a rumour that Neil would instead remain in London and join the proposed 'Jewish Regiment'.[23] Neil was forced to deny that this was so and stated that he was re-joining his existing regiment, the RBH, in Palestine.[24] Quite how this false rumour came about remains unclear but may have been part of a final mission by Lloyd George to keep Neil in London. That this attempt was made is undocumented but almost twenty years later, when Neil's daughter married, the *Scotsman* carried a piece, headlined 'Neil Primrose Memories Recalled' in which it was written that the Prime Minister invited himself to dine alone with Neil and Lady Victoria at Great Stanhope Street just prior to his departure and "argued for more than 2 hours against his decision. Neil smiled and went."[25]

The source of the account was, it was said, Lady Victoria herself. Neil was certainly in London for his final few days in England. He was reported at a House of Commons lunch along with the Prime Minister on Wednesday August 15th.The lunch was given by the Liberal War Committee, in honour of the Premier of New South Wales, and Neil's old friend Sir Henry Dalziel presided.[26]

That Neil withstood this further episode of Prime Ministerial pressure is not surprising, as although over four months had elapsed since he wrote it, nothing had occurred to change the reasoning of his resignation letter of April 2nd. He had also expressed himself publicly in words that were reported to his constituents:

I am uneasy. I am of military age and I feel I ought to be doing my duty as a soldier. I could not stay at home and see older men going out to the front.[27]

The name of the ship that Neil joined at Folkestone is not recorded but it is clear that he was not entirely surrounded by strangers. His cousin Evelyn, who had been on extended leave following his father's death, was with him on the voyage to Alexandria.[28] As the ship pulled out into the English Channel they both would witness for the final time England's diminishing shoreline.

37

DEATH IN PALESTINE

The regimental war diary[1] records Neil rejoining on September 7th and he arrived in the midst of an extraordinary episode in the RBH's history – its commanding officer Lt. Colonel John Pascoe Grenfell[2] had been caught breaching the censorship regulations and was facing court martial. The offending letter, that the army censor had opened, disclosed that the main focus of the attack was to be Beersheba (and not Gaza) and had contained criticisms of his brigade commander, Brigadier Pitt. The letter was addressed to Lord Burnham[3], the RBH's honorary colonel, and proprietor of the *Daily Telegraph* – although General Allenby subsequently made it clear that it was the content and not the intended recipient that forced him to take disciplinary action.[4]

The Court Martial which had the unusual job of trying Colonel Grenfell convened on September 14th and after three days its sentence of "a severe reprimand" was handed down.[5] This of itself was not particularly harsh but it inevitably led to Grenfell resigning his command and proceeding back to England in disgrace. As the regimental war diary records, Grenfell "handed over command of the Regiment to Major, the Hon. F.H. Cripps"; but the adjutant's rather crisp and concise words belie what actually happened. Fred Cripps was ordered ashore from the Alexandria steamer on which he was about to sail home on leave, before the Court Martial even convened, and in anticipation of the inevitable verdict.[6]

Whether Neil ever reflected in writing on the Grenfell court martial is unclear, but its outcome left Neil under the command of Fred Cripps, two years his junior and whom he had known well since their time together in Oxford. The new second in command of the regiment was Evelyn, who was younger still. Neil, even though only 34, was starting to look venerable.

During September and October the 6th Mounted Brigade of which the RBH formed part were based at Shellal on the Wadi Ghuzze, to where the British had extended the Rafa railway in order to bring up supplies. From Shellal the mounted yeomanry rode out into the dry and scorching desert on scouting patrols, to assess the location and strength of the enemy around Beersheba. General Allenby was extremely hands-on in his planning and he personally visited every part of the front, so it is certain that Neil would have spent time with his brother Harry in advance of the attack that commenced on October 31st.

This was the driest time of year and obtaining access to water was a key part of Allenby's plan. Beersheba had seventeen water wells and capturing those rather than the place itself was the key objective of the opening battle.[7] At night on October 27th the Mounted Division moved out of Shellal and proceeded south-east to the oasis at Khalasa. At Khalasa the force paused before moving, again at night, north-east to the hills east of Beersheba where they assembled at zero hour (5am) on zero day October 31st. The journey from Khalasa was 25 miles and the column, fifteen miles long, moved unseen through the empty desert. This element of surprise was vital as the Turks had not expected any attack on Beersheba from the east and had relied upon the desert for protection. This huge flanking operation by the cavalry would decide the battle.[8]

However it was the Mounted Division's Australian Light Horse who launched the successful attack on the eastern side of Beersheba; the mounted yeomanry spent the day in reserve and largely inactive at Khasim Zanna.[9] With Beersheba captured, the Ottomans could no longer hold Gaza and the ruined town was evacuated on November 7th.[10]

General Allenby's plan was to keep the Turks moving backwards and so prevent them digging in and establishing another defensive line in the Judean hills. Initially this plan seemed to be working but by November 12th the Turks had established a semi-circular line of twenty miles surrounding and protecting Junction Station. As the name implies this was an important railway junction where the Haifa-Jerusalem railway met that to Beersheba. For Allenby to capture it would not only deny the enemy supplies by rail but would also open up the road to Jerusalem to the east.

This new defensive line took in the villages of El Mughar (five miles west of Junction Station) and Katrah, located on top of a ridge, some 236 feet high. By late morning of November 13th Neil and the rest of the RBH were by the Wadi Jamus, waiting for the infantry to take the ridge. As they were struggling to do so under machine gun fire, Brigadier Godwin took the decision to use the mounted yeomanry to attack the ridge. The RBH were to take the right part of the ridge and the Dorset Yeomanry the left.

At 3pm in a scene more redolent of 1817 than 1917, Trumpeter Sergeant Gurney sounded the order to move.[11] The crest of the ridge was 4,500 yards away. The first 2,000 were taken at a trot but the remainder was taken at a gallop with swords drawn. The RBH were arranged in three squadrons and Neil's C squadron in the centre between B at the front, and A at the rear. The Turkish infantry on seeing what was galloping towards them broke cover and ran. At the crest the combat was carried on dismounted with hand-to-hand fighting to complete the seizing of the ridge.

Captain Jack Young MC of the Bucks Hussars wrote the following account of the regiment's action at El Mughar which subsequently appeared in the press:

We charged in line over two miles of perfectly flat plain, swept by shells and machine gun fire. Our men and horses were mad with excitement. The enemy, about 3,000 strong, were in an almost impregnable position, on top of a long and very steep ridge, 200ft high. We went straight to the top and into them. We captured all their machine guns, enormous quantities of ammunition, two guns and 1,200 prisoners, and we never stopped to count the dead.[12]

Colonel Fred Cripps later wrote that it was fortunate that the Turks had posted their machine guns at the top rather than the bottom of the ridge. For if the latter had been done, the RBH would not have made it up the hill but would have been massacred on the plain below.[13]

Although RBH casualties were relatively light, El Mughar was not taken without cost – four officers and 46 other ranks were wounded and six other ranks were killed. In addition over 120 horses were lost. Among the most severely wounded officers was Evelyn. Just before the charge took place, Evelyn had confided to Trooper Lawrence that being Jewish (and a Rothschild) he feared capture more than death, and asked him to stick by him and make sure he wasn't.[14] Evelyn was wounded by a bullet to the head, shortly before his squadron started the ascent uphill. Although swiftly evacuated by road, and then rail, to the Citadel Hospital in Cairo, he was to die of his wounds four days later.[15]

General Allenby's verdict was that El Mughar had been "a most dashing charge" and after it, the Turks were in general retreat towards Ramleh and they gave up Junction Station.[16] The night of November 14th was spent by the RBH bivouacked in a field by the village of Abu Shushe. The day had not been an easy one for Neil and not only because of Evelyn; during the charge his horse had been shot from under him[17] and his army servant, riding just behind him in the charge, had been killed.[18]

The next morning the RBH moved from Abu Shushe to a new Jewish settler village named Ekron.[19] These new villages had been funded with Rothschild money to provide homes for Russian-Jewish emigrants and as such Evelyn's fears of mistreatment as a prisoner of war may have been well founded.

Fred Cripps writes that the best house in Ekron was taken for the RBH's officers' mess and that night they dined on roast goose, cooked for them by the Russian householder's wife. During the day of November 14th Neil needed to find a replacement horse. He knew that the horse used by his dead servant, which was liver-coloured and called 'Buttons', had come from the Ascott stables. Buttons had survived the charge but had bolted. Neil gave Trooper James Lawrence the job of locating it. It was found in the Berkshire Yeomanry lines, before being retrieved for Neil's use next day.[20]

Late that night at Ekron orders were received to go into action at dawn next day. At the mess briefing Colonel Fred Cripps spotted that Neil was over-tired and falling asleep:

I ordered Neil who was completely done and had a touch of fever to hand over his command to his next junior. He looked me straight in the face and refused. My only alternative would have been to put him under arrest. Next morning he was on parade. I told him he had no right to be there – he smiled and said nothing.[21]

That day's action was to be at Abu Shushe, once the location of the great biblical city of Gezer[22] and sitting on top of a ridge 756 feet high. The ridge is a prominent natural feature that dominates the road below and here a Turkish rearguard had established itself to cover the main road from Ramleh to Jerusalem.[23] As at El Mughar the mounted yeomanry were to be sent in to clear them.

The RBH departed Ekron at 6am on November 15th and were in a sheltered and concealed position below Abu Shushe by 8.30 when the attack commenced. Just as two days earlier the RBH were in front but this time their advance was far more measured due to the steep incline. It was initially made on foot and only the final few hundred yards were covered by a mounted charge.

Very soon after the commencement of the attack Neil was leading his C squadron on foot over the rocky terrain, when he was hit by a concealed machine gun firing from the mouth of a cave.[24] It seems that Neil's squadron was the first to proceed out of their sheltered position on foot, and under fire, as Colonel Fred Cripps would later write that Neil "would most certainly have been recommended for the DSO had he survived".[25] Captain Jack Young, who was close by, described it thus:

as he was standing up coolly giving orders to his men, he was shot through the head by machine-gun fire at very close range.[26]

As Neil lay unconscious and dying, his squadron, now led by his second in command, continued on before re-mounting and galloping over the ridge and into Abu Shushe with their swords drawn. It was a rout and all over by 10am, 431 enemy dead were counted and 360 prisoners were taken.[27] Neil was the only officer casualty of the engagement, although one trooper was also killed and seven were wounded.[28] Captain Young's account continues:

We went part of the way dismounted, and then led our horses up, and charged again. Probably if we had not we should have been wiped out as they outnumbered us six to one. But they hate the sight of our swords, and just as we reached the crest ... they cleared. It was a wonderful sight. Neil Primrose was killed ... We buried poor Neil this morning. He was a very gallant fellow. It has taken the stuffing out of us a bit.

After this second significant defeat in three days, Turkish resistance was crumbling and Ramleh was occupied that afternoon.

221

38

A NOBLE SACRIFICE IN A GREAT CAUSE

Later that day the RBH themselves moved into Ramleh, taking Neil's body with them and it was there in the morning of the next day that he was buried with military honours in the garden of the Latin Convent.[1] By cruel twist of fate, just before the interment, Harry Dalmeny arrived to ask Colonel Cripps about Neil; word having reached him that he had been badly wounded the day before.[2] As a result he participated in what Fred Cripps later called "the solemn little ceremony". It was certainly not little by Western Front burial party standards. The entire regiment paraded and the bearer party consisted of six of Neil's fellow officers. As well as Harry, Brigadier Godwin and General Barrow, the Yeomanry Mounted Division commander also attended.[3]

Later that day, Harry had the unenviable task of writing to Lady Victoria with the news of Neil's death and burial, that was later circulated around the Primrose and Rothschild families:

> Lord Dalmeny wrote to Lady Victoria Primrose saying the Bucks Hussars had behaved gloriously … on November 15th they were advised to charge again, this time up a hill, they galloped a certain distance, dismounted, and took cover, then they received order to go forward on foot, Neil rose to lead his men and was hit in the head by a machine gun bullet. He was unconscious at once and died in half an hour.[4]

General Allenby's army had a large press contingent attached and so news of Neil's death travelled fast. The *Evening Standard* of November 17th broke the story before Neil's widow had even been informed. The following telegram from the Prime Minister rapidly followed:

Heartfelt and deepest sympathy with you in your great sorrow. Your husband's many friends, of whom I am proud to be one, will weep with you over his fall. But it is a noble sacrifice in a great cause.
Lloyd George

Given this chronology it was Monday, November 19th before his death was fully digested in print. That morning *The Times* concluded of him:

None of the younger generation in the House of Commons had shown quite the same promise as Mr Neil Primrose … he had held three important Government offices during the war and seemed to have a whole world of political achievement before him. He has made the great sacrifice on the eve of his 35th birthday, and the House of Commons is the poorer, both in capacity and character for his loss.

The *Westminster Gazette*[5] covered his death extensively and made an interesting comparison with another Prime Minister's son killed in action a year earlier.

If he dropped the position of Chief Whip to the present Government it was certainly from no lack of competence or acceptability. It was due I think wholly to the very honourable feeling that a young man ought to be on more active service than that which offers in the Whips Room … Like Raymond Asquith he deliberately declined the sheltered posts which he might have occupied without reproach.

Among the numerous newspaper tributes easily the most interesting on account of both its authorship and content was that of the Attorney General, F.E. Smith, which first appeared in that day's *Evening Standard* before being widely re-produced elsewhere. The *Standard* called it "striking" and in its exclusive focus upon Neil's relationship with Thomas, it most certainly was:

The love which these two men had for one another was extraordinary. The death of Robartes and the glory of his unquenchable courage was always in Neil's thoughts. He was it seemed to many of us never quite the same after his friend's death.

They were old Oxford friends who kept alive in London the intimate fragrance of Oxford memories ... You might well have been excused if you had written them off as exquisites, the triflers of a racecourse, or the leading members of a fashionable club.

Then the War came and for a time the two were separated though in the end again they were to come together.

Perhaps equally significant is what F.E. left out – he makes no reference at all to Neil's marriage to Lady Victoria. Without it, is the reader left in any doubt of the implication that Thomas was the real love of Neil's life and now, quite fittingly, the two of them are re-united in death? In 1917 Evelyn Waugh's *Brideshead Revisited* was still decades away from even being conceived and yet F.E.'s reference to "the intimate fragrance" of Oxford memories is surely of the same mould. Continuing the comparison, Neil and Thomas, unlike the fictional Charles and Sebastian, kept their relationship going and remained inseparable for over a decade after leaving the university. Of course F.E. does not say expressly that the two were lovers but given the context of F.E.'s close interaction with Neil in France, while Thomas remained stranded in England, there seems little doubt that F.E. had believed them to be. Of course both were now dead and beyond reproach, let alone the law's reach, but the irony of the Government's chief law officer writing such a public tribute to their male love, cannot have gone entirely un-noticed.

Later that day, the Prime Minister paid tribute to Neil in the Commons:

The House knew his bright and radiant spirit well. To his intimates he was one of the most loveable of men we ever met. He had ability far above the average, and, in spite of the reserve and shyness which held him back, his future was full of hope ... he chose deliberately the path of danger. He fell charging at the head of his troops, at the very moment of victory, and Members of this House will, I feel certain, join me in an expression of sympathy with those whom he has left behind to mourn him.[6]

Asquith followed[7] and made the following, perhaps appropriately, brief tribute – "there are few who can realise better than myself how much of hope and of promise there was for his future." Four days later, The Other Club met and drank a toast 'To the Memory of the Brave' in affectionate memory of Neil.[8]

Rosebery was in Scotland when he first received news of Neil's death on Saturday November 17th. Earlier that autumn he had received the news that his nephew Lt. Col. George Hope[9] was missing in action at Passchendaele (his body was subsequently found) and now Rosebery joined both of his sisters in having a beloved (and in Lady Mary's case only) son killed in action. On November 22nd he released the following statement to the press:

Ever since my son's death I have been so overwhelmed with friendly letters and telegrams that it is hopeless to think of acknowledging them. The mere opening takes a great part of the day.[10]

Some letters had to be answered and Rosebery answered the King's letter of condolence by return on November 20th:

Neil was everything to me, not that he was a favourite, for favouritism in families breeds sorrow. But he had lived with me so much the longest and we had so many tastes in common that he had become my greatest friend and confidant. But I have no right to complain. Hundreds of thousands of others have borne and are bearing the same and I glory in his death for your and for his country.[11]

Another royal correspondent to be answered was the King's aunt Princess Louise, who had seemingly mentioned F.E. Smith's tribute in her letter, drawing the following rather testy response from Rosebery:

I am not quite sure that his comfort of association with others is as complete as it sounds. But in a very short time I hope to remember nothing but my son's delightful life and glorious death, and to be a consolation in some degree to his dear little widow.[12]

Just two days after news of Neil's death reached London, that of his cousin Evelyn in a Cairo hospital was reported and at Neil's London memorial service, held at St Margaret's Westminster on November 26th, those attending were asked by Canon Carnegie to remember Evelyn alongside Neil.[13] Queen Alexandra was the only member of the Royal Family to send a representative, but the political elite attended in force – Mr and Mrs Lloyd George plus two former and two future Prime Ministers (Balfour and Asquith, Bonar Law and Churchill). Rosebery remained in Scotland and attended a second memorial service at St. Giles's Cathedral in Edinburgh two days later.[14] Lord Dalmeny was in Palestine and neither Neil's widow nor either of his sisters attended. As such Neil's closest relatives at the London service were Lords Crewe and Derby. The band of the Grenadier Guards played the National Anthem and sounded the last post and reveille. The Archbishop of Canterbury ended the service by giving the benediction.

The memorial service was to have an interesting and at least initially, important footnote; Lord Lansdowne met the Foreign Secretary, Arthur Balfour, at the service[15] and apparently, after it, they discussed his proposed 'peace letter' which duly appeared in the *Daily Telegraph* three days later. The letter, which provoked a storm of controversy, called for a negotiated peace and an end to the ceaseless slaughter, of which Neil was merely the latest highly prominent example.

39

ONE OF THE MOST LOVEABLE OF MEN

Randall Davidson, the Archbishop of Canterbury, was an old friend of Rosebery's and following the London memorial service he wrote to thank the Archbishop for giving the blessing. In his letter Rosebery was in uncomplaining mood and looking back to his last seeing Neil at The Durdans in August:

I had enjoyed all Neil's life and could not have enjoyed much more. Indeed I never expected to see him again. The bitterness of death was almost over when I parted with him. It is the poor little widow who is to be pitied.[1]

Rosebery was of course right that he had had a great deal of Neil's company, whereas Lady Victoria had only the briefest marriage and even that had been significantly interrupted by Neil's military service. However the indications are that in private Rosebery's grief was profound and he apparently now spent many hours writing up his memories of Neil: his baptism, his first day at school, and their foreign travels together.[2]

Rosebery told his sister "I cannot write much or at all"[3] and he took until January 22nd 1918 to acknowledge Herbert Fisher's letter of condolence. Writing from 5 Randolph Crescent on heavily black bordered paper, Rosebery conveyed to Fisher that:

I am anxious even this late to thank you for your tender and moving sympathy when Neil died. You knew him so well and he loved and admired you so truly, that your letter went straight to my sore heart. I have not been able to answer many letters but I must intrude upon your heavy positions to acknowledge yours.[4]

Derby, while much more pre-occupied than Rosebery, described his grief to Lord Esher on November 25th:

The last ten days are the worst I have been through, and my dear Neil's death coming on top of it all, has for the moment completely knocked me out ... He was one of the most loveable of men I have ever come across, and one cannot but feel the glory of his death, an example to many men of his age who ought to be fighting, but let Parliament or other shield save them from doing so[5]

Lord Derby never forgot Neil's bravery and sacrifice. After the war he commemorated Neil by having a two-light memorial stained glass window placed in St. Mary's Church, Knowsley. A winged angel is shown in each: one representing fortitude, and the other self-sacrifice.

Alas Neil's family were not to be left alone to quietly grieve as a series of unwelcome ripples in the pool swiftly followed the shock of his death. The first of these related to Neil's place of burial, when a report in the *Jewish Chronicle* claimed that he had been buried in the Jewish Cemetery at Ramleh.[6] Rosebery, who ever since their birth had been perhaps over-sensitive about his children's Christianity, immediately got the report corrected in *The Times*, which stated on December 20th that his place of burial at Ramleh was "the garden of the French Convent". The next day's *Daily Mirror* then put the matter beyond doubt by publishing a photo of Neil's grave with a large wooden cross over it. This story and another in the *Zionist Review* that claimed both Neil and Evelyn had died for Zionism were published in the context of the recent Balfour Declaration[7] but this context did not pacify Jimmy de Rothschild who sent the following rebuttal to the newspapers on December 19th:

Both these officers only fought in Palestine because their regiment happened to be sent there from Egypt after the defeat of the Senussi. They did not choose to go to Palestine and ... nothing would have been more distasteful to them both than to think they were fighting for the Zionist cause.

228

I only express the wish that the Jewish press should leave the memory of these gallant officers in the peace they have so well earned.[8]

Far worse was to follow and from an unexpected quarter, a High Court libel action, and this story also linked Neil and Evelyn in a most unwelcome way.

The alleged libel had been published by the arch-demagogue and independent MP, Noel Pemberton Billing, in his far-right newspaper *Vigilante*. Billing's extraordinary claim was that the existence of a homosexual British establishment lay behind the British Army's lack of victory. German agents, he claimed, had compiled a list of 47,000 men and women in social, political and financial circles, in a 'Black Book'. Those named had been or were at risk of being blackmailed on account of their 'perverse' love lives.[9] Doubtless no one would have paid the story any attention but for the erotic dancer Maud Allen, who Billing named as being in the Black Book, suing him for libel. In that more chaste age, even Billing could not say outright that Maud Allen was a lesbian, but instead charged her with being a follower of "the cult of the clitoris".

Lord Blake has called the ensuing trial "among the most discreditable episodes that have occurred in the English courts in modern times".[10] Certainly the trial judge completely lost control of his own court, and Billing, appearing in person, dominated the entire trial; and successfully won over the jury.

The trial opened before Mr Justice Darling[11] on May 29th 1918 and on the second day, Billing called his first witness (and probably his own mistress) Eileen Villiers-Stuart. Her sensational evidence was that Neil, along with Major Evelyn de Rothschild, had shown her the Black Book. She told the Court:

we had taxied down to The Hut Hotel in Ripley and were having tea. The book was brought there to show me by special request. Mr Neil Primrose brought it.

She went on:

Mr Neil Primrose had been told about the book at a luncheon party in May 1915. He did his utmost to get a copy and did so.[12]

Mrs Villiers-Stuart went on to say that not only were Mr and Mrs Asquith's names in the book, and Lord Haldane's, but when he asked her to leave the witness box, that Mr Justice Darling's was there too. She then insulted the judge by saying "we have to win this war and we are not going to do so while you sit there doing the work of the Hun."

Villiers-Stuart returned to the witness box on Monday June 3rd and now embarrassed counsel for Maud Allen, Ellis Hume-Williams[13] KC, by saying they had met socially and discussed the Black Book intently in "April or May 1916". At this, Hume-Williams handed over to his junior Travers Humphreys[14] to conduct her cross-examination. This resulted in the further evidence that the visit to The Hut Hotel "was after March 1915 – probably late Spring or early summer" and in answer to what office Neil then held "I think he was Liberal Whip".[15] Otherwise he got absolutely nowhere and in his question "Do you think Mr Primrose brought the book to you to disclose that his chief, Mr Asquith, was in the book?" seems to have, amid the high drama, forgotten who he was representing.[16]

Billing then re-examined her, and Mrs Villiers-Stuart now introduced the entirely fresh evidence that she had known Neil since before she was married[17] and she was a personal friend of his and "in his confidence on many matters". She finished by saying that because Neil and Evelyn knew of the Black Book, they had been murdered, by their own men. Mr Justice Darling now summed up, amid farcical scenes, and after an hour and a half the jury acquitted Billing.[18] Rosebery was incensed that Neil's name had been dragged into this scandalous pantomime and that he was powerless to defend him. He raised the matter with Lord Curzon who brought it up at the War Cabinet on June 4th but it was concluded that little could be done about Billing.[19] His hapless tool Eileen Villiers-Stuart was investigated by Scotland Yard and found to be a bigamist. Within weeks she was arrested and charged.[20] In September she was tried at the Old Bailey. Following a deal with the prosecution, she withdrew her not guilty plea in return for filing a sworn statement that her evidence at the libel trial was entirely false, and that she had been coached and rehearsed to give it by Pemberton-Billing. On changing her plea she was sentenced by the Recorder of London to nine months, without hard labour.[21]

Over a year later her husband Percy Bray, a motor mechanic of Putney, divorced her on the grounds of her adultery with her putative second husband Captain Villiers-Stuart. From Bray's evidence to the Divorce Court, as reported, it is clear that his wife was working as a prostitute when they met and secretly married in 1913.[22] They then only lived together for a few weeks, possibly as a cover for her pregnancy, before separating.[23]

At the Old Bailey trial it emerged in evidence that she was also a fantasist, who before her 1917 bigamous marriage had invented an upper class sounding name – Eileen Alys Rhoda Fox-Bray – and had claimed her father was a gentleman rather than the commercial traveller he in fact was.[24]

In the light of all this it seems bizarre that the Maud Allen libel trial and Mrs Villiers-Stuart's discredited and unchallenged evidence has led to so many wild conspiracy theories. It has even been alleged, on an entirely unclear basis, that she was Neil's long-term mistress and gave birth to his child.[25] Of course it seems likely that Neil did encounter some dubiously louche characters during his long bachelorhood, but he certainly had the means to pay for a rather higher grade of companion than the woman who was to become notorious as Eileen Villiers-Stuart.

As to their now infamous outing to The Hut Hotel in Ripley, it seems fantastically improbable and in one respect impossible. In May 1915, Neil was newly married and not Chief Whip but Under-Secretary at the Foreign Office. He was fully occupied with work and had little spare time for his wife, let alone for this jaunt. Also if they did go, as she described, why take a taxi when Neil had a car and could drive himself? But more importantly, Evelyn de Rothschild simply cannot have been there, as he was on active service with his regiment in Egypt. As is recorded on his personal War Office file[26] Evelyn had left Avonmouth on the *Minomiaee* on April 6th 1915 and would not see Neil again before April 1916 when they were re-united in time to mark Passover in Cairo.[27]

Billing was not only homophobic but also anti-Semitic.[28] When preparing his defence, he needed to use, and abuse, two safely dead officers, and Neil and Evelyn were convenient choices because of their recently publicised Jewish heritage. In Billing's warped and hate-fuelled mind they were not only convenient but also legitimate targets.

How much of this was pieced together by Neil and Evelyn's distraught family is unclear. Wisely they resisted further fuelling the fire by commenting in public; but the allegation that Neil and Evelyn were murdered by their own men could not be ignored by their regiment. Within days of the trial ending the following appeared in *The Times* of June 7th 1918 under the heading "AN UNQUALIFIED DENIAL":

The following letter has been received by Colonel Lord Burnham, Hon. Colonel of the Royal Bucks Hussars, from Lieutenant-Colonel the Hon. F.H. Cripps DSO, who was in command of the regiment during the Palestine campaign: –

My dear Colonel, – In the recent trial a statement was made that two officers in the regiment were murdered from the rear in the Palestine campaign, I desire to give an absolute and unqualified denial to this foul suggestion against the honour of the regiment and of two of my brother officers, who fell under Turkish fire while leading their men with great gallantry on two different occasions. Both Major Evelyn de Rothschild and Captain the Hon. Neil Primrose were near me when they fell, and in tribute to their memory I wish to make the most positive statement in contradiction of the abominable suggestion made at the recent trial. I hope that for the honour of the regiment you will make my statement as widely known as possible.

Yours sincerely, Fred Cripps, Lt.-Col.

EPILOGUE

In Neil's Wisbech constituency news of his death had evidently been hard to bear.[1] Some of his constituents kept his name alive by naming their new-born sons and daughters, either Neil or Primrose, depending on their gender.[2] Quite quickly, his Wisbech Liberal supporters had to undertake the distressing, but necessary, task of selecting a candidate to succeed him.[3] They unanimously chose 24-year-old Lt. Colin Coote, then on active service in Italy, to do so. The Conservatives, out of respect, declined to field a candidate and so he was elected unopposed and took his seat in January 1918.[4] Colin Coote's father was chairman of the regional East-Anglian Liberal Association and Neil had, after his 1910 elections, stayed with the Coote family at Stukeley Hall in Huntingdonshire.[5] In his 1971 book *The Other Club* Colin Coote would pen the last tribute to Neil from those that had known him, when he wrote:

Those whom the Gods love die young and the cream at the top of the milk is drunk before the milk itself.

In the December 1918 General Election the Wisbech seat was re-named and slightly re-drawn as the 'Isle of Ely'; Coote was again returned. He lost in the 1922 General Election, leaving politics for a distinguished career in journalism and ultimately becoming editor of *The Daily Telegraph.*[6]

Both of Neil's sisters were devastated by his death and Lady Peggy, whatever her differences with Neil over the ending of the Asquith premiership, remained in mourning and entirely unseen until late March 1918. Her re-emergence to attend a war related charity concert at the Palace Theatre did not go un-noticed in the press.[7] Ten days earlier, Lady Sybil had a poem on the death of Neil accepted by the *New Poetry Review.*[8] In explaining the poem's genesis she described her own grief – "at first everything is drowned in grief, and then the conviction of nearness – his unseen presence grows until there seems only the veil of earthly vision between us."

> Then spoke a whispered voice,
> Quite suddenly as I despaired:
> "There is no death – believe, rejoice.
> Why if you only dared
> Break through the hedge
> Of creeds grown like a thicket round
> The simple truths, your soul, unbound,
> Will know and feel,
> Unseen he moves as near you as you will.
> His spirit lives the same, and loves us still.

Harry, Lord Dalmeny, unlike his sisters, was too busy to mourn much in Palestine with General Allenby. He was at Allenby's side when his victorious army entered Jerusalem in December 1917 and he did not finally return to England until the end of 1918. On relinquishing his appointment Dalmeny left the army with the rank of Lt. Colonel.[9]

In April 1918, Neil's will was published and there was much press comment on his 'fortune' of £135,205 12s 10d.[10] Neil left his old political friend Sir Henry Dalziel £200, Fred Cripps and two other army officers £1,000 each and Jimmy de Rothschild £2,000. Rosebery inherited Neil's books, papers and photographs.[11] The rest, including Postwick and Great Stanhope Street went to Lady Victoria for life, and then to his daughter Ruth.

Both Rosebery and her other grandfather Lord Derby drew increasing comfort from Ruth who was, of course, destined to live entirely without memory of her distinguished father. Ruth was also to become motherless in November 1927 when Lady Victoria (by then re-married)[12] died following a hunting accident. Lord Crewe writes that Ruth spent "much time with her grandfather at The Durdans[13] – a fairy presence brightening gloomy days" and although Rosebery did not live to see her married, Lord Derby would give her away when she married the Hon. Charles Wood[14] in St Paul's Cathedral.[15] Their wedding reception, echoing that of her parents twenty-one years earlier, was also held at Derby House. Her new father-in-law was

Viscount Halifax, Lord Privy Seal in Stanley Baldwin's final administration, and soon to be Foreign Secretary under Neville Chamberlain.

In November 1918, just before the armistice, Rosebery suffered a severe stroke following a day's shooting at his Midlothian estate[16] but before this he had set in motion the commemoration of Neil in stone and marble in each of the churches where they had worshipped together. The memorial Rosebery placed in Christ Church, Epsom[17] is of a simpler design, but those erected at St. Mary's, Mentmore and in St. Giles' Cathedral, Edinburgh[18] mirror exactly the design of the memorial Rosebery had put up in memory of Thomas at Lanhydrock in 1916. The same Derbyshire alabaster is used for each; the gap in the broken pediment is this time filled with Neil's arms, and below the inscription is carved his regiment's crest. Evidently Rosebery wanted them commemorated in identical form and in Neil's case perhaps to re-set his son firmly in an aristocratic context; far from any hint of radical politics and David Lloyd George. In December 1918 Rosebery sent his design for Neil's alabaster memorial tablets to Herbert Fisher and was pleased to receive his approval and "a proof of your constant affection for Neil."[19]

Rosebery slowly recovered from his stroke but would remain partially paralysed for the rest of his life. Once recovered as much as he ever would, he made clear his preference to see Neil commemorated in silent stone and marble than in print. In October 1921 he corresponded with Herbert Fisher on John Buchan's privately printed 1919 memoir 'These for Remembrance' that sensitively memorialised the lives of six of his dead friends (Tommy Nelson, Bron Lucas, Cecil Rawling, Basil Blackwood, Jack Wortley and Raymond Asquith). Although the book was not commercially published during Rosebery's life he was still scandalised, telling Fisher it "surprises me more than I can say, as the 'stale remainder of biscuit' as Dizzy would have called it, is very revolting."[20]

Perhaps unsurprisingly, given those trenchant lines, in the same month of 1921 Rosebery declined to allow F.E. Smith (who had become Lord Birkenhead in that year's Birthday Honours) access to Neil's letters and papers, as the following letter he dictated shows:

My dear Lord Chancellor,
  My daughter, Lady Crewe, tells me that you have resumed the idea of writing about Neil. It seems incredibly kind that you should do so

when there are so many calls on your time. I wish I could be more helpful but everything I have relating to him is at The Durdans where I do not expect to be for some time to come. But even then I doubt if there is any letter of his worth publishing. I know that you from your intimate knowledge will be able to give a perfect picture of my boy and I am quite safe in your hands.

Believe me with much gratitude.

Archie Rosebery[21]

In consequence, Lord Birkenhead wrote the chapter on Neil in his 1922 two-volume work *Points of View* largely from memory. Perhaps unsurprisingly, it was subsequently said that in it he had failed to fully do Neil justice.[22] It is also interesting that his reference to Neil's relationship with Thomas is toned down very considerably from the tribute he wrote for the *Evening Standard* in 1917. Whether this was done to avoid upsetting Rosebery, or on account of his own more elevated position is unclear, but whichever, their love was not allowed to speak its name, and was now safely characterised as 'brotherhood'.

They were brothers at Oxford; they were brothers in the House of Commons; they were to die brother-like in the same cause.

The final and most simple memorial to Neil that Rosebery had arranged was placed in Postwick Church[23] in February 1919.[24] Its poignant inscription records that Neil " … truly loved this place of which he was the beneficent Squire for too short a time. This tablet is erected by his sorrowing father."

By now the entire country was engaged in memorialising the Glorious Dead and ensuring that their names did indeed live for evermore. Neil's name would be carved upon a variety of memorials ranging from Eton and New College, Oxford, to the Wisbech Working Men's Club and Institute. In central London he is commemorated at both of his clubs – Brooks's and the Reform Club. His name is also on the London County Council memorial; as owing to the war his six-year term as an L.C.C. Alderman was extended[25], meaning that he still held the position at his death. In Scotland Neil's name is on the Cramond Kirk war memorial in Edinburgh, and on the Stone of Remembrance in Temple, Lothian.

On May 21st 1929 Rosebery died at The Durdans, to the sound of the 'Eton Boating Song' playing on the gramophone at his side, in accordance with his exact wishes.[26] As one era closed, another era opened - nine days later on May 30th Jimmy de Rothschild was elected Liberal MP for the Isle of Ely, the successor to Neil's Cambridgeshire seat. Jimmy, easily Neil's closest surviving friend, would keep Neil's memory alive and hold on to the seat until 1945.

The 1929 General Election had been the first in which men and women voted on equal terms, and Jimmy's election was followed by the opening of the Primrose Hall, in March, Cambridgeshire. Jimmy's wife Dollie de Rothschild cut the ribbon and Lady Sybil was present.[27] The Hall was named by the March Women's Liberal Association and it was to serve as their headquarters. Plainly they had forgiven Neil for his pre-war opposition to women's suffrage.

In the Commons chamber itself Neil's heraldic shield is one of 42 that commemorates each MP killed on active service in two World Wars. The First World War shields are located under the gallery at the opposite end of the Chamber to the Speaker's Chair[28] – Neil's is the third of nine to the left of the central doorway and Thomas's is the third of ten to the right of the doorway. So the two 'inseparables' are there still, not far apart, and at the very fulcrum of our parliamentary democracy.

He Lives By Love[29]

*

His life was lovely and pleasant and he died in Glory

They go from strength to strength every one of them in Zion appeareth before God[30]

*

Now he is dead far hence he lies in the lorn Syrian town and on his grave the shining eyes of Syrian stars look down[31]

*

He was the light of our eyes and the joy of all who knew him[32]

*

NOTES

ABBREVIATIONS USED IN THE NOTES

Addison, 1924	Christopher Addison, *Politics from Within 1911-18* (1924)
Addison, 1934	Christopher Addison, *Four and a Half Years* (1934)
Birkenhead	Viscount Birkenhead, *Points of View* (1922)
BMMT	Buckinghamshire Military Museum Trust
Brock, *Asquith Letters*	Michael and Eleanor Brock (ed), *H H Asquith Letters to Venetia Stanley* (1983)
Brock, *Diary*	Michael and Eleanor Brock (ed), *Margot Asquith's Great War Diary* (2014)
Campbell	John Campbell, *F E Smith* (1983)
Cleveland	Duchess of Cleveland, *In Memory of Col. The Hon. Everard Henry Primrose* (1886)
Coote	Colin Coote, *The Other Club* (1971)
Crewe	Marquess of Crewe, *Lord Rosebery* (1931)
Cripps	F H Cripps, *Life's a Gamble* (1957)
CUL	Cambridge University Library, papers of the 1st Marquess of Crewe
Hazlehurst	Cameron Hazlehurst, *Politicians at War* (1971)
Holden	Paul Holden, 'A Very English Gentleman', *Journal of Liberal History 66* (2010)
Hounslow	E J Hounslow, *Fighting for the Bucks* (2013)
Hughes	Matthew Hughes, *Allenby in Palestine* (2004)
Jenkins	Roy Jenkins, *Asquith* (1964)
Johnson	Rob Johnson, *Great War in the Middle East* (2016)
McKenna	Neil McKenna, *The Secret Life of Oscar Wilde* (2003)

239

McKinstry	Leo McKinstry, *Rosebery Statesman in Turmoil* (2005)
Morton-Jack	George Morton-Jack, *The Indian Army on the Western Front* (2014)
MS Fisher	Bodleian Library, papers of H A L Fisher
NA	National Archives
NLS	National Library of Scotland
Oxford DNB	*Oxford Dictionary of National Biography*
PA (BL)	Parliamentary Archives, Bonar Law papers
PA (LG)	Parliamentary Archives, Lloyd George papers
PHA	Petworth House Archive
Pope-Hennessy	James Pope-Hennessy, *Lord Crewe* (1955)
RA	Royal Archives
RAL	Rothschild Archive London
RAW	Rothschild Archive Waddesdon
Rhodes James	Robert Rhodes James, *Rosebery* (1963)
RIBA	Royal Institute of British Architects
Roberts	Brian Roberts, *The Mad Bad Line The Family of Lord Alfred Douglas* (1981)
Sturgis	Matthew Sturgis, *Oscar a Life* (2018)
Taylor	A J P Taylor (ed), *A Diary by Frances Stephenson* (1971)
Thorpe & Toye	Thorpe and Toye (ed), *Diaries of Cecil Harmsworth MP 1909-22* (2016)
Young	Kenneth Young, *Harry, Lord Rosebery* (1974)

NOTES TO THE PROLOGUE

1   *Oxfordshire Telegraph* December 3rd 1890
2   *Morning Post* November 26th 1890
3   November 26th 1890
4   McKinstry p.198
5   Crewe vol.2 p.369-70
6   John Davis, 'Fifth Earl of Rosebery', *Oxford DNB*
7   McKinstry p.72
8   Rhodes James p.84
9   (1844-1935); married 8 October 1885 to Henry Hope of Luffness (1839-1913)
10 Rhodes James p.82
11 McKinstry p.71
12 Rhodes James p.85
13 McKinstry p.74-5
14 Crewe vol.1 p.119
15 Rhodes James p.86
16 Baron de Rothschild in the nobility of the Austrian Empire (1818-74)
17 (1831-77)
18 Rhodes James p.82
19 Nicola Pickering, 'The English Rothschilds and the Vale of Aylesbury', *The Rothschild Archive, London, Annual Review 2009-10*
20 Crewe vol.1 p.116
21 McKinstry p.94
22 Rhodes James p.80
23 March 12th 1877
24 McKinstry p.74
25 Rhodes James p.81
26 Disraeli's private secretary, later Lord Rowton.
27 McKinstry p.71
28 Crewe vol.1 p.119
29 Rhodes James p.1
30 Rhodes James p.9
31 Rhodes James p.10
32 Rhodes James p.11
33 McKinstry p.15
34 McKinstry p.15
35 George Renaud (1814-1901) Fellow of Corpus Christi College Oxford (1834). Ordained to curacy of Hatfield, Herts (1838). (Cleveland)
36 PHA 5577
37 Rhodes James p.16-17
38 Crewe vol.1 p.13
39 Lee's school when in Brighton had so many aristocratic pupils that it was commonly known as the House of Lords (*Morning Post* November 26th 1897)
40 McKinstry p.18

41   William Johnson Cory (1823-1892). In 1872 he suddenly resigned from Eton and subsequently changed his surname to Cory. His *Oxford DNB* biographer Tim Card (2004) writes "he was dangerously fond of a number of boys" and his subsequent change of identity may suggest that a paedophile scandal lay behind his resignation from Eton

42   McKinstry p.20

43   McKinstry p.24

44   Rhodes James p.35

45   McKinstry p.15

46   Crewe vol.1 p.22-23

47   Frederick Wood, younger son of Lord Halifax

48   Crewe vol.1 p.24

49   Crewe vol.1 p.16

50   Crewe vol.1 p.33

51   Rhodes James p.37

52   Rhodes James p.37

53   Rhodes James p.37

54   Cleveland. Also in this book (p.11) the Duchess writes of her "low opinion of Eton as a place of education."

55   Rhodes James p.42

56   Rhodes James p.44

57   Crewe vol.1 p.33

58   Henry Liddell (1811-98), Dean of Christ Church 1855-91, father of Alice.

59   Rhodes James p.44

60   McKinstry p.33

61   McKinstry p.37

62   Crewe vol.1 p.38-9

63   Rhodes James p.47

64   Rhodes James p.51

65   Rhodes James p.49

66   Crewe vol.1 p.40

67   2nd Earl Granville (1815-91) served as Colonial Secretary 1868-70 and then Foreign Secretary 1870-4

68   Crewe vol.1 p. 41

69   Rhodes James p.52

70   Crewe vol.1 p.47

71   Henry Wyndham, 2nd Baron Leconfield (1830-1901). Married July 15th 1867 Constance Primrose

72   Rhodes James p.54

73   McKinstry p.50

74   Crewe vol.2 p.616

75   Rhodes James p.57

76   McKinstry p.63

77   McKinstry p.61

78   Crewe vol.1 p.99

79   Crewe vol.1 p.62
80   McKinstry p.59
81   Crewe vol.1 p.55
82   Crewe vol.1 p.57
83   McKinstry p. 56

1   FAMILY REASONS OBLIGE ME TO HURRY TO SCOTLAND

1   Crewe vol.1
2   *Aberdeen Press and Journal* March 19th 1910
3   Young p.17
4   Colonel the Hon. Everard Henry Primrose (1848-1885) first entered the British Army 1868 as ensign and Lt. Grenadier Guards – the Duke of Cleveland purchased his commission. In 1879 he was appointed military attaché at Vienna. He was promoted colonel in December 1882 and was for a time the youngest colonel in the British Army. He resigned from the Embassy in Vienna in September 1884 in order to serve in Egypt/Sudan and died of typhoid fever while on active service with the British Army in the Sudan. In July 1886 his mother produced a 257-page book containing his letters to her and his sisters. Significantly the book reproduces no letters to or from Rosebery, who presumably refused to co-operate
5   *Edinburgh Evening News* January 23rd 1883
6   Neil was after the 3rd Earl of Rosebery (1728-1814). James was a Rothschild family name. Archibald after the 1st, 4th and 5th Earls
7   Reverend E Field
8   PHA 9669
9   PHA 9669
10   McKinstry p.109
11   McKinstry p.128
12   *Daily News* December 31st 1909
13   January 5th 1886
14   *Leighton Buzzard Observer* August 6th 1889

2   TOO HAPPY AMONG CHILDREN, BOOKS AND HOUSES

1   McKinstry p.135
2   Cleveland p.241
3   At his death he was 36 and unmarried. *The Times* April 9th 1885
4   Caroline Shaw, 'Egyptian Finances in the 19th Century: a Rothschild Perspective', *The Rothschild Archive, London, Annual Review 2005/6*
5   Rhodes James p.181
6   McKinstry p.159
7   Crewe vol.1
8   PHA 5572
9   McKinstry p.180
10   Nikolaus Pevsner, *London* vol.1 p.559

11   Crewe p.148. In 1882-3 the Roseberys sold 107 Piccadilly to the Savile Club and
      moved to Lansdowne House. The Savile Club remained in the Piccadilly house until
      1927 when it moved to Brook Street.
12   Crewe p.308
13   RIBA 99268. In 1940 a similar design was proposed for the site but the development
      was delayed until 1951-2
14   McKinstry p.180
15   McKinstry p.175
16   January 14th 1890
17   *Oxford DNB* Sir Francis Wylie (1865-1932)
18   Balliol College, Jowett Papers, Group IV Class B11 [17]
19   PHA 5577
20   Now the fashionable hotel and restaurant
21   March 25th 1890
22   *Bucks Herald* May 17th 1890
23   PHA 5572
24   McKinstry p.197
25   PHA 5609
26   PHA 5572
27   McKinstry p.198

3   **I AM HERE WITH NOBODY AND NOTHING BUT THE CHILDREN**

1   *Morning Post* November 26th 1890
2   Rhodes James p.227
3   PHA 5572
4   McKinstry p.200
5   Crewe p.373
6   January 6th 1891
7   PHA 5573
8   McKinstry p.201
9   PHA 5573
10   Crewe p.375
11   PHA 5573
12   PHA 5573
13   (1864-1940); born Punjab, India son of Colonel W G Waterfield. Educated at Eton
      and New College, Oxford. BA (non-honours pass degree) 1887. I am grateful to the
      Archivist at New College, Mrs Jennifer Thorp, for this information
14   *Evening Standard* August 20th 1892
15   John Joliffe (ed) *Raymond Asquith: Life & Letters* (1980) p.50
16   Balliol College, Jowett Papers, Group IV Class B11 [20] – [21]
17   William Robert Wellesley Peel (1867-1937) eldest son of Arthur Wellesley Peel
      (1829-1912) who served as Speaker 1884-95. Previously Liberal Chief Whip 1873-4.
      The Prime Minister Sir Robert Peel was his grandfather
18   *The Times* August 22nd 1891

19   Crewe p.332
20   (1867-1949); ordained priest 1895. Subsequently a Canon of Canterbury, Vicar of
        Folkestone, and then finally Rector of Stowting, Kent
21   PHA 5573
22   *Cheshire Observer* October 31st 1891
23   *Leighton Buzzard Observer* November 17th 1891
24   PHA 5573
25   *Bucks Herald* January 16th 1892
26   PHA 5574
27   Crewe p.384-5
28   *Glasgow Evening News* June 30th 1892
29   July 24th 1892. PHA 5574
30   Gladstone had suffered a bad eye injury in Chester just before coming up to
        Edinburgh
31   July 10th 1892. PHA 5574
32   Crewe p.393
33   McKinstry p.194-5
34   McKinstry p.234
35   Crewe p.413
36   (1853-1930); educated at Charterhouse and Trinity College Oxford. 1st class BA
        Modern History 1876. Assistant Master at Charterhouse School 1876-84. *The Times*
        November 29th 1930
37   PHA 5574
38   Miss Vibert was dismissed by Rosebery in July 1897 much to both girls' distress. She
        was replaced that autumn. PHA 5575
39   McKinstry p.260
40   Young p.20-21
41   PHA 5574
42   *Leighton Buzzard Observer* August 15th 1893
43   McKenna p.343
44   McKinstry p.360
45   (1814-1896) Roberts p.65-67, 210-211, 345
46   Roberts p.61
47   The *Globe* November 29th 1892
48   Lady Monkswell's diary quoted in McKinstry p.363-4
49   (1852-1925); entered the Foreign Office 1870
50   *London Gazette* June 23rd 1893
51   *Evening Standard* July 5th 1893
52   John Davis, 'Marquess of Queensberry (1844-1900)', *Oxford DNB*
53   McKinstry p.359
54   McKinstry p.265
55   McKinstry p.267
56   McKinstry p.294
57   McKinstry p.294
58   Crewe p.443

59   PHA 5574
60   Crewe p.473

4   I HAVE TRIED EVERY OPIATE

1   *Derbyshire Courier* June 23rd 1894
2   *Morning Post* September 1st 1894
3   *West Middlesex Herald* September 19th 1894
4   McKinstry p.356
5   McKenna p.425. See also Robert Bickers, 'Sir Edmund Trelawny Backhouse (1873-1944)', *Oxford DNB* (2008)
6   PHA 5574
7   He did get away from London to Scotland and stayed with the Queen at Balmoral October 13th-15th 1894. The *Graphic* October 20th 1894
8   Sturgis p.511
9   Claudia Renton, *Those Wild Wyndhams* (2014) p.163
10   (1837-1907); equerry to the Prince since 1876
11   McKenna p.424
12   McKinstry p.363
13   McKinstry p.361
14   McKenna p.424
15   McKinstry p.362
16   McKenna p.423
17   McKinstry p.364
18   McKinstry p.362
19   McKinstry p.362
20   *The Times* October 27th 1894
21   Sturgis p.524
22   PHA 5574. December 10th 1894
23   2nd Baron Tweedmouth (1849-1909)
24   McKinstry p.329
25   McKinstry p.336
26   *Leighton Buzzard Observer* December 18th 1894
27   PHA 5575
28   *Derby Daily Telegraph* January 17th 1895
29   PHA 5575
30   *The Times* January 17th 1895
31   *Evening Standard* January 19th 1895
32   PHA 5575
33   *The Times* January 29th 1895
34   Rhodes James p.370
35   McKinstry p.345-6
36   PHA 5575
37   McKinstry p.344
38   McKinstry p.346

39   McKinstry p.303
40   McKinstry p.380
41   PHA 5575

5   ETON

1   Crewe p.490
2   Crewe p.511
3   McKinstry p.382
4   PHA 5575
5   *Glasgow Herald* August 12th 1895
6   September 21st 1895
7   Crewe p.24
8   *Eton College Chronicle* May 31st 1902
9   *The Times* February 8th 1881
10   April 8th 1926
11   *Eton College Chronicle* May 20th 1926
12   McKinstry p.391-2
13   *Dundee Advertiser* September 18th 1897
14   *Daily Telegraph* June 1st 1898
15   *Morning Post* December 23rd 1898
16   *Leighton Buzzard Observer* April 10th 1894
17   *Cambridge Daily News* February 22nd 1899
18   Crewe p.533-4
19   Rhodes James p.398
20   McKinstry p.368
21   The *Globe* March 27th 1899
22   She was aged eighteen and the widowed Lord Crewe was 41
23   *Evening Standard* April 21st 1899
24   Pope-Hennessy
25   *Eton College Chronicle* May 20th 1926
26   School Clerk's Register entry dated August 4th 1899 records Neil's departure "to go into diplomacy." I am most grateful to the Eton College Archivist for providing this information
27   His new housemaster was Philip Williams
28   *Eton College Chronicle* May 12th 1899
29   *Eton College Chronicle* September 27th 1900
30   Young p.23
31   *Eton College Chronicle* September 27th 1900
32   *The Times* April 8th 1926
33   Crewe p.615
34   The pair spent six weeks together in Switzerland during the summer of 1900. PHA 5576
35   *Coventry Evening Telegraph* December 31st 1898
36   *Glasgow Herald* September 5th 1898

37   *Edinburgh Evening News* August 22nd 1901
38   Crewe p.610
39   *St. James's Gazette* April 15th 1901
40   *Abergavenny Chronicle* April 19th 1901
41   Crewe p.611
42   PHA 5576
43   John Joliffe (ed), *Raymond Asquith: Life and Letters* (1980) p.49
44   *Sussex Agricultural Express* January 12th 1901
45   (1872-1952) 3rd Baron Leconfield
46   (1877-1963) 4th Baron Leconfield
47   R S Rait revised by A C Curthoys, 'J E Sewell (1810-1903)', *Oxford DNB*
48   Alan Ryan, 'W A Spooner (1844-1930)', *Oxford DNB*

6   OXFORD FRESHMAN

1   September 8th 1901. PHA 5576
2   *Aberdeen Press and Journal* October 14th 1901
3   MS Fisher 57 ff.22-23
4   The Liberal leader Henry Campbell-Bannerman delivered his famous speech attacking the British Army for using "methods of barbarism" in South Africa on June 14th 1901. His words rapidly caused a significant split in the party
5   *Daily News* December 17th 1901
6   *Scotsman* January 15th 1902
7   *St. James's Gazette* January 15th 1902
8   February 24th 1902
9   *Bucks Herald* March 1st 1902
10   Born May 22nd 1880
11   Thomas matriculated at Oxford in October 1899. I am grateful to Judith Curthoys, Archivist, Christ Church, Oxford for this information
12   Thomas was in Miss Evans's House between January 1894 and July 1899. *Eton College Chronicle* November 11th 1915
13   *Eton College Chronicle* May 12th 1899
14   *Pall Mall Gazette* April 1st 1902
15   *Lincolnshire Echo* November 22nd 1901
16   Crewe p.634-5
17   May 23rd 1902
18   Alan Ryan, 'Herbert Fisher (1865-1940)', *Oxford DNB*
19   RAW JDR2/1/477/14
20   *Oxford Times* June 28th 1902
21   RAW JDR2/1/477/15
22   Crewe p.633

7   HE HAS NO IDEA OF WHAT WORK IS

1   Crewe p.635

2	The *Scotsman* September 24th 1902
3	*Pall Mall Gazette* September 27th 1902
4	MS Fisher 57 ff.1-2.
5	Holden
6	*Warwick Advertiser* November 22nd 1902
7	Holden
8	*Bucks Herald* December 20th 1902
9	*Edinburgh Evening News* January 8th 1903
10	*Edinburgh Evening News* January 12th 1903
11	*London Gazette* February 11th 1902
12	*Daily News* January 10th 1903
13	*Daily Telegraph* January 30th 1903
14	*Bucks Herald* March 7th and 21st 1903
15	RAW JDR2/1/477/16
16	March 30th 1903
17	May 30th 1903
18	National Trust, Lanhydrock Collection
19	MS Fisher 57 ff.3-4
20	*Oxford DNB* entry by Philip Williamson
21	Born in Edinburgh July 1st 1880
22	Humphrey Carpenter, *The Brideshead Generation* (1989) p.89
23	*Oxford DNB* entry by John Jones
24	I am most grateful to Miles Young, Warden of New College, for supplying me with both an image of the chalet's visitors' book entry for August 1902, and for the photograph
25	*St James's Gazette* January 29th 1903
26	*The Times* August 6th 1903
27	*London Gazette* August 25th 1903
28	*Yorkshire Evening Post* September 21st 1903
29	October 2nd 1903
30	*Western Daily Press* May 18th 1904
31	RAW JDR2/1/477/24
32	*Bucks Herald* December 19th 1903
33	December 21st 1903
34	*Luton Times* December 18th 1903
35	RAW JDR2/1/477/26
36	MS Fisher 57 ff.9-10
37	MS Fisher 57 ff.1-12
38	February 16th 1904
39	*Evening Standard* March 1st 1904
40	MS Fisher 57 ff .3-14
41	(1864-1940); youngest child of 10th Earl of Wemyss. First married 1930
42	Crewe p.635-6
43	*Oxford Times* June 4th 1904
44	*Morning Post* June 21st 1904

45   RAW JDR2/1/477/28
46   *Daily News* September 16th 1904
47   *Edinburgh Evening News* October 1st 1904
48   RAW JDR2/1/477/35

8   BULLINGDON NIGHTS

1   The *Sportsman* October 29th 1904
2   November 9th 1904
3   November 11th 1904
4   November 11th 1904
5   November 16th 1904
6   *Life's A Gamble* (1957)
7   RAW JDR2/1/477/39
8   ibid 477/40
9   ibid 477/42
10   ibid 477/44
11   ibid 477/46

9   YOUR FRIEND IS EVEN MORE DELIGHTFUL

1   *Morning Post* June 26th 1905
2   June 27th 1905
3   I am grateful to Mrs Jennifer Thorp, Archivist, New College, Oxford, for providing
      me with Neil's 1905 degree result
4   *Sporting Life* June 20th 1906
5   The *Cornishman* September 14th 1905
6   RAW JDR2/1/477/50
7   ibid 477/51
8   ibid 477/53 & 55
9   ibid 477/55
10   ibid 477/58 & 61
11   ibid 477/64
12   Rhodes James p.454
13   RAW JDR2/1/477/64
14   Rosebery papers, NLS, MS 10119 f.99
15   RAW JDR2/1/477/65
16   Died December 4th 1905, aged 22 (born October 2nd 1883). Educated at Eton and New
      College. Son of Albert Brassey MP
17   RAW JDR2/1/477/66
18   Rhodes James p.457
19   RAW JDR2/1/477/67
20   Located at 13 Boulevard des Italiens. The restaurant had a long history having opened
      in 1802 and being named in honour of the Treaty of Amiens. It closed in 1913 when
      the site was redeveloped

21   RAW JDR2/1/477/68
22   ibid 477/69
23   ibid 477/70
24   January 25th 1906
25   RAW JDR2/1/477/72
26   Obituary, 6th Earl of Rosebery, *The Times* June 1st 1974
27   Young p. 38-9
28   March 15th 1906
29   A separate page postscript to RAW JDR2/1/477/74
30   *Derby Daily Telegraph* April 10th 1906
31   RAW JAR 8/9/8
32   March 19th 1906
33   March 20th 1906
34   RAW JAR 8/9/10
35   *Nottingham Evening Post* March 13th 1909
36   RAW JAR 8/9/10
37   *The Times* May 19th 1906
38   *The Times* June 19th 1906
39   *The Times* July 21st 1906
40   June 23rd 1906
41   June 25th 1906
42   *Lancashire Evening Post* June 25th 1906
43   *Cornish & Devon Post* June 30th 1906
44   *The Times* July 21st 1906
45   *The Times* July 25th 1906
46   July 21st 1906
47   RAW JDR2/1/477/74
48   ibid 477/75
49   ibid 477/81
50   John Davis, '5th Earl of Rosebery', *Oxford DNB*

10   HE HAS SUCCEEDED TO A FORTUNE

1   (1791-1846)
2   *The Palgrave History of Anglo-Jewish History* (2011)
3   *Dundee Advertiser* August 19th 1889
4   The *Globe* August 22nd 1905
5   RAW JDR2/1/477/65
6   *Dundee Evening Telegraph* 23rd March 1908
7   RAW JDR2/1/477/76
8   English Heritage listing entry
9   RAW JAR 8/9/11
10   Lord Fitzroy Somerset, 1st Baron Raglan (1788-1855)
11   English Heritage file BP 445: Lord Raglan
12   *Yorkshire Post* July 30th 1902

13   (1875-1931); later 5th Baron Stanley of Alderley. Liberal MP for Eddisbury 1906-10. His sister was Venetia Stanley

14   *Evening Standard* January 17th 1907

15   (1874-1914); Liberal MP for Glasgow Bridgeton 1906-10

16   John Burns MP for Battersea. President, Local Government Board 1905-14

17   *Pall Mall Gazette* January 26th 1907

18   January 25th 1907

19   *Kentish Mercury* February 22nd 1907

20   February 27th 1907

21   William Legge, 7th Earl of Dartmouth (1881-1958) styled Viscount Lewisham 1891-1936

22   MS Fisher 57 f.24

23   *London Evening Standard* February 28th 1907

24   The outgoing Council consisted of 83 Progressives, 34 Municipal Reformers and one Independent. The new Council was made up of 79 Municipal Reformers, 38 Progressives and one Independent. *Kentish Mercury* March 8th 1907

25   *South London Chronicle* March 8th 1907

26   Rhodes James p.462

27   MS Fisher 57 f.25

28   John Knight's Primrose Soap was pale yellow in colour and in 1903 when awarded the Royal Warrant was sold as Royal Primrose soap. It was manufactured at a huge factory in Silvertown, West Ham

29   *Shoreditch Observer* March 13th 1909

30   *Daily News* November 17th 1909

31   *Norwood News* April 17th 1909

32   March 13th 1907

33   (1882-1942); Conservative MP for Aylesbury 1910-23

34   I am most grateful to David Wills for supplying me with this information

35   In the 1906 General Election 26 Labour MPs were elected. In January 1910 the number elected increased to 40

36   *Cambridge Independent Press* April 26th 1907

37   Lord Clifden had purchased the estate in 1894 from the creditors of the bankrupt 'Champagne Charlie', 5th Earl of Hardwicke

38   RAW JDR2/1/477/79 & 83

39   Obituary 6th Earl of Rosebery, the *Cricketer* July 1974

40   October 5th 1907

41   October 24th 1907

42   The *Sportsman* July 13th 1907

43   Theodosia Louisa Augusta Acheson (1882-1977)

44   She was previously married to the Duke of Manchester

45   Crewe p.49

46   RAW JDR2/1/477/81

47   4th Earl (1841-1922); increasingly impoverished he sold the library of Gosford Castle in 1878 and the remaining contents in 1921

48	I am grateful to Paul Holden, House and Collections Manager, Lanhydrock, Cornwall for providing these details
49	(1884-1968); seventh and youngest son of the 5th Earl of Cadogan

11 NEIL HAS FOUND A CONSTITUENCY

1	Throughout the period 1885-1918 the seat always returned a Liberal MP
2	March 18th 1908
3	Beck stood unsuccessfully in Chippenham in January 1910 but was elected MP for Saffron Walden in December 1910
4	MS Fisher 57 ff.26-27
5	*Cheltenham Chronicle* April 11th 1908
6	*Cambridge Independent Press* April 10th 1908
7	He resigned due to ill health on April 3rd 1908 and died nineteen days later before surrendering 10 Downing Street
8	*Daily News* April 29th 1909
9	*Evening Standard* July 24th 1909
10	PHA 5578
11	*Daily News* October 29th 1909
12	*Cambridge Independent Press* October 30th 1909
13	*Daily Telegraph* December 2nd 1908
14	*Evening Standard* December 4th 1908
15	*Evening Standard* November 6th 1908
16	Young p.45
17	*Daily News* February 1st 1909
18	*Evening Standard* February 4th 1909
19	February 6th 1909
20	March 15th 1909

12 THE END OF THE OLD STRUCTURE OF SOCIETY

1	PHA 5579
2	RAW JDR2/1/477/88
3	Rhodes James p.465
4	McKinstry p.507
5	(1853-1919); MP for Camborne 1885-95
6	(1858-1944); MP for SW Norfolk 1906-23. Kt. 1914
7	*Isle of Ely and Wisbech Advertiser*
8	*Daily News* August 14th 1909
9	*Peterborough Advertiser* August 19th 1909
10	The *Globe* September 9th 1909
11	*Yorkshire Post* September 10th 1909
12	October 5th 1909
13	*Evening Standard* October 8th 1909

14   This objection was perceptive as the proposal was dropped in 1910 and this form of land tax has never been enacted
15   Howard Coote
16   *Daily Telegraph* October 7th 1909
17   The *Globe* October 15th 1909

13   YOU ARE ALL THAT IS LEFT OF THE FAMILY NEST

1   (1890-1966); Her brother William Grosvenor (1894-1963) became the 3rd Duke of Westminster in 1953
2   *The Times* February 9th 1909
3   McKinstry p.497
4   RAW JDR2/1/477/87
5   The *Globe* April 16th 1909
6   Young p.63
7   June 23rd 1909
8   RA GV/PRIV/GVD/1909: July 17th
9   *Daily Telegraph* March 27th and July 17th 1909
10   *London Gazette* March 16th 1909. Commission dated February 10th 1909
11   BMMT, *The Last Charge* (2017) p.26. Natty was promoted Captain in 1885
12   *London Gazette* October 31st 1890
13   *London Gazette* October 12th 1909
14   *London Gazette* October 4th 1904
15   *London Gazette* January 5th 1906
16   *London Gazette* October 27th 1908
17   *Bucks Herald* March 20th 1909
18   *Bucks Herald* May 15th 1909
19   Cripps p.67
20   Cripps p.64

14   TAKE TO HEART LORD ROSEBERY'S ADVICE

1   *Wisbech Standard* January 7th 1910
2   Pope-Hennessy p.90
3   RAW JDR 2/1/477/92
4   *The Times* January 6th 1910
5   *Wisbech Standard* January 21st 1910
6   RAW JAR 8/9/6
7   RAW JDR 2/1/477/94
8   Thomas Agar-Robartes was re-elected MP for St Austell with a majority of 3,087
9   RAW JDR 2/1/477/93
10   *Nottingham Evening Post* January 26th 1910
11   Neil had 5,279 votes, Garfit 5,079
12   RAW JDR 2/1/477/95
13   *Grantham Journal* February 12th 1910

14   RA GV/PRIV/GVD/1910: March 2nd
15   March 11th 1910
16   *The Times* March 19th 1910
17   *Wisbech Standard* March 25th 1910
18   Hansard April 11th 1910 vol.16 cc921-4
19   Hansard March 14th 1910 vol.5 c140
20   *The Times* April 11th 1910

15   THE COUNTRY LOVES A LITTLE INDEPENDENCE

1   Pope-Hennessy p.89
2   Hansard June 28th 1910 vol.8 cc866-872
3   *Dundee Evening Telegraph* July 7th 1910
4   *Dundee Courier* July 12th 1910
5   Hansard July 27th 1910 vol.19 cc2129-2249
6   Hansard August 3rd 1910 vol.19 c2714
7   RAW JDR 2/1/477/96
8   Birkenhead vol.2 p.129
9   *Polo Monthly* September 1910
10   September 13th 1910
11   RAW JDR 2/1/477/99
12   RAW JDR 2/1/477/98
13   RA GV/PRIV/GVD/1910 September 24th

16   A VERY FORMIDABLE OPPONENT

1   RAW JDR 2/1/304/4
2   RAW JDR 2/1/477/101
3   November 15th 1910
4   Hansard November 18th 1910 vol.6 c760
5   November 25th 1910
6   November 25th 1910
7   RAW JR 8/9/2
8   RAW JDR 2/1/477/104
9   December 3rd 1910
10   The *Cornishman* December 15th 1910
11   1885-1918
12   December 17th 1910
13   Viscount Cecil of Chelwood, *All The Way* (1949) p.117
14   RAW JR 8/9/2

17   TORY MAGISTRATES

1   Jenkins p.248
2   (1858-1944); MP for SW Norfolk 1906-23

3   RAW JAR 8/9/1.
4   Jenkins p.249
5   The Isle of Ely was not a County and so in its case the office of *Custos Rotulorum* was held separately from the Cambridgeshire Lord Lieutenancy.
6   RAW JAR 8/9/2
7   *The Times* April 26th 1910
8   Hansard April 20th and 27th 1911 vol.24 cc1026-7, 1961-2
9   RAW JAR 8/9/2
10   *The Times* April 10th 1911
11   *Yorkshire Evening Post* July 15th 1911
12   John Robert Clynes (1869-1949), Home Secretary 1929-31
13   Lord Beaverbrook. *Men and Power* (1956) p.296
14   RAW JAR 8/9/3
15   Chris Wrigley, *Winston Churchill: A Biographical Companion* (2002)
16   Campbell p.268
17   The accolade of youngest original member goes to the Conservative Lord Winterton MP (1883-1962) Neil's contemporary at New College and three months younger
18   Coote
19   Coote
20   McKinstry p.513-4
21   November 19th 1917
22   MS Fisher 57 ff.46 and 56

18   A TRUER UNITY BETWEEN ENGLAND AND IRELAND

1   *The Times* January 18th 1912
2   July 13th 1912
3   I am grateful to Sean Naidoo for providing this information that came to him from the Reform Club Librarian
4   *The Times* August 12th 1912
5   *Yorkshire Post* August 9th 1912
6   *Cambridge Independent Press* January 24th 1913
7   Hansard February 14th 1912 vol.11 cc1-4
8   PA (BL) 26/1/68
9   Hansard May 7th 1912 vol.38 cc304-10
10   RAW JDR2/1/304/1
11   Hansard June 18th 1912 vol.39 cc1567-74
12   Defeated by 97 votes
13   April 11th 1914
14   *Evening Standard* November 19th 1917
15   Hansard July 31st 1912 vol.41 cc2138-41
16   *The Times* August 3rd and 5th 1912
17   *Buchan Observer* January 2nd 1912

19   MARCONI

1   Hansard February 11th 1913 vol.48 c750
2   Letter of April 25th 1913, RAW JDR 2/1/304/3
3   RAW JDR 2/1/304/2
4   ibid 304/3
5   ibid 304/4
6   Michael Tanner, *The Suffragette Derby* (2013)
7   *The Times* February 29th 1912
8   June 5th 1914
9   Hansard June 19th 1913 vol.54 cc641-2
10   PA (LG) C/10/1/54
11   *Pall Mall Gazette* November 8th 1913
12   PHA 5580
13   RAW JDR 2/1/304/5
14   *Western Times* January 29th 1914
15   Hansard February 10th 1914 vol.58 cc110-14
16   Brock *Asquith Letters*

20   HAS THE IRISH GOVERNMENT SHOWN ANY SIGN OF EXISTENCE?

1   RAW JDR2/1/304/6
2   Jenkins p.340
3   Hansard April 6th 1914 vol.60 cc1738-42
4   June 20th 1914
5   PHA 5580
6   MS Fisher 57 ff.70-71
7   *The Times* May 15th 1914
8   *Birmingham Daily Gazette* May 26th 1914
9   The *Scotsman* June 12th 1914
10   May 30th 1914
11   Near Larkhill, Wiltshire
12   June 12th 1914
13   Augustine Birrell MP (1850-1933). Chief Secretary for Ireland 1907-16
14   *Sheffield Independent* July 30th 1914
15   (1863-1942); MP for Huddersfield 1906-18

21   MOBILISED

1   Birkenhead vol.2 p.129
2   RAW JDR 2/1/352/2
3   His father Baron Edmond de Rothschild (1845-1934)
4   RAW JDR 2/1/352/1
5   August 7th 1914
6   *London Gazette* October 27th 1908

7   *London Gazette* January 14th 1913
8   (1864-1924); his younger brother was Lt. Col. John Pascoe Grenfell
9   *London Gazette* October 9th 1914
10 Cripps p.99
11 (1847-1922); she inherited Waddesdon Manor 1898
12 2nd South Midland Mounted Brigade
13 *Luton Times* August 28th 1914
14 *London Gazette* August 21st 1914
15 Young p.69
16 *Newcastle Daily Chronicle* September 16th 1914
17 with Royal Assent given September 18th 1914
18 PHA 5580
19 ibid
20 ibid
21 Hazlehurst p.178
22 *Gloucester Journal* September 19th 1914
23 Cripps p.99
24 NA WO 374/55314
25 Secretary of State for India September 1910 – May 1915

22   INDIAN TROOPS

1   Hansard November 18th 1914 vol.18 cc92-101
2   Hansard February 16th 1915 vol.18 cc508-13
3   NA PRO 30/57/69/5
4   NA PRO 30/57/69 /4
5   Birkenhead p.130
6   CUL C.41.1.103
7   Morton-Jack p.143
8   Campbell p.386
9   Campbell p.382
10 CUL C.41.1.101
11 Campbell p.388
12 Campbell p.387
13 CUL C.41.1.103
14 Morton-Jack p.171-2
15 *Northampton Mercury* December 11th 1914
16 In a letter of August 20th 1914 Rosebery told his sister "I am not King of Spain and could not endure such a Gibraltar. And so the beautiful home of 250 yrs … comes to an end and all our happy associations of 60yrs are in the dust." PHA 5580
17 Rosebery found the conversion of Dalmeny into a hospital not without pain. In January 1915 Rosebery visited and found Hannah's bedroom, where she had died, painted white ready for use as an operating theatre. He told his sister "It was an outrage and a pang." PHA 5581

18   Paul Holden, Lanhydrock Church Eulogy, September 27th 2015.
      lanhydrock.wordpress.com
19   CUL C.41.1.104
20   5 km north-west of Bethune, Pas-de-Calais.
21   Morton-Jack p.266
22   Campbell p.387
23   MS Fisher 57 ff.72-3
24   Campbell p.389
25   Hansard February 16th 1915 vol.18 cc508-13
26   Campbell p.383
27   *Supplement to the London Gazette* February 17th 1915
28   Birkenhead p.130
29   *Manchester Courier* December 24th 1914

23   UNDER-SECRETARY TO THE FOREIGN OFFICE

1   Hazlehurst p.131
2   Brock, *Asquith Letters* p.385
3   *The Times* January 25th 1915
4   Brock, *Diary* p.74-5
5   RAW JDR 2/1/477/109
6   *Oxford DNB* entry by Roger T. Stearn (2015)
7   *Sheffield Independent* January 9th 1915
8   Cripps p.99
9   November 11th 1915
10   RAW JDR 2/1/304/7
11   NA FO 800/95/4
12   NA FO 800/100/132
13   Brock, *Asquith Letters* p.395
14   Brock, *Asquith Letters* p.408
15   PA (BL) 36/3/12
16   *Manchester Evening News* February 8th 1915
17   February 9th 1915
18   Guy Locock (1883-1958). Foreign Office 1906-18. Private Secretary to successive
      Under-Secretaries 1913-18
19   RAW JDR2 /1/304/7

24   NEIL IS SHAPING EXCELLENTLY

1   Parliamentary Archives, Strachey S/7/8/26
2   Hansard February 10th, 15th, 17th 1915 vol.69 cc546-8, 873-4, 1101-3
3   Hansard February 22nd and 24th 1915 vol.70 cc4-6, 248-51
4   Hansard February 10th 1915 vol.69 c576
5   Hansard February 15th 1915 vol.69 c888
6   Brock, *Asquith Letters* p.444

7	Brock, *Asquith Letters* p.498
8	April 9th 1915
9	*Daily Record* March 9th 1915
10	Brock, *Asquith Letters* p.463
11	*The Times* March 24th 1914
12	Brock, *Asquith Letters* p.463-4
13	RAW JDR 2/1/304/9
14	McKinstry p.522
15	MS Fisher 57 ff.74-5
16	Hansard March 10th 1915 vol.70 cc1518-31
17	*Manchester Courier* March 11th 1915
18	*Manchester Evening News* March 25th 1915
19	*Surrey Mirror* March 23rd 1915
20	British Library Mss Eur F118/67/8-9
21	RAW JDR 2/1/304/10
22	NA WO 95/4293
23	Now the Oriental Club, Stratford Place, W1
24	There is a 1915 Sunbeam in the National Motor Museum Trust collection at Beaulieu, Hampshire. It was purchased in 1915 from London dealers Day & Day
25	*The Times* April 15th 1915
26	Hansard April 27th 1915 vol.71 cc653-661
27	Hansard April 27th 1915 vol.71 cc573-4
28	NA FO 800 100 134
29	Hansard June 9th 1915 vol.72 c267
30	The *Cornishman* May 20th 1915, *West Briton and Cornwall Advertiser* June 7th 1915
31	NLS Acc. 8365/35

**25	THE PRIME MINISTER'S DIFFICULT TASK**

1	Hansard May 19th 1915 vol.71 c2392
2	May 28th 1915
3	Brock, *Diary* p.146
4	Cecil, *All the Way* p.129
5	*Daily Chronicle* May 27th 1915
6	May 29th 1915
7	PA (BL) 50/3/65
8	RAW JDR 2/1/304/11
9	*Daily Record* June 8th 1915
10	PA Lloyd George (LG) D/5/2
11	June 23rd 1915
12	*Cambridgeshire Independent Press* June 11th 1915
13	*Nottingham Evening Post* July 13th 1915
14	MS Fisher 57 ff.76-7
15	RAW JDR 2/1/6/11
16	RAW JDR 2/1/6/12

17   Cripps p.105-6
18   Cripps p.101
19   (1883-1962); 6th Earl

26   GALLIPOLI

1   Cripps p.102
2   Cripps p.102
3   Cripps p.104
4   RAL 000/2019/15/2

27   HE HAS LEFT AN EXAMPLE I SHALL TRY TO LIVE UP TO

1   Holden
2   RAW JDR 2/1/355/337
3   *West Briton and Cornwall Advertiser* July 10th 1916
4   *Supplement to the London Gazette* January 1st 1916 p.30
5   Information provided by Paul Holden, Lanhydrock
6   NLS Acc. 8365/35
7   RAW JDR 2/1/355/336
8   RAW JDR 2/1/304/13
9   *Evening Standard* November 19th 1917
10   (1883-1966); in 1930 he inherited his father's title and estates. The 7th Viscount sold
     Wimpole in 1938 and in 1953 donated Lanhydrock to the National Trust
11   Commonwealth War Graves Commission Lapugnoy Military Cemetery
12   RAW JDR 2/1/355/337
13   *Newcastle Journal* October 4th 1915
14   October 4th 1915
15   PHA 5581
16   NLS Acc. 8365/35
17   Mark Amory, *Lord Berners the Last Eccentric* (1998) p.88
18   I am grateful to Paul Holden for this information. *The Times* reported his death from a
     fall from the third floor window of 37 Grosvenor Square, London, being the result of
     a nervous breakdown
19   Holden
20   October 14th 1915
21   PHA 5581
22   July 8th 1916

28   MUDROS

1   Peter Hart, *Gallipoli* (2011)
2   RAW JDR 2/1/304/13
3   Edward Frederick Lawson, 4th Baron Burnham (1890-1963), managing director of the
    Daily Telegraph

4 1st Baron Burnham (1833-1916), proprietor of the *Daily Telegraph*
5 Hounslow p.62
6 NA WO 374/19327
7 Hounslow p.62
8 NA WO 95/4293
9 Trevor Royle, *The Kitchener Enigma* (1985)
10 RAW JDR 2/1/304/14
11 Disastrous 1809 occupation of Walcheren (Netherlands) at the mouth of the river Scheldt. 4,000 troops died of disease (106 in combat) and thousands more suffered sickness. The campaign which achieved nothing had an estimated cost of £8 million
12 MS Fisher 57 ff.78-9

29 **THE SENUSSI**

1 *Times History of the War* ch.CXLV
2 Johnson
3 Hounslow p.75
4 RAW JDR 2/1/304/14
5 *Times History of the War*
6 The 15th Sikhs. *Times History of the War*
7 *Times History of the War*
8 RAL 000/360/12
9 BMMT. Interview carried out by Ian Beckett May 22nd 1981
10 *Times History of the War*
11 BMMT. Interviewed by Ian Beckett
12 BMMT. Captain C H Perkins MC. Interviewed June 18th 1980 by Ian Beckett
13 ch.CXLV p.317
14 BMMT. J Bertram Clark trooper RBH. 1980 questionnaire
15 *Times History of the War*
16 Hounslow p.79
17 Johnson p.70
18 Hounslow p.88
19 *Times History of the War*

30 **LEAVE**

1 RAW JDR 2/1/304/16
2 *Yorkshire Evening Post* April 22nd 1916
3 RAW JDR 2/1/61/2
4 MS Fisher 57 f.81
5 PHA 5581
6 *Dundee Evening Telegraph* May 9th 1916
7 *Daily Record* May 10th 1916
8 *Daily Mirror* May 16th 1916
9 (1863-1943); Chancellor of the Exchequer 1915-16

10   Hansard May 15th 1916 vol.82 c1134
11   NA WO 374/55314
12   The *Sportsman* May 13th 1916
13   *Northampton Chronicle and Echo* May 27th 1916
14   *Hull Daily Mail* June 2nd 1916
15   Cripps p.109
16   *London Gazette* June 3rd 1916, *Buckingham Advertiser & Free Press* June 10th 1916
17   Brock, *Diary* p.267

31   MUNITIONS

1   July 11th 1916
2   July 13th 1916
3   Arthur Hamilton Lee (1868-1947). Subsequently 1st Viscount Lee of Fareham. Donated Chequers, Buckinghamshire for the use of future Prime Ministers
4   Addison, 1934 vol.1 ch.XV
5   NA WO 95/4445
6   *London Gazette* June 21st 1916. Despatch from Army HQ, Cairo
7   Interviewed May 22nd 1981 by Ian Beckett, BMMT
8   Iskenderun, Turkey
9   *Portsmouth Evening News* August 25th 1916
10   Cripps p.101
11   Addison, 1934 vol.1 ch.XV
12   Christopher Addison (1869-1951) subsequently 1st Viscount Addison. Liberal MP for Hoxton 1910-18
13   Addison, 1924 vol.1 p.224
14   December 29th 1916. The reported meeting was held on December 2nd at St. Wendreda's Rectory, March, Cambridgeshire
15   Hansard October 26th 1916 vol.86 c1471
16   *Yorkshire Post* September 30th 1916
17   Hansard November 8th 1916 vol.87 c188
18   Hansard November 14th 1916 vol.87 c613
19   War Committee October 3rd 1916. *Newcastle Journal* October 4th 1916
20   War Committee November 17th 1916. *Yorkshire Post* November 18th 1916
21   British Library Mss Eur F118/67/10
22   Chris Wrigley, 'Arthur Henderson (1863-1935)', *Oxford DNB* (2004)
23   Addison, 1934 vol.1 ch.XV
24   *Yorkshire Post* November 23rd 1916
25   Hansard December 4th 1916 vol.88 c646
26   Hansard December 4th 1916 vol.88 c683

32   REGIME CHANGE

1   Lord Beaverbrook, *Politicians and the War* (1960) ch.XXXIII
2   Robert Blake, *The Unknown Prime Minister* (1955) p.328

3   Beaverbrook *Politicians and the War* p.459
4   Addison, 1924 vol.1 p.269-70
5   K O Morgan (ed). *Lloyd George Family Letters 1885-1936* (1973) p.184
6   Brock, *Diary* p.302-3
7   Addison, 1924 vol.1 p.275
8   Montagu was offered and declined the post of Financial Secretary to the Treasury and so remained outside the Lloyd George ministry until appointed Secretary of State for India in July 1917
9   PA (LG) F/42/11/1
10 (1855-1937); MP for Manchester Gorton 1906-23
11 Addison, 1934 vol.1 ch.XV
12 (1874-1928) *Oxford DNB* entry by Marc Brodie
13 PA (LG) F/42/11/2
14 Addison, 1924 vol.1 p.276
15 PA (LG) F/42/11/3
16 PA (LG) F/42/11/4
17 RA/PS/PSO/GV/C/K/1048A/1

33   LIBERAL CHIEF WHIP

1   McKinstry p.522
2   Fisher was not yet in Parliament but was subsequently returned unopposed as MP for Sheffield Hallam in a by-election. He made his maiden speech on the education estimates April 19th 1917
3   MS Fisher 62 f.88
4   Taylor p.134
5   *Cambridge Independent Press* December 22nd 1916
6   Sir William Clarke (1847-1930) Kt. 1914
7   PA (LG) F/42/11/5
8   Taylor p.136
9   RAW JDR 2/1/304/17

34   I MUST REJOIN MY REGIMENT

1   January 13th 1917
2   John Grigg, *Lloyd George War Leader 1916-18* (2002)
3   *Western Times* February 3rd 1917
4   *Hull Daily Mail* February 5th 1917
5   Taylor p.140-1
6   The *Scotsman* February 5th 1917
7   *Shields Daily News* February 5th 1917
8   *Derbyshire Advertiser and Journal* February 9th 1917
9   Taylor p.141
10 Taylor p.148
11 PA (BL) 81/4/14

12   Michael and Simon Asquith (ed), *The Diaries of Lady Cynthia Asquith 1915-18* (1968) p.278
13   *Liverpool Echo* March 13th 1917
14   PA (LG) F/42/11/6
15   PA (LG) F/48/1/4
16   Thorpe & Toye
17   PA (LG) F/42/11/7
18   John Turner, *Lloyd George's Secretariat* (1980)
19   *Daily Telegraph* February 28th 1917

35   TRAFFIC IN TITLES

1   British Library Mss Eur F118/67/11-12
2   Taylor p.151-2
3   *Shields Daily News* April 23rd 1917
4   Taylor p.153
5   Taylor p.156
6   LG F/42/11/8
7   (1869-1948); Elected Liberal MP for Droitwich 1906. Under-Secretary at the Home Department Feb-May 1915, when, like Neil, he was dismissed on the formation of the Asquith Coalition
8   Thorpe & Toye
9   Thorpe & Toye
10   Turner, *Lloyd George's Secretariat*
11   (1875-1937); Liberal MP 1911-22 and 1923-9. Chief Whip 1917-21

36   A PRIVY COUNCILLOR

1   Hounslow p.92-3
2   Cripps p.114
3   Sir Archibald James Murray (1860-1945). Commander in Egypt Jan 1916-June 1917
4   Hughes
5   Harry arrived in Egypt ahead of Allenby on June 29th 1917. PHA 5581
6   May 11th 1917
7   (1868-1930); First Commissioner of Works 1916-21. Subsequently 1st Baron Melchett
8   *Cambridge Daily News* May 17th 1917
9   MS Fisher 57 f.86
10   *Bucks Herald* June 2nd 1917
11   McKinstry p.522
12   MS Fisher 57 ff.87-8
13   RA/GV/PRIV/GVD/1917: June 13th
14   *Leeds Mercury* June 22nd 1917
15   *Derby Daily Telegraph* June 29th 1917
16   *Western Mail* July 5th 1917

17	Hansard July 4th 1917 vol.5, c1253
18	Hughes p.51
19	Johnson p.193
20	Crewe vol.2 p.650
21	Originally made for the Duke of Chandos and Cannons Park, Middlesex. Purchased and moved to The Durdans, Epsom circa 1747
22	thedurdansliverystables.co.uk
23	There never was a Jewish Regiment but de facto Jewish Battalions (38th to 42nd) were formed as part of the Royal Fusiliers. During 1918 James de Rothschild served as an officer with the 39th (Service) Battalion. NA WO 374/19328
24	*Birmingham Daily Post* August 14th 1917
25	The *Scotsman* April 27th 1936
26	*Pall Mall Gazette* August 15th 1917
27	*Wisbech Standard* November 23rd 1917
28	NA WO 374/19327

37   DEATH IN PALESTINE

1	NA WO 95/4506
2	(1869-1948)
3	(1862-1933); 2nd Baron Burnham. Subsequently (1919) created 1st Viscount
4	Hughes p.88
5	NA WO 95/4506
6	Cripps p.114-5
7	Johnson p.195-6
8	*The Times History of the War* ch.CCXXVI
9	*The Times History of the War*
10	Johnson p.197
11	Trooper Philip Pitcher. Interviewed July 9th 1980 by Ian Beckett, BMMT
12	*Evening Despatch* January 2nd 1918
13	Cripps p.116
14	Trooper James Lawrence. Interviewed May 22nd 1981 by Ian Beckett, BMMT
15	NA WO 374/19327
16	*The Times History of the War*
17	RAW 94.1988.91
18	Trooper James Lawrence. Interviewed May 22nd 1981 by Ian Beckett, BMMT
19	Cripps p.117
20	Interviewed by Ian Beckett, BMMT
21	Colonel Cripps DSO as quoted in the *Scotsman* April 27th 1936. A different but similar account is given in Cripps's autobiography, *Life's a Gamble* (1957)
22	1 Kings 9.15-17
23	*The Times History of the War*
24	Coote
25	Birkenhead p.132
26	*Evening Despatch* January 2nd 1918

27   *The Times History of the War*
28   NA WO 95/4506

38   A NOBLE SACRIFICE IN A GREAT CAUSE

1   NA WO 95/4506
2   Cripps p.119
3   NA WO 95/4506
4   RAW 94.1988.91
5   November 19th 1917
6   Hansard November 19th 1917 vol.99 c865
7   Hansard November 19th 1917 vol.99 c867
8   Coote
9   George Everard Hope born November 4th 1886. Educated at Eton and Christ Church Oxford. Commissioned Grenadier Guards 1909. Military Cross October 24th 1914. Missing and presumed killed October 10th 1917. Buried at Ramscappelle Road Military Cemetery
10   *Aberdeen Press* November 24th 1917
11   RA GV/AA 48/144
12   RA VIC/ADDA/17/1943
13   *The Times* November 27th 1917
14   *The Times* November 29th 1917
15   Simon Kerry, *Lansdowne: The Last Great Whig* (2017)

39   ONE OF THE MOST LOVEABLE OF MEN

1   Crewe vol.2 p.650
2   McKinstry p.523
3   PHA 5581
4   MS Fisher 57 ff.90-1
5   R S Churchill, *Lord Derby* (1959)
6   The *Scotsman* December 19th 1917
7   Lord Balfour's letter to Lord Rothschild dated November 2nd 1917
8   RAW JAR 8/9/14
9   Karina Urbach, *Go Betweens for Hitler* (2015)
10   Blake, *The Unknown Prime Minister* p.378-9
11   (1849-1936); Judge of the King's Bench Division 1897-23. Subsequently 1st Baron (1924)
12   The *Globe* May 30th 1918
13   (1863-1947); Unionist MP for Bassetlaw 1910-29
14   (1867-1956); appointed Senior Counsel to the Crown, Central Criminal Court 1916
15   *The Times* June 4th 1918
16   *Illustrated Police News* June 6th 1918
17   *Leeds Mercury* June 4th 1918
18   Churchill, *Lord Derby* p.375

19   McKinstry p.525
20   *Daily Mirror* June 20th 1918
21   *Nottingham Journal* September 17th 1918
22   *Derby Daily Telegraph* November 17th 1918
23   *Pall Mall Gazette* June 26th 1918
24   *Liverpool Echo* September 14th 1918
25   Philip Hoare, *Wilde's Last Stand* (1997) p.106
26   NA WO 374/19327
27   RAW JDR 2/1/304/8
28   Urbach, *Go Betweens for Hitler* p.119

EPILOGUE

1   *Wisbech Standard* November 23rd 1917
2   I am grateful to the late Mr Brian Payne of Wisbech St. Mary for providing this
      information.
3   *Cambridge Independent Press* December 7th 1917
4   The *Scotsman* January 16th 1918
5   Coote
6   (1893-1979) Managing Editor of the *Daily Telegraph* 1950-64. Kt. 1962
7   *Sheffield Daily Telegraph* March 25th 1918
8   *Yorkshire Evening Post* March 15th 1918
9   *London Gazette* January 14th 1919
10   *Yorkshire Post* April 15th 1918
11   *Cambridge Independent Press* April 19th 1918
12   Lady Victoria married Malcolm Bullock (1890-1966) on June 10th 1919. She met him
      at the British Embassy in Paris where her father served as Ambassador 1918-20.
      Captain Bullock was the Embassy's Military Secretary 1918-20 and they were
      married in the Embassy's chapel. Their only child Priscilla was born February 28th
      1920. Malcolm Bullock served as a Lancashire Conservative MP 1923-53 and in
      1954 was made 1st Baronet
13   Ruth inherited The Durdans on the death of her aunt Lady Sybil Grant in 1955.
      epsomandewellhistoryexplorer.org.uk
14   (1912-1980); son and heir of 3rd Viscount Halifax. Subsequently 2nd Earl of Halifax
15   The *Scotsman* April 27th 1936
16   McKinstry p.525
17   *Pall Mall Gazette* August 29th 1918
18   The *Scotsman* February 13th 1918, *Hull Daily Mail* August 23rd 1918
19   MS Fisher 57 f.96
20   MS Fisher 57 ff.99-100
21   LG F/4/7/31
22   The *Scotsman* April 27th 1936
23   Neil's name is also listed on the Postwick Church War Memorial Cross
24   *The Times* February 22nd 1919
25   Andrew Saint (ed), *The London County Council 1889-1965* (1989)

26	McKinstry p.531. The words of the Boating Song were written by his Eton College tutor William Johnson in 1862
27	*Lincolnshire Echo* May 4th 1932
28	I am grateful to Mr Richard Kelly of the House of Commons Library for providing this information
29	Inscription on Neil's CWGC gravestone at Ramleh
30	Psalm 84.7. Inscription St. Giles' Cathedral, Edinburgh
31	Inscription, memorial at St Mary's, Mentmore
32	Inscription, memorial at Christ Church, Epsom

INDEX

'NP' is used as an abbreviation for Neil Primrose, and 'TAR' for Thomas Agar-Robartes. Military names and ranks are given as they appear in the source documents. They may therefore not reflect the full career of the individual.

Similarly civil honours and titles are given as their predominant form in NP's lifetime.

270